For my parents
Lucy and Malcolm Woods

CONTENTS

PREFACE

'. . . And I will make a man of you, my son.'
If – Rudyard Kipling

'I am a tainted wether of the flock,
Meetest for death:'
Merchant of Venice, Act IV, scene I

In this book I have attempted to do justice to the courage and imagination of the Headmaster and Governors of Ellesmere College in giving me access to a historical source of rare sensitivity and insight: letters written by parents to the Headmaster of the school between 1929 and 1950. These letters demonstrate, with simple candour, the concerns of a small group of parents in bringing up their sons: what their aspirations were, their plans, fears and problems. They help us to understand what they wanted for their sons' futures, how they attempted to realise their aspirations, why they sent their sons to a public school and what the alternatives were. They show, sometimes very dramatically, how parents' plans changed during and after the war. They also illustrate some of the differences between social groups as diverse as clergy, widows and farmers in bringing up their sons. Some of the most fascinating and elusive evidence is about the sons themselves and the effects of their schooling on their models of masculinity, sexuality and attitudes to women.

Access to this archive, so generously given, solely on the condition that anonymity was preserved, has enabled me to place what might appear at first sight to be the narrow concerns of an insignificant and privileged minority into the three much wider contexts of education, social structure and gender and thereby to draw from this evidence a universe of meanings about the way in which parents like those in the study brought up their sons during the period under review. The first context, that of education, concentrates upon the development of secondary education for boys, the expansion and reform of the boys' grammar and public schools in the inter-war period, the disruption of education during the Second World War, the 1944 Education Act and its aftermath.

The second context, the social structure, focuses on such issues as the rising standards of living among the expanding middle classes in the 1930s and the impact of the Second World War on the social and occupational structure through developments like the expansion of scientific and technical professions, wider opportunities for women's employment and greatly increased prosperity in agriculture. The immediate post-war period brought a desire for better social conditions. The Labour government, elected in 1945, presided over social reform which changed the market in secondary schooling for boys, though in an atmosphere of continuing austerity.

The last context, gender, has long interested writers seeking to interpret boys' experience of public school life. The transition from boyhood to manhood and the proper model of masculinity are crucial aspects of Tom Brown's quest during his legendary schooldays. Reinforcing the prescription of such proper models of masculinity preoccupied Rudyard Kipling and, more influentially for boys, Baden Powell. This transition is the primary focus for many of the book's arguments.

In the twentieth century public school models of masculinity and methods of socialising boys into them have been subjected to intense critical assessment by a succession of public school men. Among the most notable were Alex Waugh, Robert Graves, and George Orwell, but the tradition is considerable, as E. C. Mack's patient scholarship has shown. I have attempted to link this tradition with a longer and wider tradition of interest in gender, in drama and literature in which gender is seen as problematic, a social and historical construction to be explored and examined.

Modern academic scholarship has been comparatively slow to examine the social and historical constructions of gender. In recent years women's studies has begun to thrust itself into the league of minor academic subjects, anxious to maintain the respectability required for acceptance into the big league. Despite the growing academic interest in women in society, masculinity and male gender roles have steadfastly eschewed study and have remained unquestioned, a fundamental and deeply interiorised set of assumptions and principles of social organisation, too sacred to be subjected to rigorous scholarly analysis. This book is an addition to the small but growing number of studies of male gender roles and masculinity which are beginning to change this. It examines the way boys were made into men at home and at school. A particular feature of the study is the examination of father–son relations and the differences between fathers' and mothers' roles and relationships with their sons. The role of schooling in socialising boys into men is carefully examined. Further and rich insights were gained about the boys themselves from recording the recollections of, and reactions to, their schooldays of men who were boys at the school during this period. Altogether the book attempts to show how boys were made into men during a period of climacteric change in British society, the models of masculinity and male gender roles within it.

ACKNOWLEDGMENTS

I wish to acknowledge the help and encouragement I had in writing this book from all associated with Ellesmere College. The Headmaster and Governors readily and generously gave me access to the school's archive, providing anonymity was preserved. David Skipper and Ted Maidment, Headmasters, Major Chambers, the Bursar, Richard Taylor; Neville Shehan and Nigel Ainscow, the Archivists, were all most helpful in suggesting further sources and possible informants. Alison Negus, my research assistant for a short time, and I were kindly received and given a wealth of information by all our Old Ellesmerian and other informants. Many provided documents, and Malcolm Lees made the invaluable contribution of all the letters he had written as a schoolboy, adding a new and rich dimension to the work.

My professional colleagues have also been unstinting in their support. My friends in the History of Education Society were most encouraging, especially those expert in the public school field. My colleagues in the Faculty of Education and Centre for Social History at Warwick University always provided stimulating and helpful discussion on seminar papers and early drafts. Invidious though it may be, I must single out Mel Lloyd-Smith and Bob Burgess, who spent much time and thought helping me. My greatest intellectual debt is to my teachers in the Anthropology Department of Edinburgh University, Ken Little, Jimmy Littlejohn, Mike Banton and Mary Bird, who carefully tutored my naive certainties towards critical assessments of social structures and meanings.

My most singular debt is to my family, especially my mother Lucy Woods and her sister, the late Hilda Booth. They were born in the first decade of this century; their father had died in their childhood and their mother took on daytime and evening jobs in order to support them. By application and part-time study both became independent professional women. By the mid-1930s my mother was driving her own car round Sheffield as a peripatetic teacher of the blind and my aunt was training as a nurse in the same city. Later she became a health visitor.

Undeterred by my mother's desperate and largely unsuccessful struggles during my adolescence to rejoin a hostile labour market at a level approaching her abilities, I determined to combine professional work, marriage and motherhood. Throughout her life my aunt provided a model for me of an independent professional woman. As a health visitor, she also fully understood the demands of bringing up a family and her concern that I should adequately combine motherhood and professional work was a deep and lasting bond. The contrast between the experience and priorities of these women and those of my father, brother and husband supplied the initial framework for my study of masculinity. My father and mother have provided the most profound and reliable support for both my enterprises, looking after their grandchildren and spending long hours in libraries on tedious archival tasks over several years. Without them it would have been impossible to carry on as a university teacher, mother, wife, researcher and writer. My husband and children have survived the consequent strains with consummate resilience.

Lastly I must thank Barbara Grey for her expeditious and patient typing of the manuscript and Alison Negus, who was in the brief time we worked together a thorough, efficient, and above all, cheerful research assistant.

1
BRINGING UP SONS IN
A CHANGING WORLD

1 INTRODUCTION

In January 1939, Richard Little, a Cheshire corn merchant, and his wife Vera were considering the future of their small son Robert. Although he was only a boy of 9, Mrs Little was anxious about the crucial years ahead of her son and 'earnestly wished to give' him 'the best start in life'. The Littles had a firm view of their son's future and wanted him to be 'educated and brought out to earn a good living'. Mrs Little had already formed the opinion that her son 'seems to have a very definite bent for engineering at present and is fairly clever in things electrical.'[1]

At this period educational qualifications were becoming an increasingly important factor in the kind of professions the Littles had in mind for their son and education was the linchpin of their plan to ensure his future.[2] Consequently it was the search for the best school at fees they could afford which preoccupied them in January 1939. Their task was far from easy. The demand for the kind of education they sought had risen steadily since the introduction of the School Certificate after the First World War.[3] Education to School Certificate standard was available only to the small minority of children who attended public or grammar schools. The public schools were mostly boarding schools charging very high fees. Grammar schools were mostly day schools, some having a small boarding department which charged lower fees than the public schools. They also had a number of scholarship places open to children from elementary schools and they were expanding in the immediate pre-war years. At the beginning of our period over 80 per cent of children in England and Wales left school at the minimum school leaving age of 14, most of them attending only all-age elementary schools.

In 1926 the Hadow report on *The Education of the Adolescent* had recommended that a variety of types of secondary schools should be established and that children should transfer to whichever was appropriate at 11 and stay until at least 15 years of age. The economic depression of the inter-war years restricted the expansion of secondary education and by 1938 63.5 per cent of pupils were in secondary departments reorganised along the lines suggested by the Hadow Report. Only those in selective schools, who could afford to stay at school until they were 16, had access to School Certificate curricula and examinations. The school leaving age was to have been raised to 15 in the week war was declared.[4]

The Littles had therefore set their sights on a grammar or public school education for their son. They had already taken steps to ensure that he would pass the examination to enter grammar school by sending him to the preparatory department at the local grammar school. But at the beginning of 1939 in order to do 'the very best for him' they began to make enquiries about sending him instead to a public boarding school for boys.[5] The boys' public schools were the most prestigious in the educational hierarchy of secondary schools. At the peak of the hierarchy was a small group of schools like Winchester and Eton with long historical traditions and high academic standards signified by their close association with the Oxford and Cambridge Colleges. To these had been added a larger number of schools like Marlborough and Clifton, founded in the nineteenth century. All were housed in imposing buildings surrounded by extensive grounds and playing fields, often in isolated rural situations.[6] They were also exclusively male, limited to the prosperous sections of society by their high fees. In 1938 the average national wage for men and women was £2. 13s. 3d. a week or £138. 9s. 0d. per annum, while the annual boarding fee at Shrewsbury School, one of the premier public schools, was £180.[7] Clearly, therefore, while many parents may have admired public school education and desired it for their sons, only the minority could afford it.

Mrs Little sought a school with more modest pretensions than Shrewsbury and wrote to the Headmaster of Ellesmere College, another public school in Shropshire. This school had been opened in 1884 by Canon Nathanial Woodard, the last of the network of schools he established to make cheaper Church of England public school education available to those among the middle classes who wanted a public school education for their sons but could not afford the very high fees of schools like Shrewsbury.[8] St Oswald's College, Ellesmere, grew slowly and in 1932 the Headmaster, Rev. Dr A. V. Billen, was elected to the Head Masters' Conference, the body founded in 1869, membership of which had come to signify recognition as a public school. In 1935 a young and energetic Headmaster, Rev. R. A. Evans Prosser, was appointed. Despite the fierce competition prevailing among grammar and public schools at that period he embarked on an ambitious programme of expansion, extending the school's buildings and improving the academic standard by offering 'bursaries' to parents, who agreed to keep their sons at the school until they had taken the School Certificate, normally at 16.[9]

Mrs Little was impressed by the prospectus and book of views that Evans Prosser sent to her. She very much wanted to send Robert but feared that the fees, at that time £120 a year, would overtax their resources,[10] especially with the growing prospect of a European war and all its attendant uncertainties. Prospective parents were often reluctant to make a prolonged commitment to expenditure on such a scale, so public school Headmasters had to persuade them to send their sons and Evans Prosser was a sagacious negotiator. His initial offer of a £20 reduction to the Littles proved insufficient and Mrs Little managed to cajole a further £5 reduction before deciding to send Robert to Ellesmere College.

Robert Little entered the Junior House in September 1939 just after the declaration of war between Britain and Germany. His progress through the school was undistinguished. He passed the School Certificate in 1945 and his parents were 'very pleased indeed'.[11] They had meanwhile changed their plans for him and decided on a career in his father's line of agriculture. In order to gain exemption from the matriculation examinations required to enter university agricultural colleges Robert retook the School Certificate examination in 1946. The Second World War created a crisis in his parents' plans for his career. Young men were conscripted, and from the age of 17½ every aspect of their lives, including their education, was subjected to a mass of complex government regulations. Parents continued to plan for their sons' careers after the war. The declaration of peace in 1945 meant a merciful release from the dangers of combat, but it brought

3

new problems for young men and their parents. Conscription continued and competition to enter careers was greatly intensified by the sudden return of large numbers of demobbed service men to civilian life.

Mrs Little used every means in her power to find a place for her son at an agricultural college and to impress upon him 'how important it is to do well this year'.[12] Contemplating his future amid the post-war maelstrom she commented dolefully that if he failed to gain exemption from university matriculation examinations and thereby enter agricultural college, 'there will be nothing left for him but conscription straight away. I feel that his seven years with you at Ellesmere (which incidentally have been happy ones) in great measure will have been lost.' She particularly resented the measures taken by the Labour government, elected in 1945, to continue conscription and organise a ballot to solve the labour shortage in the mines. She told the Headmaster 'The present government are making things so very difficult and so upsetting for young men and boys and parents also.'[13] Robert Little did his military service after he left Ellesmere and applied for agricultural college again in 1949 and in 1974, like a number of his contemporaries, he was working in the United States.[14]

In this case study we see the way in which a family with a secure and comfortable income from an agricultural business sought to bring up their son during the Second World War. Viewed through the evidence of Mrs Little's letters to her son's Headmaster, giving their son 'the best start in life' was an important family enterprise, requiring long-term planning, to which a considerable slice of the family's resources was devoted for a number of years. Mrs Little's preoccupation with enabling her son to earn 'a good living' required a financial and educational strategy. She wanted him to pass examinations, enter higher education and pursue a career in the same line as his father. To achieve this Robert was sent to an expensive public boarding school, despite the fact his mother forecast that they would have to 'sacrifice much'.[15] The Second World War and its aftermath caused a crisis in the Little's carefully laid plans for their son and Mrs Little responded frenetically, approaching agricultural colleges and increasing her pressure upon her son and his school.

Robert Little's experience of youth, family life at home and his education at public school viewed from his mother's letters differs widely from other accounts of youth and education during the same period. A vivid description of a quite different experience of wartime youth and education from the son's viewpoint has been given by the writer Ted Walker, some five years younger than Robert Little, in his autobiography *The High Path*. Ted's father was a carpenter who had left Birmingham in the 1930s, with his tools on the back of his 500cc Ariel motorbike, to seek work on the South Coast.[16] The Walker family had settled in Shoreham, where Nathanial Woodard, the founder of Ellesmere, had begun his educational work in the 1840s and sited the flagship of the Woodard schools, Lancing College. Like the Littles, the Walkers wanted to give their son a good start and took a keen interest in his education. Lancing College, evacuated to Ludlow during the war, was quite outside their ken and they pursued their plans at home. Mrs Walker taught Ted to read before he went to school and his father extended Ted's general knowledge through devices like quizzes on the capitals of foreign countries while shaving at the kitchen sink.[17] The Walker family finances were regulated by means of an assortment of cocoa and tobacco tins, one of which was Ted's 'Start in Life' fund. He imagined it would provide him with a set of tools for whichever of the building trades he entered in the tradition of his father, grandfather and great-grandfather.[18] During the war his father was working in the shipyards on warships using rare hard woods and bringing home good money.[19] He had identified Ted as a clever boy possessing few manual skills, who would pass to the grammar school, and the 'Start in Life' fund was earmarked to provide a bike as a reward for passing the scholarship exam.[20] It was initially appropriated, however, when Ted was 10 to pay a language tutor, the elderly but enthusiastic Mr Jupp, who taught Ted first French and then German by the direct method for three shillings a session every Sunday evening.[21] Ted passed the scholarship exam and went to Steyning Grammar School, which in Ted's judgment enjoyed a reputation commensurate with its imposing architecture rather than its mediocre scholarship.[22] He excelled in English and French, going up to Cambridge in the 1950s, and subsequently became a writer.

Ted Walker's and Robert Little's upbringings differed in several important ways, but both families concentrated on education as a preparation for a career. Robert's father had his own business and the family lived in a house with the imposing title of 'The Cedars', which at least suggested spacious living. Ted's father was a skilled tradesman and the family's living space was restricted to the narrow confines of a small rented flat. Ted went to the local elementary school and passed the 11+ examination to the nearby grammar school, while Robert attended a public boarding school. Both families benefited from the greater prosperity of the war years and were able to devote 'spare' resources to their son's education.

Ted Walker's view of his boyhood given later in his autobiography differs from Mrs Little's contemporary account of her son's upbringing in her letters to his Headmaster. In Ted Walker's retrospective account social class was a clear framework for his experience at the grammar school, which he entered just at the time when the 1944 Education Act was being implemented and fees in local authority grammar schools were being abolished. Steyning Grammar School had hitherto prided itself on its social tone, due largely to the presence of fee-paying boarders who comprised a third of the school. Ted, a working-class boy with a free travel pass and entitlement to a third of a pint of milk a day, was among the group who were tolerated socially at the school for their one important academic contribution – bright minds.[23]

The Second World War figures very differently in the two accounts. It loomed large in Mrs Little's letters as a fearful catastrophe with dire consequences for her son's future career. Although Ted Walker lived on the south coast, one of the most dangerous areas of the country which suffered frequent devastating attacks, his account in retrospect stresses the benefits of his father's satisfaction with his work and the extra money that it brought. He participated in the war and the defence of his country vicariously, practising arms drill with his pop gun, beside his father in his Home Guard uniform.[24]

Perhaps the most striking difference between the two accounts is the importance in Ted Walker's of his close emotional relations with his family, his developing sexuality and love for Lorna, who later became his wife.[25] While sexuality is not normally found in parents' accounts, it does occur in autobiographical accounts and clearly forms a very important part of the experience of growing up which must be understood and integrated into the other experiences of youth. The difference between parents' and their children's accounts of their upbringing is not simply that between prospective planning and retrospective assessment, it is a much more fundamental one of potentially differing purposes and of parents' authority over their children. Carolyn Steedman's comparison of her own and her mother's upbringing shows that until her mother's death she and her sister were quite unaware that they were illegitimate, and of their part in their mother's plan to persuade their father to marry her.[26] Clearly, therefore, accounts of upbringing differ, depending upon the viewpoint and time of the account.

One man whose contemporary and retrospective accounts may be compared with that of his parents' plans is Malcolm Lees, now a Civil Servant, younger than Robert Little and Ted Walker, who entered Ellesmere College in May 1945. Malcolm's father, Herbert Lees, was a civil servant, living in Chandler's Ford in Hampshire with his wife, Lilian, and their only son. In the autumn of 1944, hopes of a victory in the European war rose after the success of the Normandy landings and Mr and Mrs Lees began to consider Malcolm's future in the brighter post-war world which everyone hoped would come soon. The war had left its mark on the family. Mr Lees had been moved about Hampshire and the family had spent 'numerous nights in shelters' in Southampton, which had disrupted Malcolm's education. He had been to five schools and there had been interruptions in the school day because of air raids. The Lees felt that as a result their son had suffered 'a complete loss of confidence' and they wanted to settle him in a boarding school in a safe area where he could stay and complete his education.[27] Like the Littles, they believed in the value of public boarding school education. As several of Mrs Lees's relations had been to Woodard Schools they decided to approach two Woodard Schools in safe rural areas. Travelling was slow and hazardous, disrupted by unexploded bombs, and the priority given to troop and ambulance trains. After several changes they arrived firstly at Denstone College, near Uttoxeter, and later the same day at Ellesmere College. The Headmaster, Rev. R. A. Evans Prosser, was all 'gusty enthusiasm', making a much more favourable impression than his counterpart at Denstone.[28] The Leeses, like the Littles, viewed the prospect of years of fee-paying uneasily. They had originally planned to save for a further year and send Malcolm away to school when he was 14. The Headmaster persuaded them to send him to Ellesmere in May 1945, when he was still only 12, a course which stretched their financial resources to their utmost limits.[29] Like all salaries, those of Civil Servants had been squeezed during the war by income tax of 50 per cent.

Herbert Lees was a keen sportsman, an ardent follower of 'The Saints', Southampton Football Club and an enthusiastic participant in village cricket. During his visit to the school he saw possibilities for his son, especially in sport, which he had never had and very much wanted Malcolm to enjoy.[30] He would come to maturity in the brave new post-war world. On 1 October 1944, with news coming through of the airborne landings at Arnhem to continue the Allied advance across Europe, Herbert Lees wrote to Evans Prosser about his son's entry to Ellesmere. 'I have every confidence in you as his Headmaster and your staff at Ellesmere fitting him to be a useful citizen in Post War Britain and a sportsman in the true sense of the word.'[31]

Malcolm Lees stayed at Ellesmere five years, from 1945 to 1950. His parents found the fees a considerable strain and twice had rises remitted after an appeal to the Headmaster.[32] He saved all his letters home and from these and recent interviews there is ample evidence that, although homesick at the beginning of every term in his early years, he, like Robert Little, was happy at Ellesmere.[33] His education was a wide one. He used the variety of opportunities afforded at the school for sport, music and drama. He endured the compulsory rugby and OTC drill, enjoyed the choir, annual Shakespeare production, and the cricket, especially away matches in his senior years. He gained School Certificate in 1950 and left to take a correspondence course in preparation for the Civil Service examinations. He was successful and entered HM Treasury, later moving to the Customs and Excise Division where he has remained.[34]

2 THE MAKING OF MANHOOD

The Littles, Leeses and Walkers planned their sons' futures carefully and then pursued their plans very actively, with the aim of placing them in suitable occupations and careers. Education was a most important part of their plans. It was, however, a means to an end, rather than simply an end in itself. For these parents the most essential characteristic of adulthood was an occupation and its associated independent economic status. In all three cases fathers' established position was a clear example to emulate. While work is central to male gender roles in contemporary British society and fathers are the most significant models for boys growing up to be men, there is wide cultural and social class variation in conceptions of work and models of masculinity.[35]

The Walkers, in contrast to the Lees and Littles, came from the skilled working classes and regarded apprenticeship in a trade as a time-honoured way to a respected position in the community and a high and in most times secure income. The difficulties of finding work during the 1930s no doubt contributed to their pleasure at their sons' academic success with the promise of greater security in the white-collar jobs to which it would give access.

Ideas about masculinity and work depend upon the social group and historical period. Robert Roberts, like Ted Walker, came from a skilled working-class background and became a writer. But his upbringing was very different from Ted Walker's. Born in 1903, he was brought up in Salford in the Edwardian period and only became a writer after a period in his father's chosen occupation. His father took a very different view from Ted Walker's of his son's wish to continue his education and enter a white-collar job. For Roberts Senior masculinity was about the dignity conferred by a skilled manual job and the rewards of respect and secure high wages which it brought. Craftsmen were the elite of working men. Becoming a man for Robert Roberts was certainly not about continuing his education and dependence upon his parents but about making a man's contribution to the household budget, while learning a trade through which he would become a member of that elite.[36]

Conceptions of masculinity and ideas about making boys into men are social constructions, conceptions of particular social groups in specific historical periods, which are negotiated and continuously defined and redefined. They therefore change and consensus cannot necessarily be assumed. Robert Roberts bitterly resented his father's insistence that he left school to become an engineering apprentice, despite its prestige in the local community. In contrast there was a happy consensus in the Walker household when Ted stayed at school, although this almost certainly cost the family more than an apprenticeship.

The Leeses' and Littles' models of masculinity and male gender roles rested on the idea of a career, with an integrated progression through school and possibly higher education followed by employment in a competitive hierarchy of positions, rising to a comfortable niche in middle life at or near the peak of the hierarchy. Apprenticeship, on the other hand, was followed by a period as a journeyman and establishment as a skilled craftsman, a position which did not change or progress thereafter.

For all these parents men were made not born. Parents' task was to decide on their goal and to bring up their sons and educate them in a way that would ensure they achieved that model. Bringing up sons was an important family enterprise to which a significant part of the family's energy and resources was devoted. Education and upbringing for boys and girls was based on the very different futures that each was expected to have in adult life.

The crucial difference was between the future financial independence of sons and dependence of daughters. Sons would become the principal breadwinners in their households, whereas daughters were expected to marry and become dependent. These differences were clearly reflected in the differential distribution of men and women in the labour market, in their incomes and education. The 1931 and 1951 Censuses shown in Table I mark the beginning and end of this study. Both show more men than women employed, with men much more widely distributed and women confined to a narrow range of occupations. Women's employment was largely that of young unmarried women. Only a small proportion of older married women were employed, mainly in the textile industry. In those twenty years there was a contraction of male employment in the primary extractive industries and an expansion of manufacturing industries and 'white-collar' professional and administrative employment. Women's employment in domestic service declined and there was an expansion of 'white-blouse' clerical employment. While women's employment expanded modestly in size and scope, it was still heavily concentrated in a small number of areas, textiles, clerical work and the two professions of teaching and nursing.[37] These trends conceal the very pronounced changes in the labour market which took place during the war when 30 per cent of the adult male labour force joined the armed

10

Table 1 Men's and women's occupations in 1931 and 1951

	1931 MALES		1951 MALES		1931 FEMALES		1951 FEMALES	
Fishermen	26 945	.18%	15 248	.09%	80	.00%	27	.00%
Agriculture	1 116 573	7.63%	961 300	5.98%	56 683	.35%	97 486	.54%
Mining and Quarrying	960 041	6.56%	589 714	3.67%	2 507	.02%	1 189	.01%
Ceramics, Glass and Cement	76 828	.53%	81 161	.51%	44 087	.27%	46 356	.26%
Gas and Chemicals	47 067	.32%	93 000	.58%	3 976	.02%	11 090	.06%
Metals and Engineering	1 556 644	10.64%	2 260 189	14.07%	142 231	.87%	197 906	1.10%
Textiles	297 741	2.03%	197 639	1.23%	581 716	3.54%	359 129	2.00%
Leather and Fur	166 673	1.14%	116 864	.73%	63 118	.38%	64 876	.36%
Textile Goods and Dress	151 420	1.03%	124 165	.77%	506 328	3.09%	437 218	2.43%
Food, Drink and Tobacco	135 898	.93%	148 897	.93%	56 243	.34%	83 914	.47%
Wood, Cane and Cork	441 942	3.02%	433 321	2.70%	7 087	.04%	13 262	.07%
Paper and Printers	159 121	1.09%	161 725	1.01%	93 136	.57%	81 058	.45%
Rubber and Plastics	57 946	.40%	84 507	.53%	32 387	.20%	40 690	.23%
Building and Contracting	645 929	4.41%	840 475	5.23%	378	.00%	1 390	.01%
Painters and Decorators	242 263	1.66%	298 566	1.86%	13 264	.08%	10 388	.06%
Management and Administrators	354 620	2.42%	406 190	2.53%	26 503	.16%	45 859	.25%
Transport	1 565 846	10.70%	1 403 722	8.74%	68 899	.42%	130 101	.72%
Non Clerical/Commerce and Finance	1 469 520	10.04%	1 227 541	7.64%	604 951	3.69%	757 771	4.21%
Professional and Technical	404 302	2.76%	714 197	4.45%	394 389	2.40%	523 057	2.91%
Defence Services	282 118	1.93%	685 813	4.27%	302	.00%	19 668	.11%
Entertainment and Sport	91 129	.62%	82 140	.51%	22 309	.14%	21 739	.12%
Personal Services	472 506	3.23%	465 624	2.90%	1 934 294	11.79%	1 464 137	8.13%
Clerks and Typists	711 172	4.86%	861 679	5.36%	570 609	3.48%	1 270 456	7.06%
Warehouse, Packing and Stores	244 702	1.67%	348 305	2.17%	146 996	.90%	181 196	1.01%
Stationary Engine Minders	162 367	1.11%	225 905	1.41%	409	.00%	1 976	.01%
Unskilled	1 292 190	8.83%	1 118 942	6.96%	197 970	1.21%	378 437	2.10%
Others	113 830	.78%	116 713	.73%	36 191	.22%	32 373	.18%
Retired and Not Employed	1 385 526	9.47%	2 003 541	12.47%	10 804 851	65.84%	11 726 417	65.15%
TOTALS	14 632 859		16 067 083		16 411 894		17 999 166	

Source: 1951 Census Report

forces and there was an increase and widening in women's employment opportunities.[38]

After the war the Royal Commission on Equal Pay found that large sections of the labour market were characterised by segregation into men's and women's work and in the areas of overlap, where the same work was done, women's pay varied from 50 to 90 per cent of that of men. The differences between men and women were greater in low-paid industrial work and less in the professions.[39] They attributed this to women's 'traditional feeling of inferiority' which had been 'shed more successfully the higher the standard of education'.[40]

Boys' and girls' education reflected the differences in their future adult roles. Consequently the education and upbringing of sons took priority. Among the upper middle classes, for example, sons were sent to public or grammar schools and university and mothers and daughters were expected to sacrifice to make this possible, in the style of the Little family. Virginia Woolf depicted the shadow which the demands of Arthur's Education Fund cast on his sisters' education and upbringing in such families in the late 1930s. Educating sons at the great public schools and Oxford and Cambridge colleges meant a correspondingly mean education for daughters: 'a schoolroom table; an omnibus going to a class; a little woman with a red nose who is not well educated herself but has an invalid mother to support; an allowance of £50 a year with which to buy clothes, give presents and take journeys on coming to maturity.'[41] Despite the wartime registration of women and propaganda urging them to join the labour force, the position of men as principal breadwinners in households changed little. The economist Gertrude Williams described the dilemma and priorities of middle-class parents after the Second World War thus,

> Most professions require a university education or a prolonged professional training, and it is no wonder if harassed parents invest all their available capital in their sons rather than their daughters even if as sometimes happens the son has less inherent capacity. It is essential for the boy to be equipped to fight his economic battle for himself, while there is a strong probability that the girl will marry and be dependent on her husband.[42]

The families in these case studies and others analysed later regarded their sons' education very much in this light. It was a social and financial investment. The battle Gertrude Williams speaks of was for financial independence and security at an appropriate social level. Bringing up their sons was about social class and gender and their interrelationship. In order to maintain or possibly improve the family's social position they had to ensure their sons were, above all, capable providers, prepared for occupations and careers, 'able to earn a good living' as Mrs Little put it. Manliness was first and foremost about being a good breadwinner, having a high, secure income from a respected occupation, preferably professional. Bringing up sons was also about intra-family relations and the implications of wider gender and class relations within families. Gertrude Williams, like Virginia Woolf, was concerned about girls' education and future occupations and remarked that

> A very large number of parents whose class consciousness
> forces them to make every sacrifice to get their sons into the
> occupations carrying good social prestige are unwilling to allow
> their daughters more than the short training that fits them to
> be shorthand typists or to enter similar categories of employ-
> ment that would be considered below the social grade of their
> brothers.[43]

The evidence from the Littles, Walkers and Leeses focuses upon the all-important role of parents and their relations with their sons, in their education and upbringing. It is the making of sons and daughters, the next generation, which is the engine which drives the continuing and changing relations of class and gender in our society. It is one aspect of this dynamic, the making of masculinity in a number of families between 1929 and 1950 which will be further examined in this study. In these interrelationships gender is conceptualised as a social construction based upon physical sexual differences, which also engender economic, political and status inequalities within households and the wider social structure. Social class is about structural inequalities of power, status and economy between groups of households. Work and family are the most important sites and indicants of gender and class differences.[44]

3 ISSUES AND EVIDENCE

This study concentrates on parents who sent their sons to Ellesmere College, Shropshire, between 1929 and 1950. It uses three types of evidence: manuscript letters written by these parents and their sons; interviews with staff and pupils connected with the school during this period; and a wide variety of printed sources giving comparative and contextual evidence about social and educational conditions during the period. The most important single source is the one hundred and eighty files of correspondence from parents to the Headmaster of Ellesmere College. It is the existence of this archive and the generosity of the Headmaster and Governors of the school in making it available which makes it possible to gain authentic evidence of the ways in which a small group of parents sought to bring up their sons and planned their education and careers. The reaction of sons to their upbringing by their parents and the school has been investigated by means of interviews about their reminiscences of their youth and schooldays and an analysis of their letters written at the time and preserved in the files. Malcolm Lees saved all the letters he wrote to his parents and these have proved particularly illuminating of one boy's experience of this school between 1945 and 1950 and his relations with his family and schoolmates. Many other sources have been used to place the experience of these parents and sons within its social context. The study concentrates on the ways these boys were brought up to be men. Unfortunately, comparative evidence of how girls were brought up to be women and the making of femininity in these families does not exist.

The study is concerned with the making of manhood and the socialisation processes in their families and school through which a small group of boys were transformed into young men. The central question investigated is: What did parents, boys and the school do to prepare the boys for manhood and what understandings of male gender and masculinity informed their actions? An equally important question is: How did these actions and understandings change during the period of the 1930s, the Second World War and the immediate post-war period? The study investigates the relations between fathers, mothers and sons, with fathers as directors and models and mothers as carers. It looks at the ways different groups – clergy, widows, and expatriates, for example – sought to bring up their sons and it examines the meanings and importance of different aspects of masculinity such as career, character, values, sexuality and emotion in the models of masculinity of parents, sons and schoolmasters. Conflicts between the groups and their models of masculinity and their consequences are elucidated. Evidence about the psychological and emotional consequences of these models of masculinity and ways of bringing up sons for fathers, mothers and especially sons are discussed.

The work is conceived within the tradition of historical anthropology, as an analysis of meanings in their social and historical contexts. Meanings in this tradition are negotiated in social interaction and depend upon shared understandings and social contexts. Mary Douglas, in her thought-provoking collection of readings *Rules and Meanings*, gives many examples of symbolic systems within which meanings are negotiated, shared and communicated. In primitive societies categorisations of plants and animals, and in Western societies distinctions of class, are frameworks of understanding which 'carry a heavy social load'.[45] Mary Douglas instances the complexities of academic dress at Oxford and its correspondence to academic status.[46] Ellesmere College also had an elaborate system of such distinctions – senior prefects wore purple gowns and Masters their university gowns, some very threadbare, for teaching and their hoods for Chapel on Sundays and special occasions. In addition there was a bewildering variety of distinctions in the boys' blazers, ties and caps which denoted their house membership and status and their success in different sports. At Ellesmere College the organisation of space, time and dress and the underlying symbolic systems were closely related to the social organisation of the school. They were a powerful means of socialisation into the social order and values desired by the school. The analysis in Chapter 3 draws upon the anthropologist Mary Douglas and Basil Bernstein's application of her work in education.[47]

While the evidence for the study is a synthesis of manuscript, oral and printed sources, the most important single source is the manuscript letters from parents to the Headmasters, Rev. Dr A. V. Billen until 1935 and Rev. R. A. Evans Prosser thereafter. These letters furnish a somewhat different type of evidence from those from which historians in the past have deduced the intentions and backgrounds of important and influential actions of great men and women. These letters yield evidence about the meanings which parents, sons and the school gave to the processes whereby boys were brought up, socialised and made into men. The use of the letters as evidence about the meaning and making of masculinity rests upon the argument that parents were legally responsible for their sons. Their letters represented their attempts to exercise guidance and control of their sons' upbringing and to communicate their wishes as responsible parents and paying clients to the school's Headmaster.

Their ability to communicate successfully with the school about these matters rested upon a universe of meanings shared with the Headmaster. This universe of meanings about boys' education, careers and masculinity was by no means absolute, but negotiated and sometimes argued over. Such matters as the importance of games caused disagreements and occasional pain and anguish. The meanings assumed by the parents and the Headmaster in their correspondence were derived from the universe of meanings about male gender and masculinity in the wider society outside the families and school. A wide range of sources have been examined to illuminate the changing meanings of masculinity and the making of men in the families and school and the wider society of which they were part.[48]

The study also draws upon traditions of social history, the examination of history 'from below' of those social classes and groups who left no individual mark, unlike the great men and women upon whom much historical study has been concentrated. Since the 1960s new areas of study and methods of investigation have been developed which have begun to illuminate the history of such previously neglected groups. Social historians have examined changing social structures and movements using a very wide variety of sources, including census evidence and newspaper accounts. Historical investigations of the family, women, work, trade unions, childhood and youth are now established as separate studies of particular groups and institutions and their relations with the social structure. New historical methods have been developed alongside these new areas of inquiry, the most notable of which are oral history and quantitative methods. As a study of historical anthropology using manuscript, oral and printed sources, the present study draws upon these rich and developing traditions, particularly those of family and gender.[49]

The main focus is upon a small group of parents, among them businessmen, professionals, farmers, clergy and widows who sent their sons to Ellesmere College between 1929 and 1950. They therefore represent a small but nonetheless very interesting group, the study of which reveals much about bringing up sons among a section of the middle classes during a period of climacteric change in the lives of young men.

The predominant concerns of the letters and the comparison of those written by different groups indicate the nature and richness of this source material. Most of the parents who sent their sons to Ellesmere College and wrote the letters to the Headmaster devoted a significant portion of their family budget to their sons' education. Many, like the Littles and the Leeses, did this in the spirit of parental self-sacrifice. Fees, and by implication the value of their sons' education, are the single most common subject in the correspondence. After fees came careers and examinations, as in the case of the Littles, where their son's subsequent career dominated the correspondence in his later years at school. Boys' health and welfare was the third most popular topic which aroused the parents' interest after fees and careers.

Although Mrs Little conducted all the correspondence with the Headmaster about her son's education, delegating correspondence to the wife in this way was a somewhat unusual practice found most frequently among the farming community and expatriates. Approximately two-thirds of all the letters in the archive were written by fathers. A small number of files contain letters from fathers, mothers and sons and it has been possible to understand the interaction within certain families about sons' upbringing from their files. They show a division of responsibility between mothers and fathers. Fathers were responsible for the fees and management of their sons' education and careers, while mothers wrote about health, welfare and their sons' clothing, a frequent source of anguish in the war years. Where husbands were absent on active service or had died, wives and widows conducted all the correspondence. Divorce was comparatively rare amongst this group at this period.

The nature and extent of the correspondence of parents with the Headmaster varied widely. By far the most garrulous correspondents were the clergy and widows. Impecunity forced them to write begging letters detailing their circumstances. Widows were sometimes shocked in the clinical sense, quite unprepared for their sudden transformation from the dependence of 'wife' to the financial and social independence of 'widow'. Their letters varied from the severely practical to the extremely pathetic. The clergy wrote volumes, their education, literacy and ardent concern with religious and educational issues encouraging them to take up their pens at length on every subject, especially money. The school, true to its founder Canon Nathanial Woodard's articles of faith, was deeply committed to High Anglican faith and practice, and the education of Anglican clergy was a recognised part of these ideals.

Farmers, in contrast, left little written evidence. Their letters were usually brief, on occasion written on the pages of old exercise books or bill heads. They sometimes made mistakes with spelling and grammar. Unlike the clergy, they rarely queried the school bill. A number of farmers delegated the correspondence to their wives, a habit also followed by some colonial officers, whose wives were able to visit England more frequently than their husbands. The files of sons whose parents were abroad are often very full, and contain their school reports and letters from guardians in England about holiday arrangements. Guardians of boys whose parents were abroad were sometimes well informed about parents' intentions for their wards and consequently wrote some useful letters to the Headmaster. The letters reveal the impact of the war on a particular group of parents and their sons away at school. Some boys whose parents were in Malaya did not see their parents throughout the war. Others lost brothers or fathers. Some contain exciting adventures; others are poignant. All give invaluable, almost unique, insight into the process whereby this group of parents planned their sons' upbringing, education and future. Their hopes and fears for them were mixed with their knowledge of careers and their assessment of their sons' possible futures. The richest evidence is that of the Lees family where a very full file of letters from both parents to the Headmaster also contains, very unusually, a draft reply from Evans Prosser about a tricky discipline problem. All Malcolm's letters from school have been preserved and several hours of interviews have been taped.

Evidence of sons' views of their education have been gathered by means of interviews with a number of other men who were boys at the school during the period. They represent the reminiscences of youth and schooldays seen from the perspective of maturity after some years of selection and reinterpretation. The men who gave this evidence were also those who were successful and were known to the school. It was not possible to contact others who had been unhappy or unsuccessful, and did not wish to keep in contact with the school. Despite these shortcomings, the oral evidence has the outstanding value of being the testimony of subjective experience and gives evidence of intimate details of life in the school at this time unavailable by other means. The manuscript and oral evidence has been checked, corroborated or modified with the evidence available in printed sources, of which the school magazines have been very valuable.

Presenting this evidence at the same time as preserving anonymity has raised certain difficulties. A public school like Ellesmere College is a small community in which notable personalities tend to be clearly remembered and are consequently recognisable. Accordingly a number of decisions have been made and devices have been used to preserve anonymity. Firstly, with only one exception, the case studies at the centre of each chapter have been chosen from among 'average' or 'ordinary ' boys rather than boys who distinguished themselves and became 'famous figures' known to the whole school for their achievements. Secondly, the names of informants and correspondents have been changed except where permission was given to publish an informant's name. Thirdly, in certain cases, parents' occupations, addresses, previous schools and other similar details have been disguised. In one case a composite case has been made from several cases in order to preserve anonymity. While such devices will undoubtedly offend certain historians, the preservation of anonymity is necessary in writing about a school in such a recent period when the reputations and sensitivities of the living must be respected.

4 1929–1950: A CLIMACTERIC PERIOD

(i) The 1930s
The period which the letters cover was one of important and far-reaching changes in the upbringing and youth of boys, brought to a crisis in the Second World War. The early years of this period, the

1930s, were a decade in which the long shadow of the First World War and the ensuing economic depression receded only slowly. While in the distressed areas unemployment remained very high, the majority of the population enjoyed rising standards of living. Two events in 1929, when the study begins, the Wall Street crash and the publication of Robert Graves' autobiography *Goodbye to All That*, symbolised the most significant aspects of the legacy of the First World War for the parents and sons in this study.

Graves's book was an expression of the deep disillusion which followed the inordinate sacrifice of the First World War. Graves had gone straight from Charterhouse to the trenches as a subaltern. It was young public school men who had led their fellows over the top and into battle and it was upon their leadership and courage that the military strategy had depended. They had died in their thousands, their life expectancy at the front measured in weeks rather than months, the long lists of names and decorations honoured on school war memorials. During and after the Great War there was fierce criticism of public school education, which had apparently induced such unstinting commitment to a code of honour glorifying inordinate and unavailing self-sacrifice. Graves wrote a searing attack on the philistinism, snobbery and warped sexuality of Charterhouse.[50] The other event of 1929, the Wall Street crash, signalled the extent of the post-war crisis in the world economy and two years later in August 1931 the British economy was plunged into crisis by prolonged and heavy losses of gold and foreign reserves, resulting in the formation of a coalition government to restore confidence and stability.

The 1930s was a period of seemingly insoluble political and economic problems and contradictions in which Britain enjoyed at best indifferent political leadership. The overwhelming desire for peace after the carnage of the Great War left a legacy of pacifism, equivocation and vacillation in the response of successive British administrations to the rise of Hitler and Mussolini, culminating in Chamberlain's disastrous appeasement policy of 1938 and 1939.[51] Successive government policies equally failed to solve the other outstanding problem of this period: the persistent high unemployment in the distressed areas of the North and South Wales, the sites of the declining staple industries, coal mining, shipbuilding, textiles, iron and steel. It was the era of the Jarrow Marches, when unemployment reached almost 20 per cent nationally in 1934, a figure which hid the effects on communities like Frizington where the mine closed and only 33 men were on unemployment insurance benefit, the remaining 515 having been unemployed so long they had run out of benefit and were kept on so-called Transitional Payments.[52] The effects of the recession were very patchy. While these difficulties were never extreme in Birmingham, the recession in trade there was sufficiently severe for Ted Walker's father, a skilled tradesman, to decide to try his luck in the south, always more prosperous than the Midlands and the North.

Average living standards rose steadily throughout the 1930s, from 100 in 1930, to 106.1 in 1932, 105.2 in 1937 and 107.0 in 1938.[53] At the same time the birthrate continued to fall. Whereas a Victorian mother of 1861–5 had 4.66 children, her Edwardian daughter in 1900–9, 3.37, her grandaughter in 1925–9 had only 2.19 children.[54] Rising living standards and smaller families were accompanied by new patterns of consumption in all social classes. Falling birthrates and increases in consumer spending were a marked feature of the expanding middle classes. Indeed in the view of the distinguished economic historian Sidney Pollard 'The outstanding social change in this period was in fact the growth of white collar workers.'[55]

During the 1930s the purchase of private houses, motor cars and private schooling by this group expanded steadily.[56] It is easy to believe, as Richard Titmuss suggested in *The Parents' Revolt*, that in this new affluence the choice between a larger family and a more comfortable life style was governed by acquisitiveness and that 'in the end material things will take precedence over children'.[57] Jeffrey Weekes's equally convincing interpretation is that under the influence of new psychological and educational theories of child-bearing and more liberal ideas of sexuality, a new family ideology developed, emphasising more kindly and amicable styles of child-rearing, freeing parents from the restrictions of Victorian and Edwardian *pater* and *mater familias*. In a wartime booklet published by the British Council, Cecily Hamilton summed up the change:

> One of the noticeable results of our smaller families is that the modern mother can be a companion to her one or two children as they grow beyond the childhood stage; unlike the Victorian

parent of 8 or 9, she is not occupied for year after year with the cares and pleasures of the nursery . . . there is a different kind of affection than in times past. . . ; a companionable friend-liness that bridges the gap between one generation and another.[58]

The evidence of the Littles, Walkers, and Leeses suggests that rising standards of living made it possible for parents to try to achieve their aim of giving their children a better start than they themselves had experienced.

(ii) The Second World War

This period ended abruptly when Britain declared war on Germany on 3 September 1939 at the moment when Chamberlain's ultimatum to Hitler about the invasion of Poland expired. On the day after the declaration the National Service (Armed Forces) Act was passed, which made all men between 18 and 40 liable for conscription. Regis-tration began with the younger age groups and proceeded slowly. Parents who had survived the First World War, feared in the Second for their own and their sons' lives. They wanted to provide for their families if they should be conscripted and for their sons' future in the hope they would survive. A Welsh solicitor who could barely keep out of debt, with two sons at the school, viewed the cost of the increased insurance he felt bound to take out with trepidation.[59] Several families in the study suffered tragic losses during the Second World War, 58 Old Ellesmerians were killed, compared with 111 in the First World War. The experience of the Second World War was less often about loss of men at the front and more about the wearying effects of restric-tions, disruption and bombing of homes and work places.

The war immediately separated many ordinary families unaffected by conscription. Taking as an example the bombing of Guernica in the Spanish Civil War, the government believed that the war would begin with prolonged and destructive aerial bombardment of large popula-tion centres to demoralise the civilian population. Accordingly, hasty plans had been made to evacuate mothers and children from densely populated areas like London and Birmingham to designated reception areas in the country. Between 1 and 3 September 1939 nearly one and a quarter million people were moved by train to safer rural areas. The transport and billeting arrangements were often chaotic. The enforced invasion of cockneys from the East End and Glasgow keelies into the tranquil homes of their recipients was scarcely less devastating than the later invasion by the Luftwaffe. Horror stories of dirty, poverty-stricken, lice-infested children, completely ignorant of table manners, toilet training and any semblance of civility, and ungrateful, gossipy mothers, whose one thought was to return to their slums, vied briefly with Hitler and Chamberlain for the headlines in the autumn of 1939.[60]

This initial evacuation affected mainly city 'slum' dwellers, while it was the threat of invasion and the Blitz later in the war which affected the better off. Some families moved to find better food and less re-strictions.[61] Indeed in 1940 Mrs Little moved her family to the North Wales coast for a spell, much to the irritation of the school authorities, who were being besieged by parents seeking a school in a safe area away from the hitherto highly prestigious 'public school belt' on the south coast.[62]

The war also disrupted family life in families who were not evacuated. Long hours of work, long and difficult journeys to work, nights spent firewatching and in the Home Guard, the bombing of homes and work places were frequent causes of disruption. Over 60 million changes of address were recorded during the war.[63] It was this kind of disruption which had affected the Leeses during the war. The irritation of the endless restrictions was one of the most palpable effects upon the lives of most of the families in the study. Many letters tell of the difficulties of getting school uniform for their sons, mostly borne with patience and humour.

In 1940 when Britain stood alone after the fall of France and before the Americans entered the war, Churchillian rhetoric and the aud-acious examples of the 'boys in blue', who successfully fought the Battle of Britain in the summer of 1940, sustained the nation after the evacuation from Dunkirk. The Blitz began on 7 September 1940 and London was bombed on 82 out of 85 nights. On 14 November the centre of Coventry was razed and the attack moved to other towns like Southampton, where the Leeses lived. Far from demoralising the nation, the bombing served to unify and strengthen it, despite heavy losses of civilian life. But the Dunkirk spirit was temporary. During 1941 and 1942 attention switched from Britain to the Eastern

Mediterranean, the Far East and the long struggle in the Battle of the Atlantic, in all of which costly and humiliating defeats were inflicted upon the British forces. To a number of families with sons at Ellesmere College the fall of Singapore, the Jewel in the Crown of the British Empire as Churchill called it, brought catastrophe. They lost everything and one father was missing for a year before the Japanese released a list of prisoners of war with his name on it. After the bombing of Pearl Harbor in December 1941 the Americans joined the war and slowly the tide was turned. In the winter of 1942 and early 1943 the Russians divided the German advance towards Leningrad and the British and Americans pushed Rommel's army back across North Africa from Alexandria. After a prolonged bombing of important German and Italian cities in 1942 and early 1943 and lengthy and bitter naval campaigns for the Atlantic and Mediterranean the Allies landed in Sicily in July 1943 to begin the campaign to recapture the European mainland. The war entered its final more optimistic phase with the Normandy Landings in June 1944. It was their success which decided Herbert and Lilian Lees to plan their son's preparation to become a fit citizen of the better post-war world that was to come after the war.[64]

While the Dunkirk spirit, the desire for post-war reconstruction and the levelling experience of restrictions and the Blitz were widely shared by large sections of the British civilian population, including the families in the study, it was the dreariness of life amid endless restrictions which dominated the wartime experience of the British population. As wartime diaries of such 'average' citizens as Nella Last make clear, life assumed a uniform greyness, punctuated by poignant events like her sons' leaves or the more prosaic salvage, war weapons and savings weeks.[65] Every aspect of life was controlled. Men and women between 18 and 45 had to register for conscription, a new experience for women. Labour was directed and women with no domestic responsibilities were directed to war production in aircraft factories, the Land Army or the Women's Services.

Food was rationed and from the middle of 1941 the weekly ration amounted to a shilling's worth of meat, about half a pound, an ounce of cheese, four ounces of bacon, eight ounces of sugar, two ounces of tea, eight ounces of fats and two ounces of jam.[66] Social life was restricted by the blackout and petrol rationing. These restrictions did reduce the differences between the rich and poor, although they did not create an equality of experience of war. Angus Calder's account *The People's War* suggests that while the East Enders had little alternative to sleeping in the Underground stations and returning to their jobs each day, the more fortunate could escape to safer areas where food and services were more plentiful. As Evelyn Waugh's trilogy *The Sword of Honour* satirises so pointedly, the privileged life of the London Clubs and Society continued, albeit with suitable wartime economies.[67]

But while the war might appear to have produced social levelling and a shared experience of equal sacrifice, perhaps its more important effects were in the rising standards of living it brought. The bland mean rises in living standards during the war produced by social and economic historians hide their very uneven distribution throughout the population, which were clearly demonstrated among the families in the study. For while one or two formerly prosperous families were reduced to penury, among them a London estate agent and a South Wales coal exporter, others who had been struggling became more secure, like the Walkers and the Littles. Yet others, whose salaries remained static like the Leeses, had their incomes reduced by the steep rises in income tax which were imposed to pay for the war. While incomes rose, consumption was damped down by restrictions and high taxes. The debate about post-war social reconstruction, which gathered momentum after the publication of the Beveridge Report in 1942, raised aspirations. Rising incomes provided the means but there were few goods available with which these pressures could be satisfied; the purchase of private education was one of the few that remained.[68]

5 POST-WAR BRITAIN

The period after the war held the promise of sweeping social reforms, born of the desire that the distressed areas of the 1930s should never return, after the apparent equality of sacrifice during the war. The foundations for social reconstruction had been laid during the war with the Beveridge Report and the 1944 Education Act. In the general election in 1945 Churchill was rewarded not for the brilliance of his wartime leadership but for his too-belated acknowledgment of the strength of the desire for reform, and the Labour party won a landslide victory.[69] Clement Attlee's government had a clear mandate to reform health, housing and social security and to implement the 1944 Education Act, but its task was very far from easy. The Dunkirk spirit of expecting little and achieving much had largely evaporated and in its place were both the greater expectations of the electorate and the huge debts incurred during the war to be repaid to America.[70] A programme of legislation was enacted, which brought widespread social reforms in public assistance, health and social welfare. Full employment continued, but a major part of the country's efforts had to be expended not on boosting home consumption of all the goods people had missed during the war, but on exports to the USA. Austerity measures continued, even increased. Bread, never rationed in two world wars, was rationed briefly in 1947.[71]

A financial crisis was precipitated in September 1949 and the pound was devalued from $4.20 to $2.80. For the new young families attempting to create a better life for their children the bitterest pill was the housing shortage, which reached epic proportions in the years immediately after the war, when the birthrate rose steeply. Public resentment at the continuing privations was especially clamorous in the severe winter of 1947 and the fuel crisis which accompanied it. While many families, like the Leeses, had planned a brighter future after the war, the reality sometimes brought resentment and disillusion, as we saw in Mrs Little's case.

Although wartime restrictions began to be lifted in the late 1940s, rationing did not finally disappear until 1954. By the end of the period under review standards of living had begun to rise sufficiently perceptibly for family life and children's upbringing to appear noticeably easier than in previous generations. In 1950 infant mortality fell below 3 per cent for the first time in Britain. The reform of health, welfare and social security aimed to create a comprehensive welfare state based on the principle of universalism. Distinctions between the services available to the rich and the poor were abolished by making them available to all free of any charge.[72]

In education the Butler Act of 1944 abolished fees in grammar schools, raised the school leaving age to 15 and introduced free universal secondary education with transfer at the age of 11. Grammar schools, like Ted Walker's at Steyning, had to close their boarding houses and abolish all tuition fees, admitting pupils solely through open competition in the 11+ examination. Its effect upon the public schools was less direct and apparent. In the short term it filled them with the sons of parents seeking an insurance policy against failure in the 11+ and preservation of the social tone sacrificed by schools like Steyning as a result of the Act. With free universal welfare services and redistributive taxation of incomes to increase standards of living among those on lower incomes, it appeared that the position of the salaried and professional middle classes, who sent their sons to public schools, was deteriorating relatively in the immediate post-war period. Research by A. H. Halsey and associates has shown that the provision of a free service of secondary education made it more attractive to those with higher incomes more able to take full advantage of it, since the most expensive stages, A level and higher education, are those after the minimum school leaving age, when the majority of working-class children leave school. Contrary to the egalitarian purposes of its architects, the 1944 Education Act eroded the protected position of working-class children, who had previously competed for special places at grammar schools open only to children from elementary schools. Halsey's survey of four cohorts of men born between 1912 and 1952 has shown that making all places available to open competition improved the chances of middle-class boys relative to working-class boys in the age cohort which entered secondary education after the 1944 Education Act.[73]

Attempts to make the public schools more egalitarian in the wave of post-war social and educational reform were also frustrated. The financial difficulties of some of the schools before the war and a growing opinion that their exclusive privileges should be made more widely available, led to the appointment of the Fleming Committee which reported in 1944 and suggested two schemes to link them more closely to the maintained sector.[74] Neither scheme was included by Butler in his Education Bill, apparently to avoid opposition from Churchill, and the Labour government also fought shy of what would certainly have proved an extremely contentious issue.[75]

This study covers a very significant period of change in British society and the making of manhood within it, in which three distinct periods may be distinguished, the 1930s, the Second World War, and the immediate post-war period. Significant changes took place in standards of living, occupations, careers, education and especially the demands upon and consequent regulation of the lives of young men. These changes affected the families in the study very closely and it is through their authentic accounts of the way sons became men that the period is viewed.

2

EDUCATING SONS AT ELLESMERE COLLEGE

1 ELLESMERE COLLEGE: NINETEENTH-CENTURY FOUNDATIONS

All the parents in the study sent their sons to Ellesmere College in Shropshire. The foundations of the school rested upon the changing requirements of parents for their sons' education in the second half of the nineteenth century, when professional, commercial and industrial occupations in the middle levels of society between the aristocracy and the working classes were expanding. The reform and growth of the state and the British Empire, greater regulation of the professions and the increasing complexity of commerce and industry fuelled the increasing importance of formal education, examinations and schools for young men in the middle and upper classes.[1] Systematic careers with formal entry qualifications, training and a progression through a hierarchy to a peak in middle life, were being recognised in a growing number of professional and business occupations. Young men, like George Eliot's *Felix Holt*, were encouraged to aspire to careers.[2]

Among the most far-reaching changes were those in the state, where government by a small number of aristocratic 'amateurs' was gradually replaced by an ever-expanding 'professional' government service recruited by competitive examinations.[3] In the upper classes Church of England livings gave way to careers in government service as the preferred future for younger sons. Whereas the acquisition of a Church of England living needed little more than influence or connections, entering government service increasingly meant passing examinations in academic knowledge. By the end of the nineteenth century the need for information about boys' schools, careers and examinations was such that the *Public Schools Yearbook*, started in 1889 with information about 30 schools, contained details of 110 schools and 13 careers by 1910.

In the eighteenth century many of the public schools were in severe decline, racked by disorder, the butt of intense criticism and consequent unpopularity. They were revitalised in the nineteenth century during the reigns of a series of great headmasters, the most famous of whom was Dr Thomas Arnold of Rugby. New boarding houses were built. Disorder was quelled by inaugurating prefect systems. Large and unwieldy lessons to the whole school were replaced by class teaching in separate rooms. Team games were introduced and a new morality emphasising regular attendance at chapel became a distinguishing mark of public school education. The established public schools expanded and new schools were founded, Marlborough near Swindon being one of the first. These new schools added modern subjects to the curriculum. Wellington, in particular, was in the vanguard, due in large part to the strong influence of Prince Albert in its foundation, but older schools resisted these developments strongly. By the 1860s the pressure for reform in education at all social levels led to three Royal Commissions on education for the upper, middle and labouring classes. In 1864 the Clarendon Commission reported on the nine leading public schools, Eton, Harrow, Rugby, Winchester, St Paul's, Merchant Taylor's, Westminster, Charterhouse and Shrewsbury. It applauded both the new and the old, welcoming the improvements which had taken place in housing the boys, the discipline, religious practice and teaching in the schools and further enhancing the prestige of the classical curriculum and the public school traditions of education. The Commission's severest censure was directed not to the schools' education but at the masters' peculation of the schools' endowments. Fulsome praise was heaped upon their role in the making of English gentlemen.

It is not easy to estimate the degree in which the English people are indebted to these schools for the qualities on which they pique themselves most – for their capacity to govern others and control themselves, their aptitude for combining freedom with order, their public spirit, their vigour and manliness of character, their strong but not slavish respect for public opinion, their love of healthy sports and exercise. These schools have been the chief nurseries of our statesmen; in them, and in schools modelled after them, men of all the various classes that make up English society, destined for every profession and career, have been brought up on a footing of social equality, and have contracted the most enduring friendships, and some of the ruling habits of their lives; and they have perhaps the largest share in moulding the character of an English gentleman.[4]

Its views on the curriculum were equally Janus faced. It endorsed the value of the classics as its mainstay while at the same time recommending that 'modern' subjects should be added to them. While the classical languages and literature should continue to hold the principal place in the course of study 'boys should also be taught mathematics, a modern language, science and either drawing or music'. The exclusion of science had narrowed 'unduly and injuriously the mental training of the young and the knowledge, interests and pursuits of men in maturer life',[5] but the introduction of modern subjects must not invade the place of the classics, for the Commission held 'the maintenance of classical literature as the staple of English education, a service which far outweighs the error of having clung to these studies too exclusively'.[6] Science could rather provide an alternative 'education for those who had little aptitude or taste for literature'.[7]

The speed of curricular reform was glacial at Eton, but more rapid in less prestigious schools. Mathematics grew in importance and some schools introduced a modern side, in which boys were prepared for the Army entrance examinations introduced by the Cardwell reforms of 1853. Knowledge of the ancient languages and civilisations, it was held, produced a liberal mind, and was therefore the best preparation for the civilising mission of government at home and abroad. It was the exacting minutiae of translation, parsing and grammatical analysis which preoccupied public school boys. Rupert Wilkinson's analysis of this intellectual style suggests that its absorption with details led to a concern with the tactics of 'muddling through', quite incapable of appreciating wider strategic issues.[8] George Davie has demonstrated that the Scots, whose university education was more 'liberal', in the sense of wider and more philosophical than the English, were at a great disadvantage in the Indian Civil Service Examinations, which were tests of the grammar of the classical languages for English public school boys.[9] While the classical languages maintained their unrivalled position as requirements for university entry and the principal competitive examinations, the public schools continued to serve the needs of upper-class parents by preparing their sons for leading positions in government service.

The changing educational requirements of middle-class parents were investigated by the third Royal Commission on education in the 1860s. Unlike the Clarendon Commission, this Commission also investigated girls' schools. The increasing numbers of 'surplus' women who did not marry and the growing opportunities in women's occupations like teaching had increased the demand among middle-class parents for a better education for their daughters.[10] The Taunton Commission had the formidable task of reporting on some 3,000 private, proprietary and old endowed grammar schools, to which the middle class sent their sons and daughters. The Commission, which reported in 1867, considered girls' and boys' education separately and was very much alive to the growing importance of education and of success in examinations to middle-class parents attempting to ensure successful careers for their sons. Unlike the upper classes, who could bestow wealth upon their offspring, the middle classes 'have only education to look to to keep their sons on a high social level'.[11] The Commission divided the middle classes into three groups according to the career and consequent type and length of education they desired for their sons. The highest stratum, men of substantial independent means, wanted a classical education to 18 for their sons in preparation for university entrance. The second stratum of business and professional men wanted a modern curriculum of languages, mathematics and science until 16 to prepare their sons to enter business, or be articled in a profession. The lower middle classes and superior artisans wanted education to 14 in very good reading, writing and arithmetic.[12]

All three groups had difficulties in finding the kind of education they required at a price they could afford. According to the Commission, the first group 'are compelled to seek . . . the education they require, in boarding schools . . . generally . . . of a very expensive kind'.[13]

The Commissioners conducted extensive investigations in three types of school – grammar, private and proprietary. They found the 789 endowed grammar schools languishing. 'Two hundred years of revolution in men's intellects and children's training, the reformation of religion and the upgrowth of science' had largely passed them by.[14] They were in urgent need of reform. The terms of their endowment, enforced by Lord Eldon's judgment in 1805, had effectively prevented modern influences from touching them. Among the most powerful opponents of the 'modern' curriculum were the schoolmasters, who saw the classics as the only vehicle of a liberal education.

Of the 2,000 private schools, a Sub-Commissioner James Bryce investigated those in Lancashire, where he found that 'honest incompetence and successful charlatanism alternate with good and solid work'.[15] The private schools had little to commend them except that their commercial nature ensured that parents' demands for modern subjects were felt and that the things upon which parents insisted were tolerably certain to be well done.[16] It was their investigations into female education which yielded the most depressing results. The education of the daughters of educated men was largely confined to accomplishments, like music, water colouring and dancing, of little value in the Commission's view. They heard evidence from leaders of the movement for women's education and the founders of proprietary schools and colleges giving girls an intellectual education.[17]

The Commission was complimentary about the small group of proprietary schools. Their foundations sprang from parents' seeking to have their children educated 'in the way they themselves preferred'.[18] According to HMI Joshua Fitch, the most successful were the religious proprietory schools which taught modern subjects, having discarded 'fancy classics' or Greek. They had the added advantage of cheap but good schoolmasters. Among the most impressive of this type of school were those founded by Canon Nathanial Woodard, the last of which was St Oswald's College, Ellesmere. Woodard regarded education as a moral mission. He believed that the middle classes were the moral leaven of society, who, if educated in the right moral principles, would become examples followed by the working classes. He was particularly concerned to rescue gin-palace keepers, but failed to understand the repugnance felt by respectable members of the middle classes towards educating their children alongside those of gin-palace keepers.[19] He was unenthusiastic about girls' education, but his associates were aware of the market and acquired several girls' schools.[20] He was an Anglo-Catholic, who had suffered the opprobrium of his bishop for hearing confession. In his schools the Chaplain and the Headmaster ranked equally, a somewhat impractical arrangement, which had to be modified.[21] They were administered by a religious society, the Society of St Mary and St Nicholas. The low stipends of the masters were augmented by their religious and educational fervour. The schools were graded according to their clientele, and the fees and curriculum appropriate to them. St Oswald's College, Ellesmere, was a second-grade school catering mainly for the farmers and clergy of Shropshire, Cheshire and the Welsh Border counties. It seems likely that the Taunton Commission adopted the idea of grading schools according to the social level of their clientele from Woodard, who was a notable witness before it. The Woodard Foundation continued to acquire schools after the founder's death and in 1929 there were 16 Woodard schools: 8 for girls and 8 for boys. The original distinctions between the grades gradually become less marked as all the boys' schools became members of the Headmasters' Conference.[22]

Canon Woodard opened St Oswald's college, Ellesmere on 8 September 1884 with seventy boys. The fees were only 20 guineas, little more than the cost of food. The college was divided approximately equally between the sons of professional men, businessmen and farmers.[23]

The picture of life at the college, recounted in the early magazines, is one of order, regularity and serious purpose in religion, study and games. The curriculum was a careful combination of traditional and modern studies. Latin and mathematics were its peak but English and modern foreign languages were also important. Competition through examinations was the cardinal organising principle of academic work at the college. The first term broke up on 19 December 1884, after four days of half-yearly examinations. The term ended with an entertainment and farce, after which the Headmaster gave an address. Carefully setting the tone of his new school, he 'mentioned the need of pulling up the standard of learning gradually but steadily in the College and after distributing the Latin form prizes to the winners, he ended by wishing us all a happy vacation in proportion to the energy with which each had worked in the half.'[24] This stress on serious application to study and the importance given to academic success won immediate recognition. In its first year three Oxford men were appointed to examine the school in all aspects of the curriculum. Rev. E. C. Lowe, Provost of the Midland Division and late scholar of Lincoln College, Oxford, examined the Latin, French and Greek. He reported 'the creditable way the examinations . . . have been done speaks well of the school . . . the papers of the higher boys are excellent, the competition close'.[25]

The school was organised into a finely graded hierarchy which emphasised the importance of academic study and examination success. Every half-year a list of college members was published in the magazine, in which each boy was accorded his particular individual status. Three principles determined a boy's place in this ranking – his age, Latin mark and whether he was a fee-paying pupil or a servitor. The latter were domestic servants who received three hours' instruction a day, a salary of £5 a year and a certificate for academic success.[26] The list of servitors was placed after that of fee-paying pupils ranked according to their Latin marks. Pupils were ranked by form, which usually accorded closely with age. Older boys enjoyed high status and younger ones very little. Within the age grading, rank was determined by Latin examination marks. By this means the virtues of competition and serious application to academic work were combined into a hierarchy regulated by educational and social principles. From the outset the college entered its senior pupils for the Oxford local examinations. At this period there was a number of different examination systems attempting to establish themselves nationally as reliable tests of education for employers. The record of 100 per cent pass and of high placings of particular candidates from St Oswald's in these prestigious national examinations was exultantly proclaimed in the college magazines.

'Modern' vocational influences upon the curriculum were strongly felt from the outset. In 1888 shorthand was introduced. On 22 October 1888 the Provost of the Society of St Nicholas presented the Oxford local certificates. After praising the staff and boys on their success, he pointed out the practical value of shorthand.[27] The Provost also gave further official encouragement to modern curricular emphases: in 1889 the subject for his English Essay Prize was Electricity.[28] Facility with the English Language won high praise at St Oswald's. In 1890 the magazine duly reprinted the school's English examiner's fulsome praise. He had found 'the spelling faultless . . .

March's essay on the Age of Elizabeth a model. . . . All candidates used appropriate language and many sentences were almost epigrammatic in their terseness.'[29] It is difficult to gauge the effects of the academic contest upon the boys. Certainly the editor of the magazine in 1890 took it in his stride.

> Tempus adest is the prevailing finding with many of us just now, for is not this the season in which we are wont to see visions and dream of dreams of long lines of examiners, racking their own brains for questions intended in no long time hence to torture ours? Oxford locals loom like a cloud on the horizon and beyond them we sometimes catch glimpses of a pleasant prospect – six weeks holiday. But we anticipate.[30]

It is clear that St Oswald's was preparing boys for the kind of newly emerging careers developing at that period through its modern curriculum, stress on serious study, examinations and competition. The evidence in the school magazines about the careers of early Old Ellesmerians is highy selective, favouring those who had entered universities. Success in other examinations also received favourable notice. In one edition in 1905, news of thirteen old boys is given. Three were at Durham University and three at Oxford. One of the latter passed eighth in the military entrance examination for university candidates. Two were in the medical profession. One was an assayer in a Birmingham firm of refiners, another a railway inspector in Buenos Aires, and another a gunner in the 1st Orkney R. G. Artillery volunteers and the last a lecturer in mining with Durham County Council.[31]

An analysis of boys' intended careers given in the Headmaster's register between 1890 and 1905 suggests a move by sons away from their father's occupations in farming and business towards the professions.[32] These intended careers show the influence of the school in the popularity of Holy Orders and the professions in general.

The early ethos of the school was a blend of religious piety, diligent study and toughness in games. Rugger and cricket, the essential tests of public school manliness, were very important from the school's foundation. In the early days teams from St Oswald's had difficulties finding suitable opponents. The process of establishing relations in the public school club, the most important of which were their sports fixtures, was a slow one. At this period Ellesmere was very much on the fringe of the emerging network of public schools.[33] It was never as obsessed by the games cult as other established schools whose clientele was more secure and less reliant on examinations.

By 1884, when Ellesmere was opened by Canon Woodard, the reform of the grammar schools as a result of the Taunton Commission was well underway. The Endowed Schools Commission was set up in 1869 to examine schemes for the redirection of endowments for systematic secondary education. In this way curricula in endowed grammar schools were widened from elementary Latin and 'less Greek', which had remained their staple from Shakespeare's day, to include modern subjects; standards of teaching were improved, examinations introduced and a larger number of schools began to send pupils to the universities. Procedures of selection and entry to grammar schools were also reformed. Nomination by school governors was abolished and examinations open to competition from elementary school pupils were introduced. A proportion of places were free, awarded on the results of the entry examinations. From the 1880s the notion was introduced of an educational ladder from the elementary schools, through the grammar schools to the universities and professions. Despite these reforms, the distribution of grammar schools, especially those for girls, remained very uneven until well into the twentieth century.[34]

As the nineteenth century progressed the demand for secondary education for both boys and girls rose, and the larger School Boards, set up after the 1870 Education Act to provide elementary education established Higher Grade schools which had a scientific curriculum and were coeducational.[35] 'Secondary' education was a very unevenly distributed market, with public, grammar, higher grade and private schools offering different kinds of education at different prices. The Royal Commission on Secondary Education, chaired by James Bryce, reported in 1895 and showed that in many areas of the country provision was haphazard and deficient. By the beginning of the twentieth century the demand for increasing regulation by the state to replace the competing administrative organisations by a single standard system could no longer be resisted. A period of extremely bitter conflict between all the different bodies providing secondary education preceded the 1902 Education Act. A more uniform system of education was created by giving control of elementary and secondary education to the municipal authorities created in 1888.[36]

The local authorities reformed and expanded existing grammar schools and built new ones where there was no previous provision. Industrial areas, which had grown in the nineteenth century, and girls benefited particularly from these developments. The curriculum of the grammar schools laid down in the 1904 Regulations for Secondary Schools was predominantly literary, modelled on the boys' public schools rather than the coeducational and scientific Higher Grade Schools. Not less than 8 hours were to be spent on English, geography, history and language, if one language was taken and 10½ hours if two were taken. Permission of the Board of Education had to be obtained if Latin was omitted. Not less than 7½ hours was to be devoted to mathematics and science, in which both practical and theoretical teaching was to be provided. The majority of this time was devoted to maths. Consequently science remained comparatively under-developed in many grammar schools. By 1929 a considerable expansion of grammar schools for boys and girls had taken place and municipal authorities had established themselves in the organisation and control of secondary education.[37]

The expansion of boys' and girls' grammar schools created a large and complex hierarchy of secondary schools dominated by the boys' public schools with the nine 'great' schools at its peak. The public schools had resisted any attempt at control following the Clarendon Commission by forming the Head Masters' Conference, a highly effective political pressure group, in 1869. As John Honey has so convincingly demonstrated, by the end of the nineteenth century the public schools formed a closely knit network in which the most important links were inter-schools sports fixtures. From the turn of the century the growing body of grammar schools increasingly followed their examples in curriculum and games.[38]

The Great War was a watershed in the history of British society and the public schools which had trained the officers and men who fought and died in it. For the public schools it was both a celebration of the heroism and leadership of the young officers who had led their country to victory in the bloodiest conflict the world had ever seen and the unleashing of a wave of bitter criticism of the unthinking self-sacrifice their upbringing and education had induced.[39]

There were 658 Old Ellesmerians who served in the First World War, of whom a third were killed or wounded. E. R. Jenkins Menlove was one 'high spirited and valiant man . . . of whom his old school should be proud'. He had taken Holy Orders after graduation from Jesus College, Oxford, and had a parish in North Wales where he preached lengthy sermons in Welsh. At the outbreak of war he was refused permission to join up. He immediately 'enlisted as a Tommy, went out on an early draft and was killed three weeks later'.[40]

2 ELLESMERE COLLEGE: FROM THE GREAT WAR TO 1950

One of the most significant developments which affected the education and careers of young men from the Great War onwards was the slowly strengthening linkage between educational qualifications and careers. An important step in this process was taken in 1918, when the School Certificate and Higher School Certificate examinations were introduced, thus increasing the central control of the large number of examining bodies which had grown up in the nineteenth century. This led to greater uniformity of standards and reliability for employers, universities and others using examination results as a means of assessing individual ability.[41]

Two important concepts were enshrined in the new regulations, that of a liberal education and of graded advanced study for university entrance. Subjects were grouped, and to obtain the School Certificate a candidate had to gain five passes in certain groups including English language and mathematics. Seven credits gained matriculation exemption which satisfied university entrance requirements.[42] This attempt at standardisation found ready acceptance with schools, universities, employers, parents and professional bodies. Entry into more and more professions required 'a good School Certificate'. Sixth forms were introduced in the public and grammar schools to prepare pupils for these examinations, which acquired the status of a 'ticket' giving admission to the next stage of systematic careers for boys and men in certain occupations.[43]

The gradual reform and introduction of statutory control in different professions since 1850 ensured that by 1929 most professions had minimal ages and educational qualifications for entry and a considerable training period. Training varied from the lengthy part-time courses in banking and accountancy to five years' university education needed in medicine. In some, promotion also depended on further examination success, as in the prestigious fellowships of the medical profession, or the successive grades in the Civil Service. Most were regulated by a council of senior members of the profession.[44]

By the 1920s the course of careers in a large number of middle-class occupations was sufficiently regular and systematic for a literature of careers guides to develop. In 1926 *The Problem of a Career Solved by Thirty Six Men of Distinction* was published.[45] It described the entry, training, remuneration, promotion, career prospects and attractions of a wide variety of openings in the armed services, business, professions, and science. It was written with considerable authority by men who had attained eminence in their fields and dedicated, rather curiously, to the Prince of Wales, who did not have that particular problem to solve. Table 2 shows the extent to which the thirty-six careers described in the guide had acquired particular professional characteristics. Business and farming were the two major areas open to those who wished to avoid the constraints of careers with competitive examinations and promotion ladders. The most important characteristics of all the careers stressed by the writers was the possibility of an independent and secure source of income, after which, service to the community was undoubtedly seen as conferring respect and social status. 'It should be the duty and pride of every successful man to assist others less fortunately placed and there are many ways in which a solicitor can and ought to help those who have been unhappy in their lives,' wrote Sir George Lewis on the satisfactions of a career as a solicitor.[46] Because service to the community led more certainly to a respected position within it, the professions were in many ways more attractive than business and farming. Alfred Salmon, Chairman of Lyons Corner Shops, was painfully aware of these niceties.

> . . . although some professions, such as that of doctor or surgeon, may appear more directly of service to the individual, it has to be remembered that the very life of a community, particularly of the present-day English community depends on commerce, so that I think no one needs to be deterred from entering the business world by fear that he will not be serving his fellow men.[47]

In choosing a career three factors were important, the size and source of income, the respect gained by service to the community and adventure. By the 1920s, the Church, once so favoured by younger sons, had to appeal solely to a spirit of self-sacrifice and service for recruits to the priesthood. The Bishop of London in his contribution to the guide bemoaned the failure of Oxford and Cambridge eights, whom he entertained before the boat race, to enter the church 'in contrast with many famous old oars in the past' 'knowing the masses of young men and boys to be won to God in London alone, where athletic prowess is so great an asset in arranging Saturday games and in winning preliminary confidence as a basis for higher things later, . . .' he confessed he 'coveted that mass of young manhood to join in the great tug-of-war between the forces of good and the forces of evil.'[48]

The army, on the other hand, offered travel and adventure. The Secretary of State for War recommended it boldly:

> The greatest attraction of the army is probably that, for a young man not too well endowed with this world's goods, it provides an unrivalled opportunity for travelling, adventure and sport. In the majority of professions the means and opportunity of seeing the world come too late, if at all. Life is short and the world is wide. He who would know the cities and races of men, and would see strange lands under strange skies, should do so young. To the young they can give so much more in the way of experience and enjoyment than to the weary globe trotter on retirement, who probably does not go to the places he always wanted to see, because his health won't stand the heat or the cold, or because his imaginative faculties have atrophied, or because, worst of all, he fears that they haven't atrophied, and that he will merely add to his store of regrets for what he has missed in life. It may be tedious to the Colonel's friends to hear the oft-reiterated story of the demise of the celebrated tiger, but, after all, the Colonel did shoot the tiger, whereas his friends have probably never had an opportunity of shooting any carnivora larger than a stoat.[49]

While the sons in the study did not always dream of shooting tigers, adventure always loomed larger in their plans than those of their

Table 2 Bureaucratic characteristics of thirty-six careers in 1926

	INCOME		EXAMS OR ENTRY QUALIFICATIONS	FORMAL TRAINING & EXAMS	PROFESSIONAL ASSOCIATION OR REGISTER	PROMOTION LADDER
	Fees	Stipend Profits or Salary				
Navy commissions		✓	✓	✓		✓
Army commissions		✓	✓	✓		✓
Metropolitan police		✓	✓	✓		✓
Civil Service – Admin		✓	✓	✓		✓
Exec		✓	✓	✓		✓
Local government		✓	✓			✓
Social service		✓				
Politics and public life						
Church of England priesthood		✓	✓	✓		✓
Roman Catholic priesthood		✓	✓	✓		✓
Non-conformist churches ministry		✓	✓	✓		
Law: the Bar	✓		✓	✓	✓	
solicitor	✓		✓	✓	✓	✓
Medicine and surgery	✓		✓	✓	✓	✓
Dental surgery	✓		✓	✓	✓	
Veterinary science	✓		✓	✓	✓	
Science		✓	✓	✓		✓

Teaching	✓		✓	✓		✓
Art: drawing and illustration		✓				
Music						
Architecture	✓		✓	✓	✓	
The stage						
Journalism						
Literature	✓					
Accountancy		✓	✓	✓	✓	✓
Banking		✓	✓	✓	✓	
Insurance						✓
The Stock Exchange		✓				
Business		✓				
The Dominions						
Engineering	✓	✓	✓	✓	✓	✓
Marine engineering	✓		✓	✓		
Farming	✓					✓
Merchant marine	✓		✓	✓		✓

parents, who favoured professional careers requiring educational qualifications. In the period between the two world wars, Ellesmere responded in a number of ways to this increasing pressure towards fitting its pupils to enter careers. In 1927 a sixth form was established to cater for the increasing number of boys staying at school to gain matriculation exemption and Higher School Certificate.[50] From the years immediately before the First World War the public schools were the subject of bitter criticisms, the most famous of which were Alex Waugh's *Loom of Youth*,[51] laying bare the philistinism, obsession with 'footer' and the honour of the house, and Robert Graves *Goodbye to All That*[52] castigating exploitative sexual relations and denigration of women.

In the inter-war period reforms were introduced in a number of public schools to widen the curriculum, reduce the importance of games and 'civilise' relations between boys. A famous experiment was introduced by A. H. Gresham at Holt School in Norfolk to promote friendships between boys of different ages and houses.[53] Robert Birley, appointed Headmaster of Charterhouse at 38 in 1935, had radical sympathies, learned at Rugby and under A. D. Lindsay at Balliol College, Oxford. He immediately made chapel voluntary and introduced several other reforms to give boys greater freedom. Breaking down the insularity of houses and age groups proved more difficult and took long and subtle diplomacy.[54]

Ellesmere College also appointed a new young Headmaster in 1935, Rev. R. A. Evans Prosser. He was not, in any sense, a radical like Birley. He had impeccable Woodard connections and qualifications, having previously served as an assistant master at Ellesmere and prepared for ordination during his period as Headmaster of Ashburton Grammar School in Devon. Although at this time the habit of Headmasters of the cloth was rapidly dying in other public schools, it remained strong in the Woodard schools. It was a crucial time in the history of the school and a momentous appointment. Ellesmere, like other independent and public schools at this period, was struggling with the effects of the economic depression. Rev. T. H. Hedworth, Headmaster from 1910 to 1927, and Rev. Dr A. V. Billen, who succeeded him from 1927 to 1935, had continued to expand the buildings and number of boys and to raise the academic standard to that required by the Head Masters' Conference. Nonetheless the school's finances were far from secure. Evans Prosser had previously joined the staff under Hedworth as an assistant classics master in 1924. He left a reputation as a 'strenuous' rugger player and coach and a 'dashing' tennis and bridge player.[55] Under his tutelage the results in the Oxford locals in Latin and Greek improved immediately. 'Voluntary' Latin classes were introduced on Monday and Thursday lunchtimes and 'boys who had hitherto led unmolested classical lives found themselves overnight to be "blithering idiots with as much chance of passing School Certificate as a ping pong ball has in Hades" '.[56]

In 1932 Evans Prosser became Headmaster of Ashburton Grammar School and in just three years he put this school on the map and prepared himself for ordination.[57] He was well acquainted with the difficulties facing Ellesmere and the kind of changes required when he was appointed Headmaster at the comparatively young age of 38. He immediately embarked upon an ambitious building programme. A large new dormitory, changing rooms, squash courts and science laboratories were all completed before the outbreak of war in September 1939. Evans Prosser was keenly aware of the school's market position in competition with local grammar schools and fully understood the importance of careers and examinations to the parents he was trying to attract. The new science laboratories were particularly important in this regard. He told the Old Ellesmerians at a dinner on 26 November 1938, in the Grosvenor Hotel, Manchester, that 'the new science building would make Ellesmere one of the best equipped schools in the country and would encourage boys to stay on and take up medicine and biology. The new dormitory would increase the capacity of the school.' This was particularly important given, as he reminded the audience 'the opposition of the luxurious secondary schools, which were being built out of the rates'.[58] He offered exhibitions if parents undertook to keep their sons at the school until they sat the School Certificate. His strategy succeeded. Indeed it is for careful financial management that Evans Prosser may have earned his most enduring reputation. In the years before the war the number of pupils expanded. The Blitz and the blackout and the consequent disruption of the grammar schools and public schools on the south coast rapidly completed the Headmaster's task. In 1942 the school secretary was able to write with some pride to the parent of an Old Boy 'The School is full these days and for a change is able to make a little profit to pay off its large debts accumulated in the past when we were spending money to make the school into a proper and complete Public School.'[59]

To the men who were boys during his Headmastership Evans Prosser was an aloof godlike figure with a tremendous presence. He was a big, physically intimidating man known as 'Beef' or 'The Ox'. He played squash for Shropshire and regularly beat any boys he played in his earlier years as Headmaster. Roy Carver 'was terrified' when he played him because he was so 'large and ruthless' and used his 'young opponent as a punchbag'. But it stood Carver in good stead later when he himself became a county squash player.[60]

'Beef' was a great walker, striding out alone, often surprising boys on their enforced rambles through the Shropshire lanes on Sunday afternoons. He was a keen disciplinarian, keeping a stern hold on the smokers and pranksters who showed their daring and insouciance by flouting authority. One day he caught David Parton and his friends smoking at 'Hill 60', a knoll two miles from the school. Parton and his friend owned up and were gated; all the rest were beaten.[61]

Before the end of the war in 1944, a new Education Act was passed, making free secondary education from the age of 11 universally available for the first time. The immediate effects of the 1944 Education Act were the abolition of fees in county grammar schools and the opening of all the places in these schools to free competition from children in the former elementary schools. This development transformed the market for parents attempting to educate their sons for professional careers by abolishing the advantage previously held by those who could afford the low fees charged for day boys at grammar schools. It made their competitive position for grammar school places more similar to the large majority of parents in the population who previously could not afford the fees, uniform and other costs of keeping their children at a grammar school. After the 1944 Education Act all children had to sit the same competitive examination upon which a place at grammar school depended. If this competition was to be avoided parents had only one alternative – independent schools, whose fees were usually very much higher than those charged at the grammar schools before the 1944 Education Act.[62]

What the blackout and the Blitz had begun in sending boys to Elles-mere, the 1944 Education Act continued, for after the Act the school was full to overflowing. Some parents had grown affluent during the war; others were worried by the effects of the new Education Act and wanted to ensure their sons' futures.

3 WHY PARENTS SENT THEIR SONS TO ELLESMERE COLLEGE

(i) The market

For most of the period between 1929 and 1950 the provision of free education by the state was limited to elementary schooling up to the age of 14, which did not provide access to the kinds of careers sought by these parents and as they could afford it they sent their sons elsewhere. The implementation of the 1944 Education Act in 1947 did nothing to ease these parents' worries. Not only did it appear to increase the competition for grammar school places, but the free secondary education provided for the majority of children was in secondary modern schools, which children left at 15 without taking any public examinations.[63] It did not give access to the careers which these parents sought for their sons.

During most of the period under review these parents' choice of secondary education for their sons may best be described as a series of very localised markets in which public, grammar and private schools, all of which charged fees, competed for pupils. Ellesmere College competed as a boarding school in a number of markets. During the Second World War, the school developed a national market but in more normal times, Cheshire, Shropshire, Staffordshire, Manchester, mid and North Wales were the areas from which most of its pupils came. The provision of secondary schools for boys varied greatly within this region. That within north Shropshire itself gives some indication of the choice before parents between 1929 and 1950.

At the peak of the local educational hierarchy was Shrewsbury School, one of the nine 'great' schools investigated by the Clarendon Commission in 1864; it had a national market from a higher social class than Ellesmere. In 1932, when Ellesmere College was first admitted to the Head Masters' Conference, Shrewsbury School had all the marks of an august and long-established educational institution, whose boys came from the higher ranks throughout the land. The school consisted of nine houses containing altogether 477 boys.

47

Entrance was always to a house, not to the school, the entrance fee for which was £67 and the annual boarding fee was £180. There were 37 assistant masters with degrees from Oxford and Cambridge. Above the fourth form the school was divided into classical and modern sides depending on which languages were taken. There were also science, history and maths sides. Special arrangements were made for candidates for the Navy, Army and Air Force examinations. The school's academic standing was signalled by its numerous entrance scholarships and the scholarships and exhibitions tenable at the Oxford and Cambridge Colleges and the long list of prizes and honours published in the *Public Schools Yearbook*. Nowhere was its superiority more apparent than in sport. There were 290 boys who were members of the Boat Club in 1933. Rowing cemented its social and educational superiority in the exclusive network of relationships between Oxford, Cambridge and Henley.[64]

There were a number of lesser Head Masters' Conference Schools in the area. Wrekin College, founded in 1880, charged 150 gns in the 1930s. In contrast to the entry for Shrewsbury School the description in the Public Schools' Yearbook stressed careers and public examinations. A distinguishing mark of this school's facilities and curriculum were the specially designed science laboratories in which 'the accommodation and science teaching are second to none'.[65] The school had a staff of 24 graduates, and 316 boys accommodated in 7 houses. The provision of endowed grammar schools in this area, like most others, was patchy and their historical fortunes mixed. Adam's Grammar School at Wem, founded in 1650 by Sir Thomas Adams, a London draper and native of Wem, had 88 boys in 1930.[66]

To the east was another old foundation, with the same name but a more self-confident history – Adams Grammar School, Newport, which had 260 boys in 1926. In 1935 it was admitted to the Head Masters' Conference and in 1943 there were approximately 300 boys in attendance, including 50 boarders. There were two courses: academic – English, French, Latin, maths, physics and chemistry; and empirical – music and art, handicrafts and practical everyday science, maths, French, English, history and geography. Fees were £10 per annum for day boys and £4 per annum for those living within 5 miles of Newport. For parents it had the very strong attractions of a choice of curricula and low fees. After the 1944 Education Act the school became voluntary aided and the fees were abolished.[67]

These endowed schools formed the oldest established secondary provision in the area. By 1929 secondary schools founded by Shropshire County Council, following the 1902 Act, were well established. County Grammar Schools had been built in some of the areas without secondary provision and control of grammar schools which were languishing, like Adams Grammar School, Wem, had been assumed by the County Council. Four boys' secondary schools were founded in the north of the county at Bishops Castle, Market Drayton, Oswestry and Whitchurch. In 1930 they had 86, 80, 169 and 148 pupils respectively, while Priory County School for boys in Shrewsbury had 245 pupils. In the same year the total number of secondary school places provided by the County Council for boys and girls in Shropshire was 3,120, and there were 500 boys at Shrewsbury School paying fees of £150 a year.

The fees in the county secondary schools in Shropshire were set at £10 per annum in 1921 and in 1926 a new scheme of free places and scholarships was established. Free places were awarded to children from elementary schools as a result of a qualifying examination at the elementary school followed by a competitive examination at the secondary school and an oral test in history, geography and general knowledge. In 1926 1,422 pupils entered the qualifying examination and 662 proceeded successfully to the competitive examination from which 36 free places were awarded. Twelve minor scholarships were also available in districts where no secondary schools had been built, of which Ellesmere was one. Serious overcrowding in the county's secondary schools was reported.[68]

As Olive Banks has shown, in her national study of secondary education after 1902, the development of alternative forms of secondary education to the grammar schools was slow.[69] Shropshire was no exception to this historical generalisation. Secondary education meant an academic education which prepared for university and the curricula in county grammar schools was predominantly literary. At this period science was very poorly developed in county grammar schools. Education authorities measured success by the number of pupils who entered university, rather than by the proportion of the school-age population receiving secondary education. Indeed Shropshire boasted that by 1928 10 per cent of its secondary leavers went to university, which was at least twice the national average of under 5 per cent. This was clearly a function of the social background of the tiny fraction of children, 1.2 per cent in 1928, who received secondary education in the county.[70] In Shropshire the vocational forms of secondary education suggested in the Hadow Report of 1926 had to await the financial arrangements made ten years later in the 1936 Education Act. Twelve senior schools had been established in the county by 1939.[71] The war intervened, curtailing any further developments of this kind in secondary education. Before the Second World War, therefore, Shropshire was 'in many ways behind the times in educational matters' and secondary education was very severely limited both in the number of places and in the type of curriculum.[72]

Though the county was a safe area, there was disruption caused not by air raids but by refugees from them. The first evacuation hastily carried out in early September 1939 provided for the immediate movement of mothers and children from the heavily industrialised evacuation areas of London, Liverpool, Newcastle and Birmingham to safe rural areas. The effects were felt mainly by elementary schools, which were closed in the evacuation areas. The much smaller number of secondary schools were paired, each school using the building for half a day and attempting to acquire alternative accommodation for the other half of the day. The strains involved were considerable. Priory Boys' High School in Shrewsbury with accommodation for 250 was called upon to share its accommodation with the 343 boys of Holt Grammar School in Liverpool. The independent schools in the county fared somewhat better. Ellesmere received pupils from the Channel Islands and then half of Lancing College, billeted on the sports pitches in marquees for a month in the summer of 1940. The consequent over-crowding produced a rash of infectious diseases and greatly intensified the problem of finding adequate food for the school, suddenly and briefly almost doubled in size.[73] The disruption caused by the war at Ellesmere was mild compared with other schools. A survey conducted in 1940 showed that secondary schools in Brighton spent 18 per cent and inland Kent 14.2 per cent of their time in air raid shelters. In the judgment of P. H. J. H. Gosden educational standards fell during the war, but the effects were very unevenly spread, being greater in elementary schools than in the public and grammar schools and greater in London and the south coast than the north.[74]

During the attacks on Liverpool and Merseyside bombers passed over Ellesmere and jettisoned some bombs nearby, but the school was able to continue its work much as before with a minimum of disruption. It enlarged its market considerably during the war and when it ended parents' uncertainty about the effects of the 1944 Education Act continued to fill the school and a waiting list was opened.

(ii) Parents' philosophy

Apart from the unusual circumstances of the war and the immediate post-war period, the reasons why parents sent their sons to Ellesmere rather than keeping them at home at a local grammar school are intriguing. Parents wanted their sons to gain qualifications and enter careers; they wanted character building, 'sportsmen in the true sense of the word' in Herbert Lees's words, and they wanted discipline and order, all of which were available at the grammar schools at a fraction of the cost and without sending their sons away from home. For these parents a public school like Ellesmere had certain notable advantages compared with a local grammar school which made it worth the sacrifice. Education at a boarding school meant complete control and supervision of a boy's life and of the influences upon him. It was a much more effective instrument of intellectual attainment and character moulding than a day school. In a boarding school every minute of a boy's day could be timetabled and used effectively. No time was wasted in travelling and habits of order and discipline were instilled through an all-embracing daily routine.[75] Many parents and schoolmasters believed that boys were inherently lazy and had to be driven. One Headmaster of a grammar school commending the parents' decision to send one of his boys to Ellesmere remarked 'the boy shirks drudgery work and the constant supervision of a boarding school education would therefore be ideal'.[76] Domestic concerns and issues could divert a boy from his prime task of preparing for manhood and a career. In his School Certificate year Mrs Little wrote several times to the Headmaster about the importance of making her son study hard at school and the difficulty of impressing upon him the importance of his studies for his future career.[77]

Boarding schools, especially those as isolated as Ellesmere, also had the advantage of confining all the influences upon a boy's character to those of school, insulating him from competing and possibly adverse influences of alternative models of boyhood and masculinity within his home and community, such as the 'elementary school manners' carefully eradicated from the tone and bearing of one of his protegés by a preparatory school headmaster.[78]

Public schools were not only a more effective means of education and socialisation than grammar schools, they also embodied the most prestigious models of masculinity and its making. Historically secondary education was the education of boys. The old foundations, both public and grammar were boys' schools, whose purpose was to educate boys to become men. In the unreformed public schools of the nineteenth century boys' characters had been developed outside the classroom unrestrained by the later rigours of games and prefects. Rebellion, bullying, fearsome ordeals, flogging, hunting and poaching all flourished as the apprenticeship of unbridled boyhood for later manly sports and pursuits. While the radicals railed against these excesses in the *Edinburgh Review*, parents sent their sons to learn how to survive this veritable trial by fire.[79]

The rise of the cult of athleticism and the reform of the public schools from the 1830s introduced a new conception of masculinity and ways of inducing it, in which complete freedom outside the classroom was replaced by frenetic organisation and control. The new ideal of manhood which evolved from mid-century was about winning at team games and the 'perfection of muscular activity', cloaked by complete concealment of emotions. It was inculcated by a school regime in which boys' leisure was 'ruthlessly timetabled and supervised'.[80] The games cult reached its zenith in the period before the First World War and declined from the 1920s onwards, mainly due to the continuing rise in the importance of examinations and careers.[81] After the Great War the model of masculinity in the public schools associated with the games cult was replaced by the ideal of service to the community. Cyril Norwood, Headmaster of Harrow, its principal apologist, placed its roots in mediaeval chivalry and its codes of knightly honour with which public school boys were imbued in chapel and on the games field. Religion gave a boy a desire to live rightly and decently and 'not to let his school down'[82] and in team games he learned to subordinate his individual will to the 'best service to the team' and 'never on any account to show the white feather'.[83]

While the development of girls' and women's education from the latter part of the nineteenth century and the expansion of the grammar schools during the same period produced a more complex hierarchy of secondary schools and types of secondary education, the public schools and their model of the making of masculinity remained at its peak. In 1938 Virginia Woolf reviewed the half-century since women had had access to education similar to that of their fathers and brothers, and thus to the professions, and concluded that women's progress had been painfully slow and their achievements meagre. Secondary and university education and professional careers remained strongly dominated by the male values of the public schools and ancient universities.[84]

The new psychological ideas about children's upbringing which were becoming more widely known in the inter-war period also emphasised this model of masculinity, and the necessary differentiation of boys' and girls' interests and education. Boys and girls were seen as rigidly stereotyped objects 'the boy' and 'the girl', rather than heterogeneous groups of individuals with an infinite variety of ways of developing and potential interests. One populariser of Freud, Hugh Crichton Miller, Director of the Tavistock Institute, described four phases of development in *The New Psychology and the Parent* in 1922.

The first was the mother phase which lasted from birth until 7 or 8 for the boy and a year longer for the girl. Both then passed through the 'school phase' and the 'father phase' but the order and length of these phases differed. The girl passed through the school phase between 9 and 15 and the father phase betwen 15 and 18, whereas the boy experienced the father phase first between 8 and 12 and the school phase between 12 and 18. Both passed into the mating phase after 18. The girl's emotional development was dominated by her maternal instinct and preparation for marriage, whereas the boy's development emphasised independence. As Crichton Miller at his simplest explained it:

> We are familiar with the phraseology of the little boy at this (the mother) stage – 'When I am a big man I shall have a motor car like Daddy'. That is the first step towards the ideal of independence. . .[85]

Both Norwood and Crichton Miller believed that it was the value of the prefect system as a training for leadership and independence, which had established the superiority of the public school model of boys' character training. To Crichton Miller the prefect system was

> the great genius of our public-school system, and of our Anglo Saxon temperament . . . here . . . in a blundering and intuitive way, we have taken the psychologically right line . . . our public school system has never been successfully copied, because . . . the authorities ultimately failed to trust the big boy.[86]

At the outset of our period the education of boys in public schools was the dominant and most prestigious model of secondary education. They were all-male institutions in which boys were made into men by men and other boys: a masculine world dedicated to the transmission of a long-established tradition of masculinity in a man's world.

The oral evidence suggests that at Ellesmere parents, masters and boys had differing ideals of masculinity and its making. Parents and masters emphasised careers and academic qualifications, whereas boys placed greater emphasis upon adventure, camaraderie and games.

Between 1929 and 1950 the more or less equal emphases on academic work, chapel and games persisted. The school attached great significance to passing School Certificate and the teaching, very mixed in quality, some of it boring and mechanical, achieved this for most boys, although some men who had been placed in C forms felt their self-confidence had been sapped by being in the 'duffers' class', where masculinity took the form of daring pranks and defiance of the school ban on smoking.[87] The ideal models of masculinity for the boy culture of the school were the games captains, explorers like Scott, Shackleton and Oates and later wartime heroes, especially the Royal Air Force. Masculinity was about physical fitness, courage and daring. Every informant mentioned the importance of games and all except one enjoyed sport at school. One Old Ellesmerian mentioned by a number of informants was J. C. Brunt, one of the school's VCs. A contemporary described him as a sportsman, not particularly bright but 'bags of guts', 'from humble background, an example of what a public school could do for a boy'.[88] Brunt won the Military Cross and Victoria Cross in Italy in 1943. He was killed a week later by a stray mortar. Later Old Ellesmerians numbered him among their heroes. The oral informants in this study evinced mixed feelings about their education at Ellesmere. They were glad of their qualifications – as one solicitor put it 'Ellesmere gave me a leg up into the professions'[89] – but many resented the compulsory chapel, the fagging and beating by prefects. Some aspects of the masculine toughening process, the compulsory team games, poor food, spartan conditions, especially the open and very public lavatories, were considered by some to be unnecessarily harsh.[90] All valued their education at the school, particularly mentioning independence.

Separate education for boys and girls was an unquestioned assumption in the Hadow, Spens and Norwood reports on Secondary Education during the period.[91] Bringing up a son was considered of such importance and wide general interest that a number of men with less orthodox views published their ideas on the subject. While they criticised the public school model they fully endorsed the segregation of the sexes and the supreme importance of making boys into men. Their main purpose was to substitute a companionable father for the despotic style of the public schools.

One of the most interesting of these critics was the popular novelist Warwick Deeping. He was critical of both public and county schools. In his novel *Sorrel and Son*, published in 1927, the tasks of bringing up a son to his true stature, to become a member of a respected profession, is the life's work and sacred duty of his father.[92]

Sorrell is a worthy officer from the Great War who manages by hard work, thrift and application to rise from hall porter to director of a chain of hotels and thereby carry out his mission in life to educate his son Kit to become a Harley Street surgeon. Deeping's model of the ideal man is one for whom work and independence are his most important aims, after which comes a true and honourable character. The main purposes in Kit's upbringing are to ensure his success in the long series of educational hurdles to a Fellowship of the Royal College of Surgeons, to provide him with suitable male models for the character of a professional man and to prevent damage from dangerous contrary influences.

Mentors and models of masculinity are provided by Sorrell himself and by an eccentric clergyman and tutor. Brief periods at the town school and a public school end because their models of manhood are derived from the rigidities of the English social class system. The boys at the town school dub Kit a 'collar and cuffs' boy and they don't 'fight clean', when honour between boys demands fisticuffs. The south-coast public school demonstrates the shallowness and superficiality of the English class structure, which Sorrell wants Kit to transcend, when the Headmaster asks Sorrell to withdraw his son because his position (as a hall porter rather than a gentleman of means) would compromise the school. Kit returns to his tutor, a true Oxford polymath and a blue who prepares him successfully for Oxford and teaches him to box. Beside the English class system the other main danger to Sorrell's attempts to create a 'new model man', whose main virtue is his dedication to honest and respected work, is the influence of women. Sorrell, a modern, comradely father, rather than a remote Victorian paterfamilias, counsels his son in friendly chats. Sex is, of course, a natural desire of men, but women all too often ensnare a man either into luxury and self-indulgence, like Kit's mother threatens to do, or into babies and domestic cares, the fate of Kit's best friend. But the patient work and eminently worthy model of Sorrell in bringing up his son is rewarded and the book closes with his death, under the care of his son and soothed by his daughter-in-law, a new career woman completely tamed by Kit, who has no interest in babies.

Another man whose account of the ideal upbringing of a putative son differed from the accepted orthodoxies of the 1930s was Oliver Baldwin, son of the Conservative Prime Minister, and himself a Labour Member of Parliament. He planned a wide acquaintance with social classes and cultures other than his own for his imaginary son. Oliver Baldwin eschewed the public schools, unlike his father, whose aim in choosing his cabinet was to make it Harrovian. His son chose a combination of local municipal school, French Lycée and foreign travel for his unborn son, with himself as mentor and model.[93]

While Deeping and Baldwin sought to substitute benevolent paternal direction for the baleful influences of the public schools and British class structure, only Virginia Woolf considered the effects of the continuing dominance of the prevailing values of masculinity and patriarchy in British society in the late 1930s. Contemplating the increasing likelihood of a second European holocaust in 1938, she believed that the continuing domination of education and the professions by competitive male values hastened war. In education independent thought was stifled and when men joined the professions they pursued their careers competitively for financial gain. She encouraged women to be financially independent but remain outside the male values of the education system and professions in opposition to the 'possessiveness, pugnacity and greed of the professions'; thus exercising their independence of mind by trying to abolish the inhumanity and folly of war.[94]

4 SUMMARY

For the middle classes bringing up sons was about making boys into men, whether in the public schools or their alternatives. The evidence adduced from parents in this study shows that they wanted an intellectual education, discipline and character training for their sons, which would enable them to enter careers leading to respected social positions. The public school model of boys' upbringing, combining academic education, organised games, house and prefect systems was the most prestigious during the period under review. It had many critics, who attacked its barbarity and snobbishness. Reforming heads like Birley and Gresham sought to civilise the public school system. The orthodoxies of separate education for boys and girls and of the domination of secondary education by men and masculinity was supported by the deeply institutionalised gender segregation and male domination of the family and occupational structure. Fathers' influence was one of the most important and lasting in the process of making boys into men. Critics of the public schools like Warwick Deeping and Oliver Baldwin believed companionable fathers were more suitable mentors and moulders of their sons' intellects and characters than the paterfamilias and public school bloods of the Victorian and Edwardian periods.

Parents who decided to send their sons to Ellesmere College chose this school from a changing market of schools, resembling a social and educational hierarchy, with the 'great schools' like Shrewsbury School at the top and village all-age elementary schools at the bottom. Ellesmere was among the lower echelons of public schools, admitted to the Head Masters' Conference at the beginning of our period. Successive

Headmasters attempted to expand and consolidate its position by meeting the demands of parents, seeking an education for their sons which would enable them to enter suitable careers. The Second World War improved its market position nationally and the 1944 Education Act ensured the continued success of the school under its vigorous Headmaster, Rev. R. A. Evans Prosser, appointed in 1935.

3

THE MAINSTAY OF THE SCHOOL

1 MODELS OF MASCULINITY

The largest single group of parents who sent their sons to Ellesmere College between 1929 and 1950 had their own businesses in Manchester, Liverpool, the Potteries and surrounding rural counties, within reach of the school. They came from a very wide variety of backgrounds and ran many different types of enterprise, including a bakery, a zoo and an engineering factory. Their business fortunes fluctuated wildly, especially during the war, when some, like builders or engineers producing on a cost-plus-10 per cent basis for the armed services, prospered. At the same time others, like a coal exporter in South Wales, whose markets disappeared with the fall of France in 1940, found it impossible to survive and withdrew their sons from the school. While the rise in incomes did enable a number of parents to send their sons to Ellesmere during or after the war, the government held down profits by a punitive tax of 100 per cent. Because of scandals in the First World War, excessive war profits were a very delicate issue and 'profiteers', 'black marketeers' and 'spivs' were regularly caricatured in *Punch*. Nowhere was a father's social position of greater interest than in his son's boarding school. At Ellesmere at the turn of the century the first questions asked of a new boy were, 'Where do you come from?' 'What is your father?' 'Does your mother wash?' 'Got any tuck?' and 'Why don't you get your hair cut?'[1] and the oral reminiscences of informants suggest that thirty or forty years later the curiosity of new boys still centred on other boys' social backgrounds, their families and previous schools.

Public school education, at least in the 'great schools', prepared the boys for public service and the professions, disdaining industry and 'trade'. Ellesmere also laid little emphasis on entrepreneurial skills useful in running a business. W. D. Gallie attended a northern public school in the inter-war period where the largest group also came from business backgrounds. He believed that 'the most general demand of the average parent was that the school should provide whatever sort of education would help his sons to maintain the status in life which he had attained, and to maintain it slightly more easily and more securely than he could.'[2] He argued that parents were persuaded to accept the ideals of public school education, which was hardly an obvious preparation for business, because education for leadership served as a myth rehearsed on speech days to comfort mothers and provide 'some kind of heroic ideal' to which fathers aspired for their sons.[3]

One Old Ellesmerian businessman entering his son for the school in the euphoria at the end of the war told the Headmaster,

> in these and future times, which are full of interesting and unknown possibilities it is my opinion that provided you can play the game and be fair, academic qualifications are not of prime importance and . . . in the future . . . if Ellesmere can . . . guide him to stand on his own feet . . . and teach him to be true and to look after others first and himself last, I shall be satisfied.

His closing remarks offered a pithy summary with which many parents would have agreed, 'I want him to be able to fight for himself and be shown the proper way to manhood.'[4] Interpretations of what this implied, however, differed. This father was unusual in being an Old Ellesmerian, which most were not, although the evidence of fathers' education is too sketchy to draw any firm conclusions about how many had been to other public schools. This father may have been similar to the traditionalists identified in Irene Fox's study of parents' choice of public school education in the contemporary period. He believed in the virtues of public school character training and like Fox's traditionalists may not have considered any other sort of education for his son. The pragmatists in her study were the majority, who were not committed to the independent or state schools and their respective ideologies. They believed their children were more likely to succeed at independent schools and could also afford to pay the fees.[5] Such parents were often more interested in careers and qualifications than character training.

Sam Laker, a businessman with an engineering factory in Barnsley, sent both his sons to Ellesmere during the war. His letters do not reveal what sort of school he had attended, although his later education became the model for his older son. He had been invalided out of the First World War and took a science degree at Manchester University as a Kitchener Scholar. It is possible that he had received a scientific education at a Higher Grade School in the period before the First World War when their provision of free secondary education became a model for the Labour and Trade Union movement crystallised in the Bradford Charter of 1913.[6] Sam Laker told the Headmaster in 1942 'Let me be clear about my intentions for Matthew – he has no easy job to fall into. He will have to make his own way. I intend him to go to University and I intend him to have a sound scientific training as a basis for this. . .'[7] Sam Laker had been attracted to Ellesmere not by the rugger pitches and housemasters but by the new science laboratories. This was typical of the growing demand, divined in 1867 by the Taunton Commission and later by W. D. Gallie for an education for middle-class sons aimed at a career.

The Lakers started to look for a school for their sons in the spring of 1939. They sent for the prospectus of Ellesmere and made a preliminary enquiry about fees – an important matter especially if two boys were to be sent. Shortly after his appointment, Evans Prosser had carefully rewritten the prospectus as part of his drive to attract more boys. It stated that 'The curriculum demanded by the career which the boy intends to follow and his general happiness are the first consideration of the School Authorities.'[8] Following the completion of the new dormitories, changing rooms and science laboratories, a book of views of the school was also produced in 1939. When forwarding the prospectus to the Lakers, Evans Prosser also mentioned the possibility of an exhibition for their son.

The Lakers were 'very impressed with the details of the school as set out in the prospectus – and encouraged by your suggestion of the possibility of securing an exhibition which would bring the fees to a figure within our means.' The letter went on to enquire anxiously if the exhibition would be based on scholarship or character, since Matthew was backward in his school work 'due to missing school in his younger days'. He was, his father added, 'a sound character', good at cricket and football, who would make a 'useful member of the community if rightly handled'.[9] Evans Prosser was able to give suitable reassurances and the Lakers visited the school, when they received a full account of the Headmaster's views about the education Ellesmere provided and the value of the discipline and order it instilled. Evans Prosser's exposition of his educational views accorded well with that of parents. A master who served under him put it memorably, 'Prosser had a nose for what parents wanted. Their main concerns were the School Certificate and discipline.'[10]

In the inter-war period the ideology of public school education was changing to reflect the increasing importance of academic qualifications, the decline in the games cult and the criticisms which had been levelled after the Great War. Cyril Norwood, the Headmaster of Harrow who harnessed games to the new ideology, was also one of the principal architects of the modern secondary school curriculum and of the belief in the value of examinations in selecting different ability groups and providing them with appropriate curricula. He used the School Certificate as a screening device for entry into the sixth form. His greatest influence may well have been outside the public schools as the Chairman of the Committee on Secondary School Curricula and Examinations which reported in 1943. The Committee's formulation of three types of mind and three curricula, grammar, technical and modern, was the basis of the tripartite system of secondary education adopted after the 1944 Education Act.[11] Evans Prosser's views had many similarities to Norwood's. He believed in the overriding importance of the academic success of the school and introduced streaming by ability. A forms did classics, B forms German and C forms French, an innovation resented by a number of parents and boys. He was a keen sportsman and regarded sport as a key means of maintaining discipline in the school and a way of cementing the network of relationships between schools, universities and old boys.

Mr and Mrs Laker were both very impressed by the school and by Evans Prosser as its Headmaster. Mrs Laker, in particular, found his views on education 'very much to her liking' and wished to find out more about the school.[12] They visited Ellesmere a second time and after a discussion with the Headmaster of their son's preparatory school decided to send him to Ellesmere in September 1939. Preparatory school Headteachers were one of the most frequent sources of advice and information about public schools used by this group of parents in finding a suitable school for their sons.

A close network of relationships between preparatory and public schools was essential to both types of school. Preparatory schools depended upon their reputation in getting boys into public schools. The Common Entrance examination from preparatory schools into public schools was introduced in 1904. It gave the public schools a more uniform and reliable indication of a boy's ability than the varying reports received from Headmasters and Headmistresses of preparatory schools. They began to concentrate thereafter on preparing pupils for this examination and ceased to take older pupils.[13] Public schools depended upon the preparatory schools for suitable pupils. Preparatory and public school teachers assessed parents and their boys by two equally important criteria, the ability of parents to pay the fees and of pupils to pass examinations. Pupils who were academically very weak or who required large fee reductions were always a matter of delicate negotiation. A preparatory school Headmaster writing to Dr A. V. Billen, Evans Prosser's predecessor, in 1934 seeking a place for a clergyman's son at £50 promised that the connection between the two schools 'would bring forth more paying propositions in the future'. The increased emphasis on academic ability and reduced emphasis on games was clearly evident in the recommendations of preparatory school Headteachers who usually mentioned the parents' circumstances, boys' academic ability and sporting abilities in that order. Having discussed the clergyman's financial circumstances and need for a low fee, this Headmaster added that the boy concerned 'would make a good standard of Common Entrance . . . a useful Rugby forward although not much class as a cricketer'.[14]

Evans Prosser's enthusiasm for filling the school and raising its academic standards by offering fee reductions to those who kept their boys at the school until School Certificate could cause embarrassment. In 1938 he was in correspondence with a headmaster in North Wales who was trying to place several of the older pupils so that he could make his school into a preparatory school. After making one offer of a generous fee reduction, Evans Prosser promptly withdrew it on seeing the boy's Common Entrance papers, insinuating that he had been misled by the preparatory school Headmaster about the boy's ability.

Anguished letters from North Wales ensued, rebutting the allegation and saying that the parents could have looked elsewhere and had accepted the offer at Ellesmere in good faith. On this point of honour Evans Prosser had to concede defeat and the boy entered Ellesmere. When he failed School Certificate his parents comforted themselves with the benefits of the character training he had received. For these and other parents the ideology of public school character training was of most use as a substitute for their sons' lack of academic success.[15]

Any doubts that Evans Prosser had about the wisdom of his offer to the Lakers when he read that his preparatory school Headmaster considered Matthew 'very backward for his age . . . would not have passed Common Entrance and seems to find difficulty remembering past work' are unrecorded. The preparatory school Headmaster's view of intellectual ability and the relationship of intellect and character are illuminating for he added that Matthew Laker was however 'a nice boy' and a hard-working member of the Association Football XI. 'There are other subjects besides Latin and French and he may have a flair for Chemistry. There is no reason why he should not do fairly well if he plods along.'[16] Like the Clarendon Commission in 1964, this Headmaster thought scientific subjects suitable for the less able.

While Evans Prosser's relations with preparatory school Head-teachers were mutually beneficial, those with the Headmasters of grammar schools and other public schools were highly competitive and he 'poached' unrestrainedly from nearby grammar schools, at the same time defending his own bailiwick fiercely against potential losses to other public schools. In a case where the parents would have incurred financial penalties if their son left the local grammar school, he agreed to meet them halfway with the fees. While there was unrestrained competition in recruiting boys from outside the public schools, the gentlemanly and uncompetitive atmosphere within them was preserved by an iron code of conduct preventing any attempt at poaching between Head Masters' Conference Schools. Evans Prosser used this code on several occasions to considerable effect, to prevent any of his pupils leaving to go to other public schools. One extraordinary parent who claimed to be a member of the aristocracy and bred corgis, when she was not writing long letters to the school in green ink, tried to move her son from Ellesmere to Lancing in the middle of the war. Evans Prosser curtly reminded the Headmaster of Lancing, at that time evacuated to nearby Ludlow, of the convention, attributing the mother's desire to move her son from Ellesmere to Lancing to snobbery.[17] It is a nice irony that he himself left an enduring reputation for snobbery, especially among the domestic staff.

There was a number of other ways in which this group of parents came in contact with the school. On Sunday afternoons in the early years of his headmastership Evans Prosser and other masters cycled out into the Shropshire countryside in search of farmers and others who might send their sons to the school. As bank managers could obviously be relied upon to meet their financial commitments, Evans Prosser advertised 'Lloyds Bank bursaries' in *The Black Horse*, the bank's house journal.[18] During the war advertisements were placed in the *Daily Telegraph*, advertising reduced fees for the sons of officers serving in His Majesty's forces.[19]

While such tactics served Evans Prosser's cause well, they were certainly not in the best gentlemanly traditions of the Headmasters' Conference. Senior members feared the spread of aggressive and cut-throat competition in the years before the Second World War. In October 1938 Leeson, the Headmaster of Winchester, wrote to his friend Holmes, Chairman of the Board of Education, about his fears that in a few years there would be 'a systematic hunting after boys by competitive bribery and reduction in fees and wholesale advertising'.[20]

Occasionally friends of the school and parents introduced new boys. In 1936 through the introduction of W. H. Thomas, a building contractor in Oswestry, Evans Prosser offered a place at reduced fees to Howard Lawson for his son Peter, then aged 12. The Lawsons' credentials were impeccable. Howard Lawson was an estate agent, specialising in sporting and country properties with a house off Grosvenor Square and an office in Mayfair, whose letters were immaculately typed by a secretary on impressively thick writing paper. It was arranged that Peter should enter the school in May 1936.[21]

2 MOTHERS, FATHERS AND SONS MAKING PREPARATIONS

Following the decision to send their son to Ellesmere, a period of eager anticipation and preparation began for the family. Sons prepared themselves as best they could to enter a new social world, a large boys' boarding school, isolated from other communities and influences, very different from the homes and small schools they already knew. Ideas about their new way of life could be gleaned from the currently popular schoolboy fiction and comics, much of which was dominated by stories from the public school world. From these sources the importance of the informal schoolboy culture, midnight feasts and pranks played on the anti-hero Billy Bunter, were learned.[22] During the period the heroes of schoolboy fiction changed. School stories like those of Henty and Vachell, about friendships and admiration between schoolboys, were replaced by heroes, first of all like those of John Buchan, and later in the period by the air aces like Captain W. E. Johns's Biggles and Gimlet.[23] Malcolm Lees boned up on schoolboy honour from the most famous of all public schoolboys, Tom Brown, and determined to defend his honour when the time came.[24]

Tom's dispatch to Rugby, in which all the Brown family had a part, is instructive. Tom, dissatisfied with his private school, made his wish to go to public school very plain. His father decided to send him to Rugby and wrote to Dr Arnold. Two weeks later the announcement expected by Mrs Brown that Tom was to go at once to Rugby was made at the breakfast table. Mrs Brown's only demur was whether Tom was old enough to travel to Rugby on his own but 'finding both father and son against her on this point, she gave in like a wise woman and proceeded to prepare Tom's kit for his launch into a public school'.[25] For Ellesmere boys betwen 1929 and 1950 the preparations were rarely as expeditiously concluded as those of the fictional Tom Brown some hundred years earlier, although the distribution of authority and division of labour in their households was in most cases similarly patriarchal. Fathers planned, made decisions and provided the means, mothers took care of the domestic domain and exercised their influence indirectly and judiciously, and sons attempted to become independent young men by 'cutting the apron strings' from their nurses and mothers and finding fit models among other boys and young men, just as Tom Brown had done.

The main work of preparation was the purchase and marking of the new boy's trunk and its contents. The list of school uniform and sports equipment for Ellesmere College at this time was lengthy, precise and costly. The uniform, much of which could only be purchased at the school shop, marked off public school boys from the rest of society. In the 1930s all boys under 15 at Ellesmere wore Eton collars, a clear demonstration of their superiority to elementary school boys with no uniforms and the caps, blazers and soft collars of grammar school boys. There was also a special Sunday uniform of black jackets and pinstripe trousers, 'Marlborough' suits. The need for adequate changes of clothing to allow laundering contributed to the cost. Twelve Eton collars were required, for example. While the school uniform bore school colours and badges, sports strips were in house colours and these items could also only be bought from the school. All uniform, including shoes, had to bear the owner's school number. After its acquisition every item required a name tape or other ingenious method of identification. Herbert Lees laboriously marked 291 on his son's shoes with small nails.[26] In most of the families in the study the trunk and clothing were the mother's responsibility, although in cases of loss, overcharging and other complaints, fathers concerned themselves and wrote suitably stern letters to the long-suffering school secretary, W. L. Sumsion.

The care of boys' clothes, especially in the laundry, caused problems for their parents. In 1938 Howard Lawson complained that his son's Eton collars had 'succumbed to the school laundry' and as Peter was due to become a senior he had 'bought the appropriate collar for that exalted degree'. He also complained that the quality of the school laundry was so poor that his son had returned his 'clean' clothes to the 'soiled linen basket without wearing it as even he, a schoolboy, considered it was not clean enough to wear and some of his clothes which were returned this term almost warranted the donning of air-raid precaution equipment before they were laundered'.[27] It was later revealed that the offending items were muddy sports strips, which had been left wrapped up in newspaper for a week.

Howard Lawson's relating the expected war to the school's laundry was remarkably prescient, for it brought a crisis both in the ability of parents to provide the uniform and the laundry to care for it. After clothes rationing was introduced in 1941, the school received a torrent of letters from parents about the difficulties of obtaining many of the items of school uniform, and the impossibility of providing such a quantity of clothes for growing boys on the amount of coupons allowed. Eton collars were abandoned. The school appealed to Old Boys for all unwanted uniform to be sold through the school. The depredations of the school laundry on such items as woollen socks continued to cause much weeping and gnashing of teeth. 'I knit my fingers to the bone', one vicar's wife complained 'and give coupons for the wool . . . I am very depressed with the washing of the stockings; they shrink them terribly . . . after one term he has a job to get into them.'[28] In January 1942 Sumsion received a packet from another parent containing a sadly shrunken object: a grey stocking which had originally measured 10 inches but had been reduced to a bare 8 inches in the laundry. Sumsion was abject but firm. He did understand the difficulties that parents were experiencing in 'securing clothes and the annoyance occasioned by such damage' but the school was also experiencing extreme difficulty in finding reliable laundry workers.[29]

Amid all these problems Evans Prosser continued to insist upon the significance of uniform in maintaining the special social identity and social segregation of Ellesmere as a public school. In July 1943 and again in July 1944 he issued memoranda to parents reminding them that 'uniformity of clothing in an institution such as a Public Boarding School is most desirable and the great proportion of parents have closely followed the school regulations. A small minority of boys, however, are conspicuously different.'[30] To enter a public school was to enter a different social world; in Evans Prosser's view it was a world marked off from the ordinary world. The boys dressed differently and lived a life of order and discipline, through which they would permanently acquire disciplined habits.

3 BECOMING A PUBLIC SCHOOL BOY

Early days in the school often left indelible impressions, which oral informants recalled vividly many years later, for few had had any comparable experience. Those who had never been away from home commenced a completely new life and those who had been away to boarding school previously were used to the atmosphere of small preparatory schools. New boys made sense of this strange social world as best they could. There were three main aspects to the jumble of confused experience which assaulted them in their early days, in their struggle to understand and give some meaningful responses to what was going on around them. First of all there was the physical layout of the school buildings and grounds; secondly the school day of chapel, classes and games; and thirdly the social behaviour and relations of the people in the school, Headmaster, housemasters, masters, prefects, maids, porters and the initially undifferentiated mass of other boys. All three aspects were larger, more complex with more people than the homes and small schools which most boys had experienced. Understanding their new social world demanded new understandings about how to cope with school and the normal intimacies of domestic life, like eating and going to bed in a new institutional context. During David Parton's first week he was quite unaware of the tacit conventions in his new school about what was considered appropriate behaviour in different parts of the school: which parts were 'public', under the watchful eye of masters and prefects, and which considered 'private', where he could be unobserved. After classes one day he undid his blazer, and sauntered out into the corridor eating an apple, to be met by no lesser figure than the Captain of School, who, realising his complete ignorance of all the unwritten prohibitions, merely 'put the fear of God' into him, merciful chastisement for which Parton was always very grateful.[31]

In this closely knit and highly prescribed social world some boys found it difficult to conform sufficiently and were unhappy at school. Among them was Peter Lawson. After two years his father reported himself 'very satisfied with his progress' but his son disliked Ellesmere, attributed by his father to 'the boyish habit of disliking every school'.[32] Peter had persistent difficulties in looking after his clothes and shoes. Sumsion, the school secretary, used conformity as a possible sanction.

I really feel that for a boy of his present age he does not look after himself as he should. We know that we have to 'nurse' the juniors and actually dress some of them to make sure that they get the right clothes, shoes etc. on them, but in no case in the senior school do we make any special arrangements for any boy, and I am quite sure that your boy would not like to feel that he was the only one when this was necessary.[33]

Lawson senior agreed that his son did 'not appear to look after himself as he should' but believed that it was one of the school's duties to 'knock some self-discipline into him in the future'. 'It is up to Ellesmere College', he concluded.[34]

Philosophers, anthropologists and sociologists have long wrestled with the problem of how human beings understand and give meaning to their experience in the way of Parton and Lawson. One important theme running through their work is that the meaning of reality is actively and consciously constructed in social and historical processes. Particular meanings are not given. They do not automatically inhere in certain experiences; rather meanings are actively imposed upon experience from previously shared understandings. Clearly Parton experienced the school corridors as places in which to relax, but the shared meanings of the Captain of School and his new schoolfellows were very different. That he should have had his blazer buttoned, been walking smartly and kept apples for consumption in the house dayroom were not rules built into the bricks and mortar of the school. These understandings, new to David Parton, derived from the rules and meanings shared by members of his new school which they had developed historically in relation to similar rules and meanings in other public schools.[35]

A second theme in much of this work, especially that of the anthropologist Mary Douglas, is that we understand and give meaning to the world by differentiating and categorising our experience, and then maintain the categories through rules.[36] Thus the school was divided into two categories, public and private, which derived from the way that behaviour was differentiated into that acceptable in public concourses like school corridors and that in dayrooms which were more private and informal, where friends relaxed and chatted. The two categories, private and public, informal and formal were maintained by rules, many of which were implicit, maintained by informal sanctions like ridicule, rather than explicit, written and codified with formalised sanctions like beating or 'gating'.

A third important theme developed by Mary Douglas and applied to education by Basil Bernstein is the powerful insight that rules and meanings are communicated through symbolic systems, which serve as economical message systems. A single symbol may convey a wealth of meaning.[37] Certain colours symbolised the school or house, subsuming every facet of its complexity into a single small emblem. Such a symbol could arouse passionate loyalty in suitable circumstances, like a hard-fought rugger match. One of the most potent ways of conveying the rules and meanings of social orderings, as Evans Prosser appreciated so well, is through the symbolism of dress. As Mary Douglas has commented about Oxford University: 'Once the rules for Oxford academic dress have been exhaustively spelled out, we have the full scheme of academic statuses and events.'[38] The same was true for Ellesmere College. The basic distinction of the school's social ordering were symbolised by the black gowns of masters, jackets or blazers for boys, nurses' uniform for matrons and overalls for domestic staff. Among the boys there was a large number of further distinctions between gowned prefects, and house prefects, captains of rugger and cricket, members of school teams and house colours, worn on ties. Older boys wore a different uniform from younger boys. These fine gradations and distinctions of dress were based on fundamental principles of social organisation, which also underlay the physical layout of the school.

One of the most important tasks for a new boy in his early days at the school was to learn his way about, from the dormitory, to the chapel, classrooms, dining room, changing rooms and playing fields. The school is set in 69 acres of land given to the Woodard Foundation by Lord Brownlow. The main bulding, opened by Canon Woodard in 1884, is a large Victorian Gothic edifice in a commanding position overlooking the Shropshire plain. By 1929 a number of smaller buildings had been built beside the original, including a swimming pool, sports pavilion, scout hut, OTC hut and camera club hut. To these Evans Prosser added considerably by the addition of the north wing, housing the science laboratories and a large new dormitory, increasing the capacity of the school by 50. It took new boys several days to learn their way round their new surroundings. In his first letter home written on his third day, Malcolm Lees told his parents, 'I think I've just about got the run of the place now.'[39]

The different groups who lived in the school were accommodated in separate areas. The Headmaster, his wife and family had a house in a secluded part of the grounds. Most other masters during this period were bachelors who had rooms in the school. The women domestic staff lived in a long corridor near the dining hall known as the Warren. The boys were divided into four houses, Talbot, Meynell, Woodard and Wakeman. Each house had an adjoining dormitory and a dayroom in different parts of the school and the boys slept in the dormitory of the house to which they belonged. The arrangement of living accommodation reproduced the social categories of the school. The Headmaster remained totally separated from the school in a sacred sanctum of his own, boys were separated from masters, and domestic staff from any contact with the rest of the school.

After 1938 when the number of boys reached 300 and New Dorm was opened, the new boys all slept together regardless of which house they were in. New Dorm, later Long Dorm, houses 50 new boys together. Their segregation was a constant reminder of their marginal status as novitiates, who had to make their way up the rungs of the hierarchy to the sixth form. It is of their first days in Long Dorm that many old boys of the school retain memories and it is in Long Dorm that we may first encounter the conflict and compromise which underlay the model of the carefully ordered world with which Evans Prosser so successfully wooed the parents. When Malcolm Lees arrived in New Dorm he and his friend Colin West 'bagged' two adjacent beds, moving a suitcase to 'reserve' them. Another boy moved one of the suitcases but Malcolm promptly replaced it, stood his ground and won.[40]

In his last year at Ellesmere, Mike Smith became house prefect of Long Dorm, a taxing job, in which prefects were known to abuse their power. Smith determined successfully never to beat the younger boys in his charge, and recalls with pride that his housemaster, Bankin Jackson, wrote to his father about his compassion, adding 'He has undoubtedly proved one of the finest prefects in Long Dorm.' He was succeeded by a gowned school prefect who was expelled for bullying.[41] From Long Dorm boys moved into house dormitories and the house became a prime focus of their social relations and allegiances. Each house had a distinctive style, organisation and reputation. When Major Terence Thornton was at Ellesmere between 1935 and 1940, the blues and the violets, Woodard and Wakeman, were the best games houses.[42]

Houses were hierarchical, presided over by a housemaster, house captain and prefects. From the house organisation, the authority of masters and older boys, especially prefects, who could beat them, new boys soon learnt that age was a paramount organising principle of the school. The social distance between masters and younger boys was preserved in three different ways, the organisation of space, speech and dress. Masters always taught in their own classrooms. The boys moved about the school from one to the other in orderly procession. Masters always wore their gowns, however threadbare, for teaching. Deference was signified by the address, 'sir', always used by boys addressing masters, however senior the boys. The domestic staff were also expected to signify their deference. Social distance between masters and the rest of the school was further demonstrated by the sanctity of the Senior Common Room which was approached by domestic staff and boys only in 'appropriate' circumstances.

After age, academic ability was the most significant ordering among the boys. The school was divided into A, B and C forms in order of ability, and within each of these fortnightly tests and termly examinations determined form placings. Being in a C form, and especially low in a C form, signified being a 'duffer'. In the view of the oral informants who had been in C forms like similar forms in grammar schools, they were the source of the most insouciant rebel culture among the boys, the friendly homes of most pranksters and smokers. In after-life C-form boys gained the reputation for business success and generous support for the school, encouraged by their favourite master, J. W. Nankivell. Meeting Mike Smith at an Old Ellesmerian meeting in 1968, he is reported to have said, 'All the educated boys are idiots – you C stream boys all make money.'[43]

As well as age and ability, gender was a cardinal principle underlying the way in which the school was organised. During this period when most of the masters were bachelors, the school was very much a male establishment to which a very few women and girls had access, and they remained on the fringes. During the war a small number of mistresses were appointed and, despite the small numbers, they had their own common room. Women were more frequent among the lowlier positions in the school, junior school mistresses, matrons, clericals and domestics. One girl, Jansis, Evans Prosser's daughter, did spend her early years as a pupil in the school alongside the boys, but her position as daughter of the Headmaster was quite exceptional. The domestic and caretaking staff, housekeepers, maids, porters and groundsmen was considerable but suffered a drastic cut during the war. Most lived in the school near the laundry and kitchens. Their status as servants was clearly marked in their work, uniform, and deference expected of them. One long-serving member put it succinctly, 'We were below stairs and kept there.'[44] During the war there was such a shortage of maids that the boys had to take turns laying tables and washing up. One oral informant resented this, considering that he was not at school to learn such domestic skills, but others found it a useful experience and valued the chance to learn to look after themselves.

Evans Prosser believed in order and discipline and he told prospective parents about the way the school inculcated them into the boys. One of the main means by which these habits were instilled was by the organisation of time in the school. The daily round of lessons, prep, chapel, games and OTC into which new boys were initiated immediately imposed an order on every aspect of their lives. Almost every minute of the day was assigned to a particular activity, ensuring that boys were always busy. Idleness was seen by many parents and Headmasters as a fundamental vice among schoolboys. Rigorous timetabling of every minute of the day made idleness impossible and at the same time was one of the most important ways of maintaining control over the boys.

During the day a hand bell and an electric bell were used to signal each change of activity. The system was essentially monastic and during Evans Prosser's headmastership in 1935–61 it changed little. In total fourteen bells were sounded throughout the day. It began with a waking and then a rising bell, after which there was a bell for breakfast followed by chapel. Lessons began after chapel at 8.55. Three lessons were followed by a quarter-of-an-hour break and then two more lessons and lunch. In the afternoons there were more lessons, games or the Corps. This pattern was unvarying except for Saturday afternoon and Sunday. In the evenings supper was followed by supervised prep. There was a period of free time before bedtime and lights out at 9.30 for younger boys and 10.30 for seniors. The school had numerous clubs and societies which met mainly at weekends; Saturday evening was popular. Superimposed on the regular rhythm of the school day and week was a calendar of events which regulated the school term and year. At the beginning of each term a printed calendar was issued. On one side there was a daily calendar. The days were distinguished by sporting events and fixtures, religious festivals and services and outstanding school events such as plays, concerts and examinations. The reverse side gave the names of gowned prefects, sports captains and the days and times of regular choir practices and chapel services. Malcolm Lees saved all the letters he wrote home in his five years at Ellesmere and the ordering of time stands out very clearly in them. The most important distinction is between time spent at home in the holidays and the school term. Many of his letters mention exactly how many days it is until 'Food and Freedom' as the holidays were known. Like other public school boys, he marked off the days on the school calendar 'with gusto'.[45] Fortnightly tests, sports fixtures like inter-house table tennis, the annual steeple chase, great events like VE day and the Royal Wedding were important markers.

For boys who came from such a wide variety of backgrounds 'finding the form', discovering the cultural and social manners and nuances of their new community could prove a minefield of potential *faux pas*. Particular ways of dressing among the schoolboy community were enforced, not by the formal means of penalties imposed by prefects, but by equally powerful informal means – the example of the most influential boys in the school. The captains of school, rugger and cricket served as models, heroes to be venerated and copied by younger boys, a feature of public schools further reinforced by the schoolboy fiction of the period. 'Form' learned as a schoolboy at Ellesmere made a lasting impression in some cases. In the 1930s one Old Ellesmerian recalled the 'form' at the turn of the century.

> . . . it was considered very bad form to do up the bottom button of your waistcoat, to show your braces under any circumstances, to use a belt with flannels, to part your hair in the middle unless you were going to enter the church, to wear bow ties, and not to have a crease in your trousers.[46]

Language and speech, with their infinite possibilities of meaning and inflexion, are very sensitive to social influence and have always been significant indicators of social origin and group membership in Britain, no more so than in the public schools.[47] Ellesmere was no exception. In 1937 A. C. Graham complained in the *News Supplement*, a wall newspaper of the period, about a group who 'classify practically every phenomenon known to experience as 'just too crude' or 'quite too utterly choice'. In the writer's view these speech mannerisms were used 'to prove to the outer world how infinitely superior they (the speakers) are to the common clay'.[48]

Rough manners and dialect speech were always conspicuous in schools like Ellesmere. One oral informant recalled the son of a Lancashire businessman who had apparently made enough money during the war to send his son to Ellesmere. Unfortunately the lad was unable to refine his speech, and his life was made so unendurable by the social denizens of the Shell form that he left after only a term.[49] Informal schoolboy culture was negotiated within the formal orderings of the school society. In the delicate matters of 'form', speech, life in the Houses and on the playing fields the powerful schoolboy culture held greatest sway. The oral evidence suggests that subverting the rules in such rebellious acts as smoking, exploiting weaker masters' lack of discipline and daredevil end-of-term pranks were seen by many boys as acts of bravado and demonstrations of masculinity.

The organisation of space, time and dress also carried important symbols and messages about the organisation of the wider society outside. In the families and social mileux from which the boys had come age, gender and social class were crucial underlying orders. One important principle of social organisation embodied in the school was that of hierarchy. The school was organised as a series of levels of prestige and authority, with new boys at the bottom. They soon learned to aspire to the status of captain of rugger or prefect and the authority and privileges that accompanied it. Few boys would have arrived at the school without some acquaintance with the kind of authority and discipline they found there, where masters and older boys could and did enforce their authority through corporal punishment, and the imposition of lines or chores of different kinds. The idea that authority of this kind was vested in older men and enforced through punishment was found in many families and schools. The reactions of new boys to the pressures to conform were varied. For the majority the easiest way to survive was to conform. Nonetheless, as in all schools at every period, reality did not completely fit the model of discipline and order outlined by Evans Prosser to prospective parents. Order was negotiated. In 1900 there was a buoyant market in lines at a penny a hundred, in the capable hands of one Calcott, who could even arrange credit, and in the 1940s one equally entrepreneurial spirit charged a biscuit for illegal entry to the house tuck cupboard, the key of which he had charge.[50]

4 FATHERS AND SONS

The orderings of school, emphasising the authority of older men and subordination of women, reinforced lessons already learned at home in the family. Fathers were the most important single influence on and model for their sons. Fathers directed their sons' careers; mothers were subordinate, their activities and interests largely domestic and their influence upon their sons indirect. In the summer of 1939, as the international crisis which precipitated the Second World War deepened, Howard Lawson informed the school that, assuming his son passed the School Certificate, he intended to withdraw him as 'the experience he would gain in the business world is likely to be more beneficial to him than staying at school'.[51] He requested the Headmaster's views on this course of action and, after several letters from Evans Prosser and a discussion with his son, he informed the school that he had changed his view and that Peter would return in September.[52] In anticipation of the outbreak of war Mr Lawson voiced his increasing concern about the effects of the looming war upon his business to the Headmaster. Peter gained his School Certificate with four credits and his father was 'very pleased', although he was surprised and disappointed by his son's failure in English after Peter had declared he had 'romped through the paper'. In the summer of 1939 the government passed a number of hasty pieces of legislation restricting rents and attempting to clarify liability for war damage to property. As Mr Lawson had feared, the outbreak of war had disastrous effects on his business and he informed the school less than a week before term started that his son would not return. He had another son to provide for and 'so far as I can see into the future and possibly the destruction of my business through International Affairs £40 per term is £40.'[53]

Evans Prosser replied immediately reminding him that he could not so easily break his contract to pay the term's fees since he had not given a term's notice.

A lengthy and bitter correspondence ensued. Peter Lawson was ill with impetigo, while his father and Headmaster argued about whether he should go back to school when he had recovered. Lawson's financial affairs continued to deteriorate and he lost £1,000 in a fortnight during September 1939.[54] Evans Prosser was not impressed, possibly fearing the effects of the war upon the school and continued to press Lawson on his legal and financial obligations. In yielding, Lawson reproached Evans Prosser,

> Remember it is not very easy for a person who has never had any financial responsibility or the management of a firm, and who is sitting comfortably in the country to visualise the conditions of a professional business in London at the present moment.[55]

Unfortunately we do not have Evans Prosser's response to this irony and the correspondence ended abruptly early in November 1939 with Howard Lawson's untimely death. Evans Prosser wrote to Peter Lawson immediately offering him assistance and advice in choosing a career and contacted Barclays Bank on his behalf.

Lawson senior had cast a long shadow over his son, for Peter replied firmly that he had set his heart on following his father's profession, a project his mother and his mentors had told him 'would be inadvisable under present circumstances'.[56] By February he had decided 'to make one final dive to obtain a post with an Estate Agent: if that fails I shall take a temporary situation in a bank'.[57] But his plans were not realised, for the *Old Ellesmerian Chronicle* sadly recorded his death in 1940, sending condolences to the mother so long invisible in the correspondence and now revealed as an object of intense pity.

While the war devastated Howard Lawson's business, it provided ideal conditions for Sam Laker. Government contracts were negotiated on a cost-plus-10 per cent basis, which emphasised production and ignored inefficiency and waste. Like Howard Lawson, Sam Laker served as the principal model and manager of his son's career. He expected Matthew to pass the School Certificate on which his future plans depended. In 1942 Laker senior wrote to Evans

Prosser about his elder son, 'He intends to make a determined effort to get his School Certificate this academic year, I am anxious that he shall – and a good one.' Laker drove his son and his school; imbued with the Dunkirk spirit, he chid his son's Headmaster:

> I know that you have difficulties, perhaps with staff and in other directions, we are all the same – I am running a factory and trying to get a quart out of a pint pot – I am getting more than a quart and am still not satisfied yet. What can be done to help Matthew now? One suggestion is extra tuition, can this be arranged? Is Matthew making as good progress as you ex-pected? His position in form indicates progress and he stands quite high on the form list, but I do not know the standard of C forms – and I do not like 'C' forms.[58]

Matthew failed his School Certificate at the first attempt. His father was still keen for him to go to university and fortunately he succeeded the second time. His father entered a correspondence with the Professor of Electrical Engineering at Manchester University and Matthew was accepted for a six months short course before his con-scription in 1944. In 1945 he was a Royal Air Force pilot serving tem-porarily with the USAF.[59]

5 SUMMARY

In choosing a school for their sons these parents were looking for both academic qualifications which would lead to a suitable career and disci-pline as the basis of their sons' training. The network of relationships between public and preparatory schools was the most common source of information and recommendations which led parents to consider Ellesmere College. The Headmaster, Rev. R. A. Evans Prosser, appointed in 1935, adopted an aggressive policy of advertising and fee reductions to fill his school in competition with other secondary schools in the gloomy financial atmosphere which prevailed in the pre-war period.

For new boys Ellesmere College was a strange social world with ways of ordering space, time, dress and society which they had to acquire and to which they had to conform. The college was a hierarchy in which older boys and masters imposed discipline by beating and sanctions. Informal sanctions, like ridicule and the fear of non-conformity, were as strong or stronger means of maintaining particular patterns of speech and dress. Nonetheless a strong anti-school culture flourished, especially in C forms.

The School Certificate was crucial in parents' concern for their sons' education. Fathers were the main model and guiding light in their sons' future. Their first lessons in manhood were learned at home, where their fathers made decisions and managed the family finances. Mothers were subordinate and domestic.

Education at a public school was about manliness: boys learning to be men from men and other boys. Conceptions of manliness varied among the parents, masters and boys. While parents emphasised academic qualifications, which would lead to independence in a secure and respected social position, the values of the schoolboy culture held the tough physique, leadership and courage of the captain of rugby as the supreme model of masculinity.

The formal orderings and discipline of the school emphasised hierarchy based on the social principles of age, gender and academic ability, similar to those found in the families from which boys came and in wider society. Strict adherence to these social rules and principles was one of the most powerful and effective means of socialisation within the school by which such social messages as the inferiority and subordinate position of women was instilled. The vigorous schoolboy culture also further emphasised masculine values in smoking and daring pranks.

4

THE POOR CHURCH MICE

1 CHRISTIAN GENTLEMEN

The place of religion and morality in conceptions of public school masculinity has always been an important one. While the parents in the study laid greatest stress on a career and independence as a way to manhood and the informal schoolboy culture associated physical toughness and daring with manliness, the great Headmasters, who were the influential expounders of public school ideology, placed Christian belief and morality at the heart of public school masculinity.

The most famous public school Headmaster of all, Dr Thomas Arnold of Rugby, coined a new ideal, the Christian gentleman, which played an important part in reforming the wild excesses of the eighteenth-century public schools. Arnold, Headmaster of Rugby from 1827 until 1842, did more than any other Headmaster to make attendance at chapel a distinguishing feature of public school education and Christian morality a mark of gentlemanly conduct. He was a prophet, whose shining religious and moral fervour was made legendary by Dean Stanley's *Life* and Thomas Hughes's *Tom Brown's Schooldays*. Arnold's views derived from the evangelical wing of the Church of England. Evil and vice among schoolboys were destructive and palpable and had to be rooted out. It was through exhortatory sermons in chapel, example and inspiration that Christian gentlemen were made from sinful schoolboys. Arnold's greatest contribution to the reform of the public schools was to trust his pupils of all ages, instituting a prefect system which was later regarded as the most significant means of leadership training in the public schools.[1] In the second half of the nineteenth century this ideology was modified to become 'muscular Christianity', in which gentlemanly virtues and

Christian morality were fused with manly physique and sportsman-ship by a number of other later masters and Headmasters, notably Thring of Uppingham and Almond of Loretto. Thomas Hughes and Charles Kingsley popularised these ideals of physical toughness, loyalty and honour in their conceptions of manliness.[2]

Nathanial Woodard's religious and educational ideas derived from very different sources. As a churchman he occupied an uneasy position on the extreme Anglo-Catholic wing of the Church of England, whose ideas were most strongly influenced by the Roman Church. Piety in religious practices, rather than moral fervour, was encouraged in Woodard schools. The efficacy of religious rites, supremely the sacra-ments of the church in conferring spiritual benefits and the crucial importance of the priestly function were the cornerstones of this tra-dition. Such notions were associated by their critics, like Charles Kingsley, with effeminacy.[3] Despite these differences, the games cult was espoused as enthusiastically at Woodward's Lancing College and indeed at the Roman Catholic Stoneyhurst College as it was at other schools.[4] In the inter-war period, as we have already seen, muscular Christianity was in decline and another great Headmaster, Cyril Norwood of Harrow School, was playing a leading role in reshaping public school ideology into the ideal of service to the community.[5] As a Woodard School, Ellesmere maintained a strong High Church tradition but, despite appeals for funds during the inter-war period, it had no chapel. Evans Prosser's priority was to extend the capacity of the school and modernise its curriculum, but the funds collected to commemorate those who died in the First World War by building a chapel had swelled only slowly.

How far boys who went to Ellesmere became Christians and gentlemen and were imbued with the ideal of service is difficult to assess. Regular chapel and high church practices at school induced rejection in some and Christian commitment and regular church attendance in others. The school attached much significance to gentlemanly conduct and Mike Smith believed that it was from the example of Evans Prosser, 'Nanki' and others that he learned gentlemanly civility: to open doors for others and say 'Good Morning'. He also believed that the fundamental lesson of the school was that 'life is about respect for others', a philosophy which has helped him lead and look after the great variety of people he now employs in his business.[6]

2 EDUCATION FOR THE CLERGY

One group with a very direct concern with the importance and effects of chapel and moral training were the clergy. Their own academic background and Church of England connections led many of them to favour the public schools for their sons' education. By 1929 the secularisation and urbanisation of society had reduced the value of country livings and the clergy had experienced a severe decline in their number, influence and incomes from the high point in the middle of the nineteenth century. Some stipends were as low as £240 and 5,000 out of 12,719 were less than £400 in 1939.[7] Consequently they found it increasingly difficult to find an education for their sons and daughters at a price they could afford. The great schools were outside their reach unless their sons were outstandingly able and won scholarships and they, therefore, applied to schools like Ellesmere. The opening statement of the College's first entry in the *Public Schools Yearbook* in 1933 said, 'The object of the college is to bring Public School Education, classical and modern on the principles of the Church of England within reach of those who are debarred by the cost from the older Public schools.'[8] Clergy were specially encouraged to send their sons by the offer of an unspecified number of Exhibitions and Nominations allocated specifically to their sons. Pressure to follow father's footsteps was strong in some clergy families and a further attraction of the school was the encouragement it gave boys to enter Holy Orders.

Clergy connected with the school as governors, or through connections in the Woodard Foundation, were often the means of persuading other clergy to send their sons. Canon Maynard Smith of Gloucester Cathedral was provost of the Midland Division of the Society and closely associated with the college. A pithy correspondent, Maynard Smith also wrote detective stories. In late November 1938, he wrote to the Headmaster about 'a little friend' of his, James Heywood, whose school was to become a preparatory school and, as James was 13, he would have to leave it immediately. Canon Smith told the Headmaster that James was 'good at games, a healthy, cheerful little chap. He means to be a priest. His brothers have turned out well. One of them is clever. I don't know about James' wits. He strikes me as entirely normal.' His father, Reverend Edward Heywood, had an income of £400 a year and no independent means. Two of James's brothers were at Keble College, Oxford, preparing to enter Holy Orders 'with grants from various sources', but, continued Canon Maynard Smith, 'I don't know how he manages to carry on'. 'Can you take James at very reduced fees? . . . Do your best.'[9] This letter was followed immediately by one from Canon Edward Heywood confirming the contents of Canon Maynard Smith's. Evans Prosser did indeed 'do his best', offering a place at a fee of £60 a year. In the Heywood household big financial decisions were a matter for consultation, with Canon Heywood taking the final responsibility. He replied immediately saying 'how much my wife and I appreciate your kindness . . . for the very substantial reduction . . . it is very generous . . . and we want to give the matter our most careful consideration . . . I cannot as yet see my way clear . . . .'[10] If her youngest son was to go away to school Mrs Heywood may well have had to manage her household on a severely restricted budget. In her polemic *Three Guineas* published in the same year that the Heywoods were pondering the funding of James's education, Virginia Woolf drew attenton to the amount of money mothers and sisters sacrificed in this way to Arthur's Education Fund as she called it, money rarely spent on their own education.[11]

It was agreed that James Heywood's fees would be paid in instalments, as the money became available, although Canon Heywood was still 'a little disturbed as to how I am to get the money, but one has to have faith in these matters and I shall hope it will turn out alright.' Perhaps in case Evans Prosser's faith was not as strong as his own he reassured the Headmaster that 'you need have no fear I shall not meet his fees.'[12]

The Heywood household was clearly a remarkable one, for all three sons were called to Holy Orders. Research on the clergy in the contemporary period has shown that the husband's life in Holy Orders also structures many aspects of his wife's life and that for the most part this incorporation into their husband's vocation is willingly accepted by clergy wives.[13] We do not know, however, how intra-family relations among clergy families have changed since the inter-war period nor, more germane to our present purposes, the effects of being born the son, rather than choosing to become the wife, of a clergyman. Certainly in the Heywood household father's influence seemed irresistible. Canon Heywood had a single plan for his youngest son's education and career, 'I have always wanted James to go to Oxford, to

Keble.' His father was not a graduate, but his two elder brothers were clear examples for James to follow. Despite his youth, James had already decided to follow his father and brothers. 'The lad has never wavered in his sense of vocation,'[14] his father reported to the Headmaster.

The war, with its ever-tightening regulation of young men's lives, threatened the Heywoods' plans in a similar way to the Littles and the Lakers. In November 1942 James was 17 and conscription loomed. Urgent decisions had to be made. Canon Heywood like other parents in the study regarded the war as a disastrous interruption in his son's life to be endured until peace and normality were restored. His main concern 'was to guard the opportunities for my son when this appalling war is over so that he may go on with his desire to take Orders.'[15]

James was weak in Latin and Evans Prosser warned Canon Heywood this might lead to his rejection in the strong competition to be accepted for ordination. Canon Heywood brushed the Headmaster's misgivings aside briskly.

> I see no difficulty in his eventually being ordained as his brother who suffered from the same weakness in languages eventually got to Oxford and is now a Curate . . . The fact of his weakness in them ought to have been dealt with at an earlier date, for his reports always noted that he was not doing well in them. The question of Greek is no impediment in this matter as many Bishops are prepared to do without it.

Canon Heywood had to accept, however reluctantly, that the war prevented the full realisation of his plans and he wrote:

> of course if there is any chance that he could go on to prepare for Ordination right away I would not think of anything else but putting him forward for it, but it seems that no exemptions for this are allowed now. The Church is going to be in a bad way for ordinands in the near future if the war drags on much longer.

If his son could not be accepted as an ordinand because of the war, at least the first part of the plan, going to Keble, could be embarked upon and Canon Heywood continued to press hard for his goal.

I have made enquiries and am told there are one or two possibilities open. The Warden of Keble suggests that he should try to get through Responsions [the preliminary examination] and at the same time apply for a Probationer Course at the University . . . I am sure the Warden of Keble would do all he can to help us. Two of my boys have been at the College. . . . I do not press this course as James may desire to go to Cambridge if his school friends are all going there. You would perhaps discuss it with him.[16]

During the war male students of medicine, dentistry, science and technology were given deferment to complete their degrees, which were accelerated to two years. Arts students had a years' deferment, but this ended in 1942, after which only women and unfit men studied Arts.[17] Short courses, prior to a commission in the services, had been established in the universities and Evans Prosser advised parents and boys to take advantage of this situation. In the early stages of the scheme entry requirements were relaxed and selection by the particular service for the course, supported by a statement from his Headmaster that a boy had reached School Certificate standard, was required in place of matriculation. Evans Prosser advised Canon Heywood to enter his son for a commission and a university short course forthwith. Discussion in the Heywood household was necessarily brief and three days later Canon Heywood informed the Headmaster that 'my wife and I now agree that we will accept your advice and would be glad if you would put him forward for a short University course, with the intention that he may go on to a Commission.' The plan enunciated so definitely three days earlier was not wholly abandoned and Canon Heywood continued.

if you think that Cambridge is the best choice for his subsequent training, we agree that you should endeavour to get him accepted there; if however there is any chance that he could go to Oxford (I mean after the War) then we would desire him to be entered there.[18]

Unfortunately James Heywood's application for a commission and University short course in the Royal Air Force was unsuccessful.[19] His father was disappointed. Looking back on his son's education at Ellesmere he was 'sorry in some ways he has not turned out one of the ' "brainy" sort' but on the positive side James had 'always been very happy' at the college and had 'qualities of character which will stand him in good stead in the days to come'. He was 'glad [James'] housemaster has found him of service in the general life of the school.'[20] While his father, like other similarly placed parents, comforted himself with the character-building ideology of public school education we can only guess at the effect upon James himself of such a setback to his father's intense desire that he should follow his two brothers to Keble. His longstanding resolve to enter the church did not weaken, for after the war he went to a provincial university and was ordained.

3 FATHERS AND SONS

The evidence from the three cases examined in detail suggests that it was fathers who were at the same time the single most important model of masculinity for their sons, and the directors of their careers. Laker, Lawson and Heywood were the providers and managers of the family finances. It was their power as providers which was the basis of the model they gave their sons and of their own ability to direct their sons' upbringing. Father as provider was a role essential to their own and their sons' understanding of their masculinity. The three fathers were in very stark contrast in the way they carried out this role. Canon Heywood struggled constantly, his high calling dignifying his efforts to make his finances adequate to realise his vision of his three sons all entering Holy Orders through Keble College, Oxford. Lawson afforded a disastrous example for his son. Once so successful, with a house and office in one of the most select areas in London, the declaration of war brought catastrophe to him, and may well have caused his death. Laker's success in the booming wartime conditions in the engineering industry clearly encouraged him in his self-confident command of his son's career and his Headmaster. The heritage bequeathed by these three fathers to their sons could not have been more different. Heywood left a shining example of faith and making a little go a long way; Laker was a model of pugnacity, hard work and success and Lawson left tarnished honour to be regilded by his son. This evidence accords well with Andrew Tolson's view that,

> As a boy there is a sense that one's destiny is somehow bound up with an image of father – his achievement at work, his status in the home. In part, fathers' 'presence' seems to contain . . . an affirmation of masculine power . . . generated out of the 'patriarchal' bond between father and son.[21]

Tolson's view, deriving from Freudian psychology and Marxist social theory, suggests that there is a fundamental distance and ambivalence in relations of sons to their fathers, who serve as authority figures in the family and are frequently absent. Consequently there is a fundamental insecurity at the basis of the male personality structure in our society. Boys strive to achieve, to do as well or better than their fathers in the competitive struggle at work. Through socialisation at school and in the peer group they learn the stereotyped masculine values and behaviour, the reaffirmation of which provide security.

The influence of their mothers on these three boys appears to have been greatest during the short-lived period of total dependency in infancy, after which it was indirect. Mrs Laker and Mrs Heywood were almost invisible, having left no correspondence, and appear only fleetingly when the decision was made to send their sons away from home to Ellesmere. The silence and invisibility of these women may hide their preoccupation with an all-consuming job outside their homes but this would have been extremely unusual. Mrs Lawson wrote *in extremis* as a widow, desperate for advice and help. These women were probably dependent upon and subordinate to their husbands. They concerned themselves with domestic matters and arrangements influencing their sons' upbringing in infancy and early childhood and only indirectly thereafter, like the fictional Tom Brown's mother. They took care of the domestic domain, 'wise' women who did not oppose the wills of their husbands and sons especially in combination and enabled them to realise their ambitions by smooth and economical domestic management.

In the period under review, manliness implied the antithesis of the womanly or womanish. By going away to school to a world of boys and men, a boy made a momentous step towards becoming a man by severing his connections with his childhood life dominated by his mother and domestic interests. It takes Tom Brown some 51 pages to make the step 'all real boys so long to make', to outwit his nurse and 'cut the apron strings' and then to join 'his equals in age and strength'

. . . so that he 'could measure himself with other boys' and live 'with those whose pursuits and wishes and ways were the same in kind as his own'.[22]

For Tom Brown and his successors the journey to school was symbolic of growing independence from the women's world. As we have seen, Tom travelled to Rugby alone despite his mother's reservations, having from the age of 4 learned ways of avoiding or opposing his nurse's restricting wishes. One recently widowed woman who sent her son to Ellesmere failed to appreciate the symbolic significance of the journey to school and accompanied her son on the train journey. He pointedly ignored her as soon as his friends got on the train and she was so upset by this she wrote to the Headmaster about it.[23]

4 FAMILY RELATIONS

As has already been remarked in Chapter 1, new conceptions of family life and parenthood developed in the period under review. Falling birthrates led to a decline in completed family size, which, with declining mortality rates among all age groups, meant that parents had fewer children, more of whom survived and they themselves lived to see their children grow to adulthood.[24] These developments were particularly marked among the middle classes, who despite a narrowing of inter-class differences continued to have fewer children than the working classes.[25] These changes were accompanied by the expansion of white-collar occupations, a vigorous extension of suburban housing and a rising consumer market. In the more ample 1930s there was a boom in private building, mainly of small self-contained suburban houses, many financed by building society mortgages.[26] Advertising, chain stores and hire purchase were the means of furnishing the houses of and clothing the small middle- and upper-working-class families in their new homes.[27]

Relations within larger Victorian and Edwardian families where the household also included servants had changed from a diversity of relations emphasising siblings to a narrower range of much closer and longer-lasting relations between marriage partners and their children. The debate about the implications of these changes has been about the marriage bond and the much-disputed trend towards more symmetrical relations between husbands and wives.[28] Of equal importance are the changes which affected children. Since the Victorian period there had been an increase in the dependency of children upon their parents with the reduction in juvenile labour and introduction of a lengthening period of compulsory school attendance. The reduction in family size and longer life expectancy meant that relations between siblings became less important, and those with parents more important. Mothers, in particular, changed their roles and developed closer relationships with their children as the number of servants and mother surrogates declined.[29] Families became smaller, closer and home centred, a development encouraged by the consumer market and conveyed by a variety of media like the annual Ideal Home Exhibition, the growing number of women's magazines and domestic science teaching in girls' schools.[30]

In ideologies of family relations and child-rearing there was a reaction against earlier harsher regimes and a growing belief in more liberal ideas, based however loosely on Freud. Hugh Crichton Miller was one of the writers who made Freud's theory of psychic development within the family available to parents. He explained the crucial significance of the so-called Oedipal period. For boys the period of dependence upon the mother was followed by 'a long period of psychological homosexuality' in which fathers and schoolmates become dominant and a mother's influence 'may become not only hampering but absolutely detrimental'.[31] After this boys switched their interests towards the heterosexual in the mating period. Boys thus had a stormy passage from mothers to schools, fathers and other boys and then back to a heterosexual interest in searching for a mate. Girls' development was less disjointed and problematic, being dominated by a single unifying theme, maternal instinct. Fathers had the delicate task of weaning their daughters from the school phase and other girls towards interest in a mate. 'A father's failure to play his part could be disastrous,' Crichton Miller warned.[32]

In the 1930s and 1940s a number of writers, including Susan Isaacs, D. W. Winnicott and John Bowlby, were interpreting Freud's ideas to parents. Rather than the Oedipal period and fathering, they emphasised infancy and mothering, seeing fathers as remote authority figures. D. W. Winnicott gave a famous series of broadcast talks during the war elaborating the importance and psychic complexity of mothering in the early development of infants, a process in which fathers could be involved by the invitation and encouragement of their wives.[33] In common with other writers at that time, his interest did not extend to later adolescent development. Implicit in these theories was a view that a mother permanently at home was 'a guarantee of a child's psychic health and a defence against delinquency and family and therefore "social" breakdown'.[34] This focus, however, was excessively myopic. In the families in the study mothers' influence was limited, and greatest during the critical first five years. Fathers were active and significant for a longer period than mothers in these boys' upbringing. Early childhood under maternal influence was only the merest beginning.

5 THE ROPERS: A CLERGY FAMILY

In one clergy family letters from father, mother and son have all survived and it is possible to understand something of the interaction within the family during the sons' upbringing. Rev. Lawrence Roper began his correspondence with the school in 1937, when his eldest son Martin was only 7 years old. In a long letter to Sumsion, the school secretary, early in 1938 he laid out his plans for his son's education at Ellesmere and beyond 'I think it will be wise for him to begin in the Michaelmas term next year (1939), when he will be about 9 years of age and should be ready for the prep school.'. Roper immediately raised the question of fees, a crucial matter in the success of his strategy.

> How are you going to deal with me in the matter of fees? Of course I should propose to keep him at Ellesmere until he became ready for some profession – perhaps the Royal Navy or medicine (or as it may work out). My little girl will most likely be entered at Abbots Bromley; while I have another boy to deal with later on – if the first goes on all right, no doubt he would follow his brother in due course.[35]

Mrs Roper was apparently more independent than Mrs Heywood. She came from an ecclesiastical and musical family. She had a part-time job and expressed her own independent views in letters to the school.

91

She had definite ideas about her son's education and the file of correspondence contains several letters from her. They are often long and
amusing, usually undated and written in an irregular hand. She wanted
Martin to have a period at the local school at which she was dancing
mistress, rather than going straight from 'dame school' to 'public
school'. She also had misgivings about her son being at his father's old
school – in the shadow of his father's reputation maybe. The Ropers
paid a visit to the school and Mrs Roper was completely reassured. She
wrote to Mr Sumsion that she and her mother, who accompanied
them, 'were so impressed with everything that my one idea is that he
must go to Ellesmere!!'[36]

The school offered to take Martin for an all-inclusive fee of £80 per
annum, £65 fee and £15 for extras, because of the long and valuable
family connection with Ellesmere.[37] Martin entered the Junior House
or 'Zoo' as the older boys called it, in May 1939 under J. W.
Nankivell. Mrs Roper's concern about her son's sudden move from
the cosy intimacy of home and 'dame school' to a larger public school
may have been mitigated by the family atmosphere then prevailing in
the Junior House under the Nankivells. 'Nanki', as he was known,
established himself as one of Ellesmere's best-loved characters. He
entered the school in 1912 and was head boy in 1922. After Oxford he
married Kathleen Lane, whose brother had preceded him as head boy
at Ellesmere. After a period in Southern Rhodesia they returned in
1935 to the Junior House at Ellesmere. Mrs Nankivell worked hard to
ensure the happiness of the junior boys and remembers reading to
them most nights in the two younger dormitories. Like clergy wives,
housemasters' wives were incorporated into their husband's jobs and
lives and undertook a variety of tasks in the domestic care of the boys
in their husbands' charge. It became an increasing strain for Mrs
Nankivell, with a son born in 1933 and daughter in 1937 to look after,
and in the summer of 1939 the Nankivells moved into a house in
Ellesmere.[38]

James Long, also an Old Ellesmerian and former master, took
charge of the Junior House. Long was a personal friend of the Ropers
who wrote to him as 'Dear Jim', and sent him small presents at
Christmas. Martin Roper was happy in the Junior House. This was
important to both his mother and father, who mentioned it several

times in their correspondence. One factor which may have contributed to the ease of Martin's passage and the alleviation of his mother's fears was the presence of other women to take care of junior boys. As at home, domestic care in the school was in the hands of women. Matrons and maids prepared the food, did the cleaning, cared for the boys' clothes and looked after them if they were ill. They took great care to try to ensure the well-being of younger boys. While conditions were spartan, the regime tough, the code of values among the boys vilified anything defined as cissy. Sympathetic ears and shoulders, especially for younger boys, existed among the women domestic staff. W. B. Gallie, in his account of his public school days, *An English School*, recalled how his first three years were characterised by an unhealthy cycle of anxiety, strain and exhaustion with spells in the sick room each term. Successive matrons and school doctors, recognising his unsuitability to the school's policy of physical toughening, did their best for him.[39]

At Ellesmere the lowliest member of the staff were the maids. Their duties began at 6.00 a.m. when they cleaned the masters' studies, emptying the grates, fetching coal, laying new fires, and bringing enamel jugs of hot water for masters to shave. The boys had no such luxury, cold water only being provided in the dormitories. The maids also polished the long, cold dormitory floors and made all the boys' beds. The bitter cold of the dormitories troubled not only the maids, many of whom were Welsh girls from Rhos, some as young as 14; the boys too felt the cold.[40] Mrs Roper complained in a very careful and qualified way about the cold dormitories. Martin had a number of illnesses during his first year, starting with chickenpox just after he arrived. Physical fitness was an important aspect of the manliness desired by the parents. Nonetheless the process of toughening a young boy into a man, which was begun in junior or preparatory departments, was often a cause of misgiving to mothers, especially in the early stages. Mrs Roper, writing in her son's second term in the Junior House said 'I am sure every care is taken of the boys but I think the extreme cold of the dormitories is perhaps too much for small boys. Martin does not usually feel the cold at all but he has said how cold it is upstairs.'[41] Great importance was attached to sympathetic ministrations of the matrons as mother substitutes and, while Mrs Roper praised the kindness of a departing matron to her son, she regretted the change of staff causing a break in the continuity of caring women.

The junior boys' uniform was distinguished by Eton collars, which were washed and starched each week in the school laundry. Ruby Purcell recalls them vividly. She started as a laundry maid in 1937 and has worked in the school laundry for 50 years.[42] All the boys' clothing was kept by the matrons, who gave out a set of clean clothes twice a week. The onset of war in Martin's second term in the junior school probably meant little to him. During his period there, which lasted until 1943, there was a number of changes because of the war. Several men left the school staff for active service and Miss Collins and Mrs Parry were appointed; their classes in weaving and handicraft 'delighted the boys'. Boys from other schools came and went, evacuated from other parts of the country. In the dayroom was a map of the war on which the progress of the Germans and Allies was charted and on Sundays they often played 'Germans and English' and added to the fort under the trees.[43]

Towards the end of Martin's first term at Ellesmere, his father raised a formidable hare by complaining that junior boys did not hear Mass every Sunday, the chapel being too small to accommodate them, and only one priest, the Chaplain, was at school on certain Sundays. Evans Prosser was also an ordained priest but he was not always available. Roper was outraged. It 'would not be tolerated in a Roman school and should not be tolerated in a Woodard School,' he declared.[44] The nub of his argument was that only by regular attendance at the mystery of the sacrament from the earliest age could later faith and practice be ensured.

Controversy over faith and practice was rarely far away in the High Church faction and consequently in the Woodard schools. Nathanial Woodard's own early career had been overshadowed by a disagreement with his bishop about confession. Mr Roper, a devout Anglo-Catholic, had apparently also been accused of 'Romish tendencies' early in his career.

Unfortunately for Evans Prosser this hare ran and ran. He received a long and anguished letter from James Long, Martin's housemaster, who while thanking the Evans Prossers for their many kindnesses and assuring the Headmaster of loyalty, elaborated his distress at some length. He was exercised that under the present arrangements a boy entering the school at 7 'is brought up for six to seven years of his life on Services and a Religion which do not even represent Nonconformity at its best'.

Evans Prosser's reply to Roper has not survived, but he must have cast considerable doubt both on Roper's view of the value of early religious training and of the desire for it by other parents, for Roper's reply of 24 January 1940 said:

> With regard to what you say concerning the wishes of the majority of parents, and the opinions of 'thousands of Old Boys' – so far as the wishes of the majority of parents are concerned, I do not think this matters very much: probably most of them are more or less pagan in outlook, and, if you were to ask them, would not very much mind if their boys had no religious teaching or practice provided for them – let alone Mass on Sundays: while the opinion of Old Boys, that the reason they do not now attend Church is explained by the fact that they had too much Chapel while at school is sheer humbug; since the reason they do not now attend Church is simply that they now have no grasp of Religion.

He concluded that the whole business was very 'painful and disappointing, but for Martin's happiness he would remove him from the school'. He concluded that his only course was to pursue the matter with higher authorities, and approached the Provost. His pressure in high places succeeded, for on 8 February 1940 he wrote of his pleasure at the Headmaster's news that new arrangements had been made about Sunday services at the school.

Whilst Lawrence Roper was able to take his mind away from the war and its consequences to agonise over his son's spiritual well-being, Mrs Roper wrestled with the much more mundane and pressing problems of running her household, despite the many difficulties created by rationing and the severe shortage of domestic help. Striving to retain her standards and life style, she wrote a series of exasperated and usually undated letters between 1940 and 1944 about her problems, in particular that of producing suitable school uniform for her four children. One to Jim Long begins: 'I do not know where to begin with my tale of woe over the clothing coupons. Martin's school things were 29 coupons. Then to save his school things in the holidays I got him karkie shorts 8 blooming coupons.' One daughter's outfit took all her parents' allowance of coupons. 'I wonder if you could wangle to get me 45 coupons for him. He grows up quickly . . . The whole thing of coupons for kids is of course grossly unfair as I know you will agree . . . Oh this . . . war. . . . I know this is no concern of yours but you will understand it is hard on the parents.' Martin 'burned the back of his new blazer and I was furious with him.' Poor Mrs Roper did, however, keep her sense of humour, by this time somewhat wry, and ended: 'I hope you have term free from illness, and that tyfus will not get to the school, you seem to indulge in all the complaints that are going. Nothing like being cheerful is there????? Yours very sincerely, Myra ● damn that blot!!'[45]

Apart from her early letters about her son's entry to Ellesmere, Mrs Roper's letters were mostly confined to domestic and welfare matters, especially her endless problems with providing the correct school uniform for her children, all of whom were big for their ages and grew rapidly. Like other parents she found the black Sunday uniform a particular problem. The church warden of the church of which her husband was incumbent was a tailor and he measured Martin for his new black coat, but the material took such a long time to come because of wartime shortages that Martin had returned to school and it had to be made without any fittings.[46]

The buoyant labour market during the war and the opening of nurseries in particularly hardpressed areas did provide opportunities for greater independence to some groups of women. The mothers in this study were largely unaffected. Like Nella Last and other women diarists during the war, they stayed at home knitting, making do amid the endless tedious restrictions and worrying about the mindless carnage around them.[47] With the Germans extending their bombing outside London and the south Myra Roper wrote a most troubled letter to Evans Prosser about the safety of her son travelling back to school with the severely disrupted train service, air raids and unexploded bombs in Birmingham where he had to change trains. The files of correspondence contain many such letters. The journey from home to the world of boys and men, which had so exhilarated Tom Brown, had become a nightmarish ordeal. At Christmas 1940 Guy L'Estrange took 36 hours to go home to Belfast via Stranraer and Larne, spending 8½ hours on Carlisle Station, a journey which required a police permit.[48]

Janet Finch's recent research on clergy marriages has shown that the division of labour and responsibilities between clergymen and their wives is very rigid despite their constant proximity.[49] Although changes have occurred in the ensuing period, Mrs Roper, like her successors, transgressed the boundaries of her domestic concerns into her husband's managerial domain only if absolutely necessary. In 1943, when her husband was ill in hospital, Mrs Roper made the decision that Martin should enter the senior school, having first consulted her husband, who 'was not really feeling well enough to tackle it'. Martin was very keen to go up into the senior school and his father felt they could not stand in his way. His mother, however, was not very enthusiastic about the move because he would need a complete new uniform at a time when the family had very heavy medical expenses. She was also concerned that he was only 12 and she wrote to Mr Long, 'I hope he will be alright in the blues. You assure me he will and if you think he can battle it, well that is that. It is no use worrying about him he must find his own feet. He had to at junior house.'[50]

In 1943 Martin Roper therefore moved into the senior school. Like his father and uncle he was in Talbot House, known after their games strip as the blues. During his time in the senior school Martin decided to enter Holy Orders, a decision no doubt encouraged by his father and school chaplain.

In 1946, when Martin took his School Certificate, his father laid his plan for the next two years and wrote a series of letters to the Headmaster about his son's future education and career, in view of the expense of educating his four children and the rise in school fees after the war. The elder daughter was at Abbots Bromley, another Woodard school near Lichfield, and he wished to send his younger daughter there and his younger son to Ellesmere.

Dear Headmaster,
The question of Martin's future is bothering me, and so I am writing to you about the course that may be followed by him during the next terms.
It seems clear that – unless there is an alteration of the

97

requirements of the Military Service Act – he will be conscripted in the early part of 1948 (he becomes 18 years of age on 5 February in that year). The ground he covers during the intervening time will have very great importance for him – indeed, it will have a determining effect upon the course of his career after he had done his military service.

You may recollect that I have entered my younger son, and I hope he will be able to enter the school next Michaelmas Terms in addition, I have two daughters – one is at St. Mary's and St. Anne's Abbots Bromley, and I hope the other will enter there in due course. All this means that my finances will not enable me to support Martin at a residential university; but I am anxious that he should take a degree. What I suggest, therefore, is that he might be able to read for the Matriculation Examination of Dublin University (unless the Higher School Certificate is accepted as an equivalent) during the next twelve months, and then – if successful – he might be able to make some headway with work for the Junior Freshman year before he went into the Army. I believe it would affect him very much, from the psychological point of view, if he had already got started on the Arts Course before he was called up, and then had only to continue it after his military service, instead of having the prospect of beginning from the bottom when he was twenty years of age.

For many years past, he has conceived the idea that he has a vocation for the priesthood, and I think this may be so; although, of course, I am not qualified to make any decision about that, and it must be left to those who have to train him. This leads me once more to ask you if he may begin to learn Greek with as little delay as is possible. If he does not begin Greek now, he will have no opportunity to do so until he leaves the Army – that is until he is twenty years of age. He should be able to pick it up with fair ease (given a competent teacher) at the present time; but it will be a more formidable task for him after his Army service. If it is feasible, it would perhaps be the best course for him to offer Greek for Matriculation.

I am sorry to bother you; but I hope you may have time to give me your observations.

Yours sincerely in Dno.,

Lawrence Roper.

It was followed on 10 January 1947 by a letter saying that Martin would have to leave at the end of the term and not work for the Higher School Certificate as his father would have liked because he could not afford the fees. In a letter of 20 January 1947 we see Lawrence Roper's ingenuity in furthering his son's education and career while controlling his budget with admirable middle-class economy. Again it is worth quoting the letter fully:

Dear Headmaster,

Since my recent letter to you, I have been told by the Abbot of Nashdom that the Community will receive Martin next May as a guest, and that one of the priests (who is qualified in Classics, and has been engaged in preparing candidates for Holy Orders), will be prepared to give him instruction in Greek.

Also, I have heard from the Registrar of the Joint Matriculation Board, to the effect that if Martin can get a credit in one of the Group II subjects, *before 1 December next* he will be granted exemption from Matriculation in any of the northern Universities. The only subject he has worked upon in this particular Group is Chemistry; but that subject requires practical as well as theoretical work, and – of course – there are no facilities for laboratory work at Nashdom; however, there is a priest there who is able to give instruction in theoretical work. It seems advisable to me, therefore, that Martin should work on the subject General Science (listed no. 18, 31.iii. in the Joint Matriculation list,) instead of Chemistry – for I understand that no practical work is required for this subject.

It appears to be vital to his future that he should get this credit before next 1 December, and before he becomes liable under the Military Service Act; so I hope you will allow him to devote a considerable amount of his time this term to General Science, as that subject will be vital to him for the next six or seven months. Of course, he should keep on with Divinity and Latin; but the only subject he will require for examination purposes in this year is the Group III subject.

According to the Registrar, after next 1 December, all the five required credits will have to be gained at the same time, in order to get exemption from Matriculation.

I am sorry to trouble you again; but this will probably be the last occasion in Martin's Case.

Yours sincerely in Dno.,

Lawrence Roper.

These two letters are very important. Firstly they are typical of the letters in the files about sons' education and future. Secondly they illustrate the vigorously pursued and carefully considered long-term plans which many of this group of parents had for their sons, supporting the view that for many of these parents, education at this public school was part of a consciously constructed strategy through which they brought up their sons and launched them into independent financial positions. Nashdom was a community of Anglo-Catholic religious men. Father Roper had found an ingenious means of gaining his ends within his financial means.

Thirdly they show the way in which these parents attempted to deal with the increasing bureaucratic regulation of the lives of young men during the war. Father Roper was greatly concerned to minimise the disruptive effects of National Service upon the crucial period of higher education, which would enable his son to enter the church. Like James Heywood and a number of others in the school at this time, Martin Roper followed his father's example and entered the church. His father was a forceful and committed High Church man who was the single strongest influence upon his son.

Ellesmere too left a strong impression upon him. During the Easter holidays immediately after he left the school Martin wrote to the Headmaster to express his gratitude for all that his days at the school had meant to him. He admitted his disappointment that his dearest wish to have been a school prefect was not fulfilled. However he closed his letter with the hope that 'in later years I may always continue in the Faith, pro patria dimicans' (the school motto: through faith in the fatherland).[51] The most important influences on Martin

Roper were his father and his school. His mother's influence was indirect and mainly concerned his interest in music which he enjoyed very much at Ellesmere.

In May 1947 Martin wrote to his housemaster from Nashdom. He was then conscripted and served part of his military Service in Gibraltar. After leaving the army, he had a short period teaching while trying to get into university and in 1952 he wrote from a school in Sussex, saying that he had scored 60 per cent in Latin in the Durham University Matric, a success he attributed to his teaching at Ellesmere. He subsequently trained for Holy Orders and was ordained.

The importance of Chapel at Ellesmere was influential in persuading a number of boys, whose fathers were not in Holy Orders, towards a vocation for the priesthood. Prebendary Richard Taylor, now in Sutton Coldfield, was at Ellesmere in 1936–8. The key influence in his life was Sharp, the Chaplain at that time. Taylor's father, a farmer, was 'slightly shocked' by his decision to enter the church, but his mother, who had charge of the family's affairs because of his father's ill-health, was happy. His father had always been determined he should not become a farmer because of the difficulties he had had in the depression of the 1920s.[52] This influence extended to a small number of boys; others had very different reactions. M. C. Cockin, another oral informant, said that in the 1940s the chaplain had a clique of 'churchy' boys who were also in the scouts and not the OTC and were considered 'cissy'.[53] Compulsory chapel was resented by several of the Old Ellesmerians interviewed. David Parton said there was too much chapel; it put him off,[54] and J. D. Carver particularly resented having to come back so early from exeats to attend chapel.[55] One parent complained of the school's 'morbid religious proclivities' when his son set up an altar at home in the spare bedroom to continue his High Church rituals in the holidays.[56]

6 SUMMARY

Religious belief and morality were important constituents of conceptions of masculinity in the public schools. Thomas Arnold's model of the Christian gentleman as the goal of public school education was being superseded by notions of service to the Community during the period under review. At Ellesmere College the emphasis upon attendance at Anglo-Catholic rituals in chapel was more welcome to the clergy in the education of their sons than the majority of other parents. While the school succeeded in recruiting a number of boys to Holy Orders, it alienated others, who found compulsory chapel and Anglo-Catholicism oppressive and alienating.

Fathers provided models of masculinity as providers and sources of patriarchal authority. During their school days, fathers devised strategies masterminding their sons' careers and managing the financing. The clergy, in particular, directed their sons' careers with the greatest care; their want of funds to execute their schemes had to be remedied by the ingenuity of their strategies and their mendacity.

Where the models and expectations of fathers and the school combined, as it did in the case of some clergy sons, the pressure upon the boys to fulfil their fathers' aspirations and plans could be intense.

The influence of the mothers upon their sons was limited to the short period of dependency in infancy and early childhood. After they went to Ellesmere it was indirect. The popular child-rearing theorists of the period, who emphasised the importance of mothering in infancy, shed little light upon the upbringing of these boys. More serviceable than Winnicott and Bowlby for understanding the experience of these boys would be a theory of fathering, addressing power relations within the family in their wider social and economic context, also able to analyse the psychology of patriarchy and its emotional legacy for sons and indeed daughters.

5

THE WIDOW'S MITE

1 WIDOWS IN BRITISH SOCIETY, 1929–50

Between the 1920s and 1950s, the period of this study, women experienced greater freedom and emancipation than their mothers and grandmothers. The New Women of the 1920s and early 1930s, flat-chested and short-skirted, liberated from the confines of her Edwardian mother's corsets, were enthusiastically portrayed by Aldous Huxley and Evelyn Waugh as 'bright young things'. Historians have noted the occupational gains made by women during both wars, when a larger proportion than ever before worked in the wide range of men's jobs vacated by men who had joined the fighting services.[1] These changes affected mainly young unmarried women. It was the reduction in family size, longer life expectancy, rising living standards and changing family ideologies which were much more significant for the vast majority of women, who were married and not gainfully employed.[2] Myra Roper may well have believed that she enjoyed greater independence and freedom than her mother or grandmother. She had a part-time job. She certainly had independence of mind in relation to her son's schooling and her own musical interests. In his later years at school she visited her son on her own on at least one occasion despite the difficulties of travel at that time.[3] This 'independence' was, however, very limited, for like most married women she was financially dependent upon and subordinate to her husband and her life was dominated by her domestic concerns. Caring for her husband and their four children was her first concern and a demanding one. During the war she may have perceived herself worse off than her forebears because of the severe shortage of domestic help, which she found particularly burdensome when her husband was ill. She was subordinate to him and only made decisions if forced to do so by his incapacity. Her role in bringing up her son was one of indirectly influencing and supporting her husband and son's decisions and providing domestic services. Independent new women like Mrs Julia Stitch in Evelyn Waugh's *Scoop* were much more likely to belong to the upper classes, who could afford it.

The labour market, insurance, public assistance and pensions continued to reinforce the dependence of women upon men. The assumptions and structure of men's independence and women's dependence upon men bore particularly cruelly upon widows, who were dependent on a bewildering complexity of social factors.[4] The existence and terms of their husband's occupational pension, his life insurance provision, the policy of Assistance Boards towards them, their own position in the labour market and the attitudes of friends, relations and charities combined to ensure that widows' capacity to continue to bring up their children and educate them in the manner already embarked upon with their husbands often became a lonely struggle. Bamford has noted one of the favourite strategies in the nineteenth century of widows with sons at public schools: coming to live near the school and sending their sons as day boys to save expense.[5]

The historical development of a national policy on widows' pensions is tortuous and protracted. The assumptions of eligibility under the new Poor Law of 1834 dictated that widows should work to support their children. Harrowing evidence of widows leaving children unattended to go to work led to a relaxation of the rules in the period before the First World War.[6] Nonetheless Lloyd George's Pensions legislation in 1908 excluded widows' pensions because of the fear that the extra cost would alienate the all-important support of working men.[7] This legislation was extended in 1925 and 1929, giving widows of men with two years' National Insurance contributions a pension of 10 shillings a week, 5 shillings for the eldest dependent child of school age and 3 shillings for second and subsequent children. In 1937 an important step was taken when the legislation was once more extended to cover certain middle-class groups by making widows of insured men earning £400 per annum or less eligible for pensions[8] and, as we have seen from the case of Canon Heywood, this included some of the men in this study.

For much of the period of the study middle-class widows from the group who sent their sons to Ellesmere were dependent upon the provision of their husbands' occupational pensions or private insurance and their own ability to supplement this by working or other socially acceptable means. Occupational pensions schemes developed slowly from the late nineteenth century, the Civil Service, railways, banks and insurance companies being among the first to have pension schemes for their clerical and managerial staffs.[9] Provision for widows in these early pension schemes was often separate from retirement pensions and it varied very widely. In a number of cases widows' funds had preceded pension funds. The police had established widows' funds from the middle of the nineteenth century, clearly influenced by the dangers of the job.[10] In 1930 tax relief on pension contributions was extended to widows' funds and unified pensions and widows' funds became increasingly common. Widows often received their husband's contributions as a lump sum with or without interest, of much less help to a young widow with children than an elderly one without.[11] Provision for widows remained very variable and as recently as 1965 a survey by a study group of the Royal Institute of Public Administration reported that lump sum payments were still the normal benefit paid to widows by private sector schemes.[12]

Widows, already the hostages to fortune of their husbands' pensions and insurance provision, found little comfort when they overcame the taboo against married women working outside the home and sought work in a hostile labour market. As we have seen in Chapter 1 both the 1931 and 1951 census returns showed that women occupied a much narrower range of jobs than men. Women's competitive position in the labour market was particularly hard for widows because of their age and marital status and the low pay attracted by women's jobs. In 1931 domestic service and the textile industry were still the biggest employers of women, in both of which pay was very low. In more highly paid women's occupations like teaching and the Civil Service women had to resign on marriage,[13] while nursing was almost wholly confined to single women, not by a marriage bar as such, but by the rule that nurses should live in at the hospital where they worked.[14]

To overcome the acute shortage of labour during the Second World War women between 18 and 45 were conscripted and the labour of those who did not join the women's services was directed.

The British war economy gradually overtook the German in its efficiency, for Germany did not conscript women. While these measures increased and widened the participation of women in the labour market, they affected young unmarried women, leaving older married women with their traditional disadvantages. It was the war's bestseller, the Beveridge Report of 1942, which finally brought a comprehensive insurance scheme with a system of benefits for widows. The 1946 Insurance Act gave a temporary widows' allowance to all widows, a widowed mothers' allowance to widows with dependent children and a widows' pension to those over 50. The Act, like the Poor Law it replaced, was once more based on assumptions about women's dependence and the primacy of their domestic responsibilities. While young childless widows received no pension and had to seek work, the dependence of widowed mothers on their husband's pension was exaggerated by a rule proportionally reducing allowances for those with earned but not unearned incomes.[15]

For many generations widows and their dependants suffered because of the conflicting demands of the Poor Law that they should work in a labour market which assumed women's dependence on a male breadwinner and paid women very low wages. Widows had long been objects of charity, their support and the care and education of their children being a concern of many charitable foundations. Ellesmere College was invariably sensitive to its responsibilities to such charitable purposes and requests for help from widows were always viewed favourably. Despite the very 'generous offers' of fee reductions made to them, widows often had great difficulties in meeting even these and had to find the fees by a combination of means, charities, relations, friends, employment and inordinate sacrifices.

2 A PROFESSIONAL WIDOW

In May 1929 Mrs Caroline Peters wrote to the then Headmaster of Ellesmere, Dr Billen, from a Woodard school for girls with boys in the junior school only, requesting a prospectus for his prep school, apparently on the recommendation of her own Headmistress. Her first letter gave the bare facts of her own position and the reasons for the enquiry:

I am very keen that my small son should come to you in September – he will then be just nine years old and I understand up to standard in his work.

I have the position of Sister on the Queen Agatha's staff and have my little girl and boy with me. This is our 5th term. My husband was killed in a motor accident three years ago. I do so hope you will be able to take Lawrence in September. I am quite sure Miss Andrew would give you any details you wished.

Yours faithfully,

Caroline Peters[16]

Mrs Peters's difficulties in bringing up two children were mitigated by two factors: she was a member of a profession and she had a powerful advocate in Miss Andrew. By 1929 nursing was a widely recognised and well organised profession. In the period before the First World War nurses had fought a vigorous campaign for a professional register which they controlled, a bill to this effect having been presented to Parliament every year from 1904 to 1914. The war made their claim irresistible and the Nurses' Registration Act was passed in 1919. Yet membership of the only profession wholly controlled by women was only a modicum of comfort for Mrs Peters, in trying to reconcile the conflicting demands of motherhood and finding a job to provide the means to bring up her children. In the nineteenth century and the First World War nursing had become established as a profession for educated girls 'of breeding', a vocation, which came before husband and family. This antipathy to married women was reinforced and institutionalised by the live-in rule and because a large part of their income was the emoluments connected with residence.[17] In 1930 the minimum salary of a staff nurse in a provincial voluntary hospital was £55. 4s. a year and a sister £72. 19s. a year plus emoluments. Salaries in municipal hospitals at that time were higher at £60. 13s. and £78. 11s.[18]

In view of the difficulties of married women in the nursing profession, Mrs Peters was indeed fortunate to secure this post. Her children were being educated in the kind of school she wanted and the whole family was being kept at the school. She had also found a most valuable adviser and supporter in her Headmistress. The alliance of these two professional women proved effective in gaining Mrs Peters's end. Miss Andrew wrote a warm and persuasive letter to her fellow Headteacher, Dr Billen, revealing much about contemporary attitudes to widows, boyhood and relations between Headmasters and Headmistresses in independent schools:

Dear Dr Billen,

Mrs Peters is 'one of the best' in every way and well worthy of any help of the utmost that you can give her. She has sacrificed very much and undertaken to work for her children herself, in order to ensure their having an education in Church Schools.

But she will barely manage it, she has her post here as almost equivalent for the education of one of her children and the other has to be provided for from her slender private means. I am sure she cannot nearly manage anything like the ordinary fees. I do hope you will be as good as ever you can to her. Lawrence is of average ability and a manly, nice minded straight little lad. I should like him to go to Ellesmere.

In a PS she added 'In character Lawrence Peters is really the pick of my boy boarders'. Miss Andrew was apparently well aware of the flattery and inducements necessary to accompany a request to take Lawrence for a low fee noted earlier. She continued:

The Peters are from Birmingham, and know lots of people . . . generous . . . and would speak out for the school, as for this one. I am trying to get two other boys to you – brothers of 9 and 7 whose parents will be home from Malaya to choose their school this year. They can pay properly!

With all good wishes for a good and happy term and kindest regards to Mrs Billen.

Hearty congratulations on the rise in numbers. I am so glad. Yours sincerely,
Nancy Andrew[19]

Dr Billen offered a place for her son to Mrs Peters but did not state the fees. Mrs Peters wrote on the 21st of May asking if he would consider £75 a year and Dr Billen replied offering her a place for £66.[20] Mrs Peters replied immediately accepting. 'The help will make a tremendous difference to me – I really am most grateful.' She promised to visit the school for the first time later that term after conferring with Miss Andrew.[21]

Lawrence Peters had a very successful career at Ellesmere. His mother hoped the school would find his voice good enough for the choir and he sang in the choir for several years. In his last year, he put an enormous amount of work into the interhouse music competition, but his house was unsuccessful.[22] He was also a keen sportsman, a member of the First Fifteen and a successful athlete. His scholastic career was distinguished and he gained School Certificate and matric exemption and he was offered a place at Barts. Mrs Peters was popular with the Evans Prossers. She presented some furniture and vestments for the chapel to the school and in 1939 she presented the Cups after the sports which made her 'very pleased and proud'. Mrs Peters was gentle and disarming in the way she assumed the role of surrogate father, planning her son's career and finding the means to carry it out. Hearing of 'the splendid way' the Headmaster 'had gained scholarships for your boys' she asked him to be 'extremely kind', and if he deserved it, help Lawrence to gain a scholarship at Barts.[23] Lawrence Peters entered Barts in October 1939 and later he served with the RAMC. Largely because of her training in one of the two women's professions and the support of Miss Andrew, Mrs Peters was able to educate her son at Ellesmere and launch him into a secure and respected profession.

3 THE MEMSAHIB

There were other widows beside Mrs Peters who sent their sons to the school, who did not belong to one of the two women's professions like her and who found it, in some cases, an almost desperate struggle to educate their sons at Ellesmere. In the middle of the first term as Headmaster of Ellesmere, in November 1935, Evans Prosser received a letter from Thomas Cooke's Scholastic Agency asking for a prospectus and letter to be sent to Mrs Daisy Dover, a widow recently returned from India. Mrs Dover's husband had been an officer in the Indian Army. She and her children were well established in the life and society of the British Raj. Her two daughters had married officers in the Indian Army and Police Force and her elder son was shortly to be commissioned in the Indian Army. Her younger son, Jeremy, was then 14 and attended a Roman Catholic College in India. He had learned to ride when he was young, was 'keen on the outdoor life and the jungle' and was 'already a good shot'.[24]

Her husband's untimely death forced Mrs Dover like Mrs Peters into the role of surrogate father, bringing up her son, planning and managing his career. She intended to educate him, she told Evans Prosser, at 'a good school in England where he could remain until the completion of his education'. She wanted him to sit the Indian Police examination and enclosed the examination papers, saying Jeremy would have to concentrate in the next few years and 'cram during the holidays'. Many of Jeremy's relations were in the Indian Army and Police Force and his older brother was at Sandhurst completing his training before being commissioned with the Indian Army.[25] Mrs Dover busily set about the tasks of securing her son's future, finding a suitable school, securing the funds to send him there and arranging a free or 'indulgence' passage home from India.

Mrs Dover asked for information about the lowest possible 'all-inclusive' fee which could be arranged. Such fees were those charged to parents who were abroad, whose sons saw them only when they came home on leave. Boarding schools took care of their every need throughout the year, arranging suitable holiday travel and accommodation, giving them pocket money and providing all their clothing. There was a number of such pupils at Ellesmere at this time, paying an 'all-inclusive' fee of £145 a year. Evans Prosser offered to take Jeremy Dover for an all-inclusive fee of £100. It was finding the means to carry out her plans and fulfil the role of surrogate father which created the greatest problems for the former Memsahib.

Mrs Dover was used to the ineluctable social order so carefully depicted by E. M. Forster in *A Passage to India*. Hitherto her position as an officer's wife had apparently ensured a comfortable life and secure future for herself and her children and she confidently expected substantial help from the Officers' Association towards the provision of a suitable education for her son. She enthusiastically enlisted the Headmaster's help in formulating a plan to submit for their approval.[26]

Attempts to establish an adequate pension and widows' fund for officers in the armed forces had a long and chequered history, having foundered on the relatively short span of most officers' careers and the bottleneck of promotions to the very senior and longest-serving ranks.[27] Sadly for widows some of the earliest and best provision was found in the Civil Service, insurance and the banks, hardly hazardous occupations, while the many more widows of men in the armed services had to rely on private insurance and charity. The Officers' Association had been formed to take care of the many needy cases this situation created. Its means were, however, barely adequate to the demands made upon it and Mrs Dover found her plans for her son in danger when at the beginning of December 1935 she heard from the Officers' Association that they were 'unable to consider payment of boarding fees' and that she was asking for help far beyond what she must expect.[28] This came as a 'great shock' to her and she wrote again to Evans Prosser, who offered to take her son for £60 per annum. The Officers' Association offered to pay £20 a term and Mrs Dover then told her son to accept the first available free passage to England.

On hearing that he would arrive at the end of March, Mrs Dover wrote to the College asking about the arrangements for buying and paying for her son's school uniform and journey to the college, enquiring if a charge on Harrods could be arranged. Clearly alarmed by these enquiries, the secretary Mr Sumsion informed Mrs Dover that there had been a misunderstanding and that the offer of fees of £60 was not an all-inclusive fee on the same lines as the original offer.[29] This information came as a 'complete bombshell' to Mrs Dover who had arranged her son's imminent arrival in England solely on the strength of what she supposed was an 'entire charge' fee of £60 and the Officers' Association offer to pay it. She was forced to reveal the full details of the penurious circumstances to which she had been reduced. Her husband had left no provision whatsoever for her and her son. She had to work for her living and she could not afford to pay her son's fees nor look after him in the holidays because she had no home. She had accepted a position as housekeeper/companion for wages which barely enabled her to keep herself. She would, she said, be overjoyed to have her son with her for the holidays but her dependence on others for her home and livelihood made it imposible.[30]

Domestic service was still the largest single source of employment for women in the 1931 census returns but it was being slowly overtaken by clerical work. The very long hours, subservience, lack of independence and remoteness of employers' homes made it increasingly unpopular, but for girls in rural areas it remained the only available occupation. Eileen Balderson, who started in service as a between maid in 1930 after her mother died, disliked the lack of freedom, but felt that free time was not a great deal of use with only 7s. 6d. a week. To her, like Daisy Dover, service had the great advantage of giving her a home. Daisy Dover's letters have an air of dignified resignation. Her menial position among her former social equals may well have sustained her view of society and her determination to prevent her son from losing social caste.[31]

Jeremy arrived in England on 27 March 1936 to find his mother working as a housekeeper for Major and Mrs O'Kelly in Marks Tey in Essex. They allowed him to stay with them until his mother found a suitable school for him. Her efforts in this direction had by this time become frenetic.[32] Finding Ellesmere quite beyond her means, she accepted an entire charge place at a grammar school for £60 a year although it 'broke her heart to send him to a school like that'. She felt that if she went on with the matter any longer she would 'knock herself up with the worry'. Her plight aroused the sympathy of 'two of her relatives, who so disliked the idea of Jeremy going to a Grammar School that they promised help (which they could ill afford)' so that she could make up the extra £40 and send her son to Ellesmere.[33] She was therefore able to inform the Headmaster on 26 April that her son would enter the college on 5 May. During his years at Ellesmere, Mrs Dover worried constantly about her son's academic progress and future career. She maintained relentless pressure on the school and her son, exhorting him to work hard. The plans for his career were changed. It was decided that he should follow his brother to Sandhurst but in 1938 the regulations for entry to Sandhurst were changed and Jeremy had to spend two more terms at Ellesmere. 'Mr Hore Belisha seems to have upset all my schemes,' she complained.[34]

Throughout his time at the college, Jeremy's mother had persistent difficulties arranging her son's holidays and paying his fees. On several occasions she had to ask that she remit part of the fee after the due date, the first day of each term. At the same time as Jeremy's extra terms at the school gave her added financial burdens an unforeseen crisis occurred in her job, pitching the hapless widow into debt, which she took several years to pay off after her son had left the school. In

July 1939 just before Jeremy left Ellesmere, Admiral and Mrs Poulson Smith, for whom Mrs Dover worked, died within ten days of each other and Mrs Dover had to close up their house and was once more homeless and penniless.

When Jeremy Dover left Ellesmere in the summer of 1939 his mother owed the school £13.10s.5d. and in 1940 it was constantly on her mind. From 1940 many new employment opportunities were offered to women as the government took unprecedented measures to solve the problems of the chronic shortage of labour in the attempt to maximise the country's war effort. The registration of all women between 18 and 45 and the direction of labour opened many men's jobs to women in engineering, aircraft production, farming, munitions and the Civil Service. While these developments have been interpreted as a general gain in the position of women in British society, detailed research by Penny Summerfield has shown that older married women were seen by employers as slower in acquiring new skills and more prone to absenteeism. There was little attempt to help married women cope with their dual role and the increasing difficulties of shopping and cooking in wartime.[35] Some older experienced single women found their job opportunities limited by the outbreak of war.[36] The opportunities for a wider range of jobs and higher pay were mainly open to young single women.

Mrs Dover found herself 'obliged to accept work on very small pay owing to the war'. It took her some two years to clear the debt to the school. Debt was an extremely sensitive matter, closely touching the *amour propre* of this group of parents. In such matters the school secretary, Mr Sumsion, pursued his quarry skilfully but remorselessly. He warmly appreciated Mrs Dover's small remittances and her debt's slow demise. 'I am sure you will be very glad to have this finished off', he told her when he finally tracked her down in 1942.[37] With fathers debt was about honour and social position. 'Surely a man in your position can find this money,' Sumsion reproached a dentist in 1939. 'Legal proceedings will only humiliate me,' was the curt reply.[38] The school never took clergy to court. One case went on for ten years and when the son came back to the school, looking 'very prosperous' having recently moved to a rich living in the Birmingham suburbs it was duly noted. 'Why cannot he help his father?' Sumsion wrote to the Provost of the Midland Division of the Woodard schools.[39]

113

Mrs Dover was indeed pleased to pay her small debt off finally in 1943. She was working in Dorset where she felt herself very fortunate. She had a 'quiet' time in comparison to other places although they had had 'some nasty moments'.[40] She was particularly pleased that her two sons were in the same regiment out in India. They were not in the same battalion, but had managed to have leave together in Poona in 1942. Both were doing well Mrs Dover had reported to Mr Sumsion; Jeremy, having failed the Sandhurst selection, had enlisted immediately in the ranks. Sumsion, a veteran of the First World War, opined 'he ought to make a fine soldier and seems to be keeping pace with promotion'.[41] Mrs Dover considered herself 'exceptionally lucky' that both her boys were in India, but her sons saw matters differently. The elder boy had taken part in the Egyptian campaign in 1940 and both were 'most disgusted not to be there – in at the "kill" '.[42]

It was four years after her son left that Daisy Dover finally cleared her debt to the school. Widowhood had reduced her from the luxuries of life in the Raj with shooting parties and servants to a life as a mendicant and servant. Despite this she clung tenaciously to her plan for the education of her younger son. In formulating such a plan and carrying it out she became a surrogate father, but without the finance of a man in the social background from which she came, and she had therefore to resort to begging from charities, relations and the school and, when all else failed, to inordinate sacrifice. Despite plunging down the social scale and experiencing the difficulties of a middle-aged widow earning a living in wartime Britain, her goal remained to educate her younger son at a public school and to get him back out to British India to a respected position.

4 THE WAR AND ITS EFFECTS

There is no evidence that Daisy Dover participated in the kind of discussions of the new society after the war which so fascinated the Mayhew family and which Paul Addison has suggested was a leading topic of conversation in wartime Britain.[43] Nor did she experience the occupational gains made by those women who entered the labour market to earn high wages and in some cases managerial authority in work which had hitherto been male preserves.

Ellesmere College also remained on the fringe of the war, largely untouched by the Blitz, and the frantic activities of the factories, ports and railways engaged in the war effort. War at the school meant grinding tedium for the majority of boys, deep anxiety and occasional heroism for a few. The blackout, a boring diet, the difficulties of travel, the scarcity of clothing, paper and textbooks were the main effects in the everyday lives of those in the school. All of those there during the war could probably remember something of a more expansive life style immediately before the war. Clothing coupons, taped-over windows, reused envelopes, dimmed lights and the frequent reappearance of Lord Woolton's sausage on the table became 'normality' which was rarely questioned or resented. The school magazine appeared only once instead of twice a year, away matches ceased and part of the golf course was cultivated as a school 'allotment'.[44] 1941 brought the most serious difficulties of the war to the school in the form of evacuees from other schools and a number of serious epidemics, but these problems were minor compared with those suffered by many others, and the school responded to the government's urgings to keep morale high and soldiered on. Treats and exeats with parents were another casualty of war. In at least one instance a rare and longed-for treat became a wartime nightmare. Putting up at the Black Lion in Ellesmere, Mr and Mrs Coryn found the food inedible, served by a waitress with filthy hands and the chamber pots in the bedroom unemptied.[45]

While the war enormously increased the difficulties of Evans Prosser and his staff in running the school, it crowned all the Headmaster's efforts of the previous five years. Ellesmere, safe in the fastnesses of rural Shropshire, benefited from the disruption of education in the grammar schools and the evacuation of the large number of public schools on the south coast. The Leeses were only one of a large number of parents who chose Ellesmere as a school in a safe area where their son could continue his education until 18 uninterrupted by the Blitz and blackout restrictions. By 1941 the school was full to capacity, the School Certificate and Higher School Certificate results had never been better, the school had its largest-ever sixth form and won its first state scholarship.[46]

One aspect of public school life that Evans Prosser was determined to uphold despite considerable difficulties of the war was the school uniform. Eton collars were only discontinued for junior boys in 1940 because of the difficulties of staffing the laundry, but apart from this minimal concessions were made.[47] The Headmaster reminded parents in 1943 and 1944 how important 'uniformity of dress was in an institution such as a public school' and pointed to the 'favourable impression' it created.[48]

The war affected the staffing of the school. Mistresses and retired masters were appointed to replace conscripted men. A sizeable group of domestic staff disappeared to help on the farms at home or join the WRNS and ATS. The want of maids generally increased the boys' responsibilities for such chores as table laying, bed making and shoe cleaning. The most noticeable change was in the dining room where instead of being waited on, the boys had to take turns to lay the tables and wait upon each other, a system resented by some boys,[49] but heartily approved by a mother who told a reporter of the *Liverpool Daily Post* that 'it trained the boys to make good husbands'.[50] The system was in fact a form of fagging, which reinforced the age hierarchy within the school. The younger boys performed services for the older boys who were in charge of the organisation and could impose domestic chores as a punishment. In his first year at Ellesmere the luckless Malcolm Lees had to polish the dormitory floor as an imposition. He sought to expedite this dreary task by standing on the polishing cloth and sliding up and down, only to be reprimanded by the prefect.[51] For boys at Ellesmere domestic tasks were the antithesis of manliness: women's work carried out by younger boys for their elders and betters, sometimes as a punishment.

While war at the school was about many such irksome and dull routines, not all the boys and their families escaped the Blitz. One widow, whose case further illustrates the position of widows and their strategies in bringing up their sons, felt the full force of the attack when the Luftwaffe diverted their attention from London to other key cities in the spring of 1941. Paul Watson entered Wakeman House in September 1938 under Mr Todd, some two and a half years after his father died. His family lived in Wallasey where he had attended a prep school. His mother had first contacted the school in November 1937 and was shown round in January 1938 by the Headmaster who made 'a very generous offer of help' by reducing the fees to £80 a year.[52] Mrs Watson was grateful and told Mr Evans Prosser she would 'be perfectly happy for Paul to be under your care and supervision', but she had to consult her late husband's executors.[53] Mrs Watson was fortunate, as she did not need to take a job or undergo the sacrifices of Mrs Dover to educate her son since his godfather, a businessman in London, offered to pay Paul's fees at Ellesmere. But her dependence on this man's generosity caused her endless anxieties about her son's academic progress and whether or not he was proving worthy of such benevolence. During the war she also became concerned about the continuing prosperity of the benefactor's business.[54]

After a term in the school Paul was put into the Remove form which 'made the boy very worried' and his mother even more so as she was 'more than anxious for him to progress'.[55] The Headmaster promptly and successfully allayed her worries about the nature of Remove forms and the work done there and she wrote back hoping that Paul would 'show us what he can do'. We do not know how much the need to impress his widowed mother conveyed itself to Paul Watson. While his progress towards a career might not be reassuring, his manly courage clearly encouraged her. In April 1939 Paul broke his front teeth while out boating with some friends, entailing daily visits to the dentist and general anaesthesia under 'gas' to crown the remaining pegs. The 'fine spirit' with which her son bore the pain and discomfort involved soothed Mrs Watson's worries over his late return to school and the expense of his treatment.[56]

On 7 September 1940 the Germans began their night bombing of London, the 'Blitz'. They bombed London every night until November. Londoners adapted their emergency services and life style, sleeping in the Underground stations and tunnels, but the Germans then changed their tactics and in the final phase of the Blitz in the spring of 1941 the Midland industrial centres and western ports like Liverpool became the major targets. Their attacks were most devastating on the morale of smaller towns, which did not expect attacks and were consequently ill prepared. The reaction of most of the population was to abandon their homes and flee to less vulnerable areas, leaving those engaged in war work to try to cope in the devastated areas and restore shattered services, as Mrs Watson found.[57]

On 16 March 1941 Wallasey was attacked and the front windows of the Watsons' house were blown out. For Mrs Watson it was a 'terrifying experience'. 'The destruction in the immediate neighbourhood' was appalling. They had no water in the house for 5 days and had to queue at standpipes in the street. The town's gas supply was cut off completely and electricity was spasmodic. Practically all the residents left and Mrs Watson had 'no friends left at all'. She and her daughter could not leave, as her daughter had taken advantage of the improved opportunities for young single women and was working as personal secretary to the local food controller, a good post which she enjoyed. Mrs Watson therefore asked if Paul could leave all his sports and corps clothes and gear at school, bringing only his essential things home because they had to be 'ready to leave at any time'.[58] She sent a small trunk to the school which 'used to be fitted to our car in the old days' for Paul to store his things. In the Easter holidays of 1941 the family slept in Hoylake and travelled into Wallasey during the day, 'all very trying and tiring'.[59]

During these holidays Mrs Watson gave notice that Paul would leave school after passing the School Certificate, hopefully, in the summer and in any case his godfather expected him to leave then. Unlike Mrs Dover and Mrs Peters, Mrs Watson had not assumed the role of surrogate father and had 'absolutely no idea what to do with him afterwards'. She was 'naturally very worried'. She consulted the Headmaster, who as we have seen was recommending university short courses as the best career route for his pupils at that time. This course of action had the advantage from the school's point of view that pupils stayed at school until they entered university. The problem for Mrs Watson was the additional expense for her son's benefactor. She deftly transferred this problem to its authors and asked Mr Todd, her son's housemaster, and the Headmaster to write to his godfather explaining the benefits of this plan, including anything they 'could say in Paul's favour'.[60] Paul failed the School Certificate in the summer of 1941. His mother was 'very disappointed', 'so much depended upon it' – 'entering the University short course for the Air Force is quite impossible'.[61] Paul retook the examination again unsuccessfully at Shrewsbury school in November 1941 and left Ellesmere at Christmas to join the Royal Air Force in the ranks.

5 SUMMARY

The widows among this group of parents faced the greatest difficulties in bringing up their sons to enter suitable careers. They had the unenviable task of becoming surrogate fathers, devising and carrying out financial and educational strategies, but without the necessary financial means. Their circumstances varied greatly depending upon their husbands' occupational pension and private insurance provision, help from charities and relations. Their position and needs contradicted social assumptions about women's dependence upon men and the all-consuming nature of motherhood which underpinned the limited participation and low position of women in the labour market. Middle-aged women, who were not members of the women's professions, attempting to re-enter the labour market, found only the low-paid menial positions open to them. Professional women with support from the school and elsewhere just about managed to educate their sons at the school, but others resorted to mendicancy, inordinate sacrifices and debt.

Their correspondence gives few indications of the ways in which these three widows coped with the emotional and psychological problems of bringing up their sons without the all-important model of the father which loomed so large for other boys. They may well have believed that sending their sons away to an all-boys boarding school to be made into men by men and other boys according to the prestigious public school models of masculinity was the very best substitute they could provide. The war, as we have already seen, brought a crisis in the plans of these parents for their sons' careers as ever more complex and rigorous regulations were introduced for young men. The absence of young men away in the armed services created wider opportunities for young women, but it did not help older widows, such as those in the study, trying to enter the labour market. Among the men in the services, at the school and among the boys' families, the war was not a universal experience of heroism and self-sacrifice in which all sections of the population shared a universal experience, the crucible of a desire for a fairer and more equal society. For those at the school and their families at home the war was a matter of surviving the tedium of irksome restrictions and inconveniences of a country at war. The school survived very considerable difficulties and hardships imposed by the presence of evacuees, rationing, increasing costs, staffing and other shortages, not least among the domestic staff. Ellesmere, in a 'safe' rural position 'had a good war'. The disruption of shared facilities in the evacuated and reception grammar schools and the position of 'the public school belt' on the south coast ensured that Ellesmere College was full and made a profit.

6

PROFESSIONAL FATHERS AND SONS

1 THE PROFESSIONS 1929–1950

The second largest group of boys in the school between 1929 and 1950, after those from the families of businessmen, was that of sons of men in the professions, solicitors, doctors, bank managers and Civil Servants. This group of occupations was expanding steadily in the 1930s and 1940s. The only profession to decline significantly between the 1931 and 1951 censuses was that of the Church of England clergy. The number of men in the Civil Service trebled from 19,378 to 59,514; those in the professional and technical categories of occupations increased from 404,302 to 714,197 and medical practitioners from 26,490 to 36,190. The largest rises were in the scientific and industrial professions. Civil and structural engineers had more than doubled from 21,821 to 53,529 and there were more than four times as many mechanical engineers, over 50,000 in 1951.[1] While the traditional professions received their remuneration in the form of fees, many of the newer and more rapidly expanding professions were salaried. While during the 1930s salaries had recovered more rapidly than wages from the depression, they received a setback at the beginning of the war when income tax rose to 35 per cent and prices and wages rose sharply. As one doctor's wife told the Headmaster in 1943, ' . . . times become harder for middle class people who have always tried hard to do their best for their country while doing for themselves and in no way being a charge on the state.'[2] Many found it hard to manage their sons' education. The salaries of Civil Servants in the executive class rose by 13 per cent between 1940 and 1944 but accelerated in the years after the war to 32 per cent by 1950. Meanwhile prices had risen 22 per cent between 1940 and 1944 and increased a further 26 per cent between 1945 and 1950.[3]

Many of the newer, expanding occupations were attempting to organise themselves in a similar way to the traditional professions of medicine and the law by electing councils to control practice, entry and training. There were two different routes into many of the professions at this period: apprenticeship and part-time study or full-time study in higher education. The more established professions were moving steadily away from apprenticeship towards a fully graduate profession. Reform of the veterinary profession, for example, had begun in the early nineteenth century with the establishment of veterinary Colleges in London and Edinburgh, followed by the granting of a Royal Charter to the Royal College of Veterinary Surgeons in 1844 and an Act in 1881 requiring the colleges to examine and maintain a Register of Veterinary Surgeons.[4] Apprenticeship was finally abolished and practice limited to graduates in 1948.

As we have already seen, the introduction of the School Certificate after the First World War was followed by its increasing use as an alternative criterion to a profession's own preliminary examination to control the standard of entry to professional training. There was a steady expansion in the entries for the School Certificate and in university places in the period under review. The war greatly increased the demand for scientific and technological research and training. During the war, as we have seen, the universities ran short courses which enabled entrants to matriculate and return after demobilisation to complete their degrees. For the parents in the study the war was at worst an interruption in, and at best a suitable introduction to, a peacetime professional career. Demobilisation caused a sudden and sharp increase in the competition for places in the universities for entrants born between 1928 and 1931 seeking places between 1946 and 1949, when up to 90 per cent of university places were reserved for ex-servicemen and women.

2 CHARACTER TRAINING AND DISCIPLINE

Success in the careers parents favoured required not only the intellectual ability to pass examinations, but also the drive and ambition to succeed in a competitive hierarchy. For professional parents academic

Table 3   Full-time students with UK home addresses in UK universities, 1946–7

	MEN	WOMEN	TOTAL
Ex-service personnel	22 356	1 879	24 235
Ex school boys and girls	21 593	14 326	35 919
Total	43 949	16 205	60 154

Source: *Universities Quarterly* (1947), vol. 2, no. 1, p. 22.

success and character training were often inseparable. Lack of ability was pardonable; lack of effort was not. Academic progress was carefully monitored, laziness being the principal vice to be eradicated. Henry Davidson, a retired Civil Servant, noted a 'steady retrogression' in his son's progress in his first four terms at Ellesmere. His form place was fifth, fifth, twelfth and twenty-second, 'a most unsatisfactory record'. In his father's view the boy did 'not lack intelligence'. Mr Davidson was particularly incensed by his son Ian's poor performance in physics, thirtieth in a class of thirty. In the holidays Ian had been coached by his father, who was 'struck by his quickness of uptake and excellent memory'. The remedy was simple: 'more drive is needed'.[5]

During the period under review there was a widely held view that the unique value of character training in a boarding school lay in the lessons learned by being a member of a community. The Fleming Committee, appointed in 1942 to examine ways of associating the Public Schools more closely with the maintained sector, found wide support for the view that community life in a boarding school taught pupils 'self reliance and confidence', 'unconsciously to give or obey orders' and 'by degrees to become fit for . . . responsibilities'.[6] Such views were common among parents, like Canon Heywood, whose sons did not fulfil their academic aspirations. They comforted themselves with the way their sons had benefited from the character training at the school.

The Headmaster's view was rather different. For him character training was primarily about instilling discipline. Insulated from all other extraneous influences, under the masters and prefects, a boy had to learn to accept authority and obey rules, a habit which once acquired would remain for the rest of his life. One case illustrating Evans Prosser's views is that of Eric Jarvis. In 1941 Eric was in the junior School and his parents were informed that he was 'idle, lazy and indolent and would not work to the extent of his capabilities, although he had ability he would not try and he was untidy and careless both in and out of form'. Eric's father was an army officer stationed nearby. The family had a house in Ellesmere and Eric was a dayboy at the College. Evans Prosser's solution was that Eric should become a boarder rather than returning home every night and weekend. In that way 'he would come under the discipline of the prefects and the masters and he will be made to do things to time'. Mrs Jarvis was unimpressed, and in a carefully argued letter she examined every possible reason for her son's behaviour, concluding that a 'good rest away' from school and home 'running wild', 'in the way of a homeopathic treatment, a little idleness might cure the wish to be idle'.[7] Unfortunately we do not have the Headmaster's reaction to this unwarranted intrusion of A. S. Neill's progressivism among the public school shibboleths. Whatever the Headmaster may have urged was unsuccessful and Eric Jarvis spent the summer of 1941 on his mother's sister's farm. One can only imagine the baneful influence this experience left from the school's point of view.

Many of the school's rules were aimed at insulating the boys from such unorthodox and dangerous influences as Mrs Jarvis's through the strict regulation of exeats, parents' visits, trips to Ellesmere and contacts with domestic staff. So effective was the insulation that Major Thornton referred to the school as a 'cocoon'.[8] D. J. Latham was not so kind, in his early days at Ellesmere finding it a 'prison'.[9]

Parents, especially mothers like Mrs Jarvis, were seen as self-indulgent and inimical to the development of the drive and will power necessary for masculine ambition and success in a career. Parents were allowed to visit twice a term. When one boy had four visits, the matter was brought to the offending parents' attention sharply and their irresponsibility in taking the boy for a drive in one of his father's lorries on the pretext of visiting his sick mother was underlined.[10] During the war visits from parents became a rare event because of petrol rationing and government propaganda to make journeys only if they were necessary. A. E. Carver's parents continued to visit by catching the train from Wolverhampton to Oswestry and cycling from Oswestry to the College. One evening they missed the last train from Oswestry and cycled all the way to Wolverhampton, arriving home at 5 a.m.[11]

Visits to the town of Ellesmere by the boys required the written permission of their housemaster. They were limited to four per term for boys over 15 only. Walks, compulsory on Sunday afternoons, had to be in the country; the shop in Tetchill, the nearest hamlet, was out of bounds.[12] As a sixth former D. J. Latham was allowed to bring his bicycle to school on condition he cycled only in the country lanes round the school and did not go to Ellesmere on it.[13] M. C. Cockin, who, as a prep school boy, was free to cycle about Lichfield, resented the enforced isolation. 'It was monastic', he said, 'and they kept it that way.'[14] As in other public schools at this period, the strongest sanctions were reserved for the prohibition of social and sexual pollution by contacts with the maids. Relations between boys and maids were punished by expulsion and dismissal respectively. Ruby Purcell remembered an episode during her early days at the school when a couple met in an upstairs lavatory until it came to the notice of a master, when retribution was immediate.[15] In the 1920s Peter Snape recalled a case in which the boy concerned was publicly flogged before his expulsion.[16]

Conformity to a rigid set of written and unwritten rules was one of the distinguishing marks of the public schools, which aroused the most common criticism of their education, that they produced a 'type'.[17] The issue of the effects on pupils of conformity to different kinds of school organisation has provoked extensive research by sociologists. John Wakeford's study of public schools in the 1960s used Erving Goffman's model of the 'total institution', where inmates led an 'enclosed formally administered round of life'. Wakeford suggested that retreat, colonisation or 'working the system', intransigence and rebellion were common adaptations by the boys to the all-encompassing regime in the public schools he examined.[18] A study of a grammar school in the 1960s by Colin Lacey concentrated on the effects of streaming and the adoption of an anti-school culture by boys in the lower streams, who found few intrinsic rewards in the school.[19] Recent research in a wide range of schools including public schools has lent support to the view that school organisation factors like rules and the distribution of authority and responsibility among staff and pupils have significant consequences for pupils. Their reactions are active and complex, bringing the models, cultural forms and experience of home to bear on school life.[20] Wakeford found strong evidence to support the views of the Public School Commission, which reported in 1968, that public schools had the advantage of a 'regulated environment' and 'high level of discipline' but boys might be deprived of affection and experience emotional losses. In the Commission's view the schools' artificial isolation, lack of privacy and strong emphasis on conformity to a narrowly defined type were their main disadvantages. Wakeford concluded from his study that, 'Not all boys behave as the staff believe they should do, even less as the staff advocate outside the school that they should do.'[21] They actively adapted to their experience at school in a large number of ways with varying degrees of visibility and subversive effects on the school regime and individual boys' psychic welfare.

The evidence from the present study suggests that there were several models to which boys conformed in their adaptation to the school's organisation and discipline and that their reactions were mediated by their family and peer-group relationships and values. The strength and nature of family and peer-group relations were crucial factors in the extent to which boys experienced emotional loss and consequently their happiness or misery especially in the early years at the school. A boy's family and 'pals' mediated the pressure to conform, influencing the pattern of conformity and its costs.

Conformity in a public school like Ellesmere involved not merely conforming to the catalogue of school rules and procedures but, equally importantly, becoming an accepted member of the competitive hierarchy of the dormitory and house with their strong informal social pressures. One housemaster at Shrewsbury School, writing to his counterpart at Ellesmere about the difficulties of accommodating Paul Watson, when he retook School Certificate in November 1941 at Shrewsbury School, described his house as 'a den of lions'. He was adamant that accommodation with a landlady in the town was preferable for an outsider, who would definitely not be made welcome.[22]

Public school socialisation and models of masculinity emphasised physical and emotional toughening within the competitive hierarchy of the school's academic and extra-curricular organisations.[23] The school was not a community of equals and, although the boys were 'like situated' in Erving Goffman's sense of being isolated together in a total institution, the internal organisation of the school was highly differentiated. The houses, games and academic work were arranged in competitive hierarchies. Experience of such a hierarchy and the ability to compete within it was an important aspect of the boys' socialisation for future career success. As Andrew Tolson argues, competitive hierarchies are characteristic of the work organisations which dominate men's lives especially those with the kinds of professional careers sought by the group of parents in this study.[24] Competing successfully within a hierarchy was an important aspect of masculinity for these boys and their parents. The methods by which the school produced tough, self-confident, emotionally independent competitors could be very stressful for younger boys and the early weeks and months in the school were often the most traumatic. New boys were uncertain of the rules and models to which they were expected to conform; younger boys especially missed their homes and parents and new friendships took time to establish. Ian Davidson, whose academic deterioration caused his father such concern, found his early months in the junior school a nightmare. He wrote a pathetic letter imploring his parents to bring him home and threatening to run away if they failed to do so.[25]

3 TOUGHENING THE SENSITIVE ORPHAN BOY

Boys who had no parents or prep school experience of the powerful forces of socialisation in such institutions arrived at the school without friends, survival techniques or models of manliness to follow. Such a boy was Lionel Mason, an orphan, sensitive and unschooled in the public school world of boys and men, having spent his childhood with a variety of elderly relations. The fortunes of war deprived him even of his uncle and guardian, Commander Parsons, a paymaster in the navy, who was abroad from 1941 to 1944. Lionel entered Meynell House in May 1941, when he was 12. A shy and serious-minded boy, he suffered agonies from his more established school mates' ragging in his first term. He had no one to turn to, finally confiding in the school doctor, Dr Caspar, who visited the school to minister to the queue of assorted schoolboy ailments assembled by the matrons twice a week.

It is not clear what medical pretext gave him a place in the queue, but Dr Caspar diagnosed his patient's illness as an acute lack of self-confidence resulting in 'a sense of impotence' in dealing with the leg-pulling. In his view the 'leg-pulling' was 'not serious' but Lionel was 'greatly hurt' by it.[26] What Lionel needed was an instant course in assertiveness to instil in him the self-confidence he had so palpably failed to acquire during the sheltered life he had led before he came to Ellesmere. It was through sport that public school boys learned such lessons about the game of life and Dr Caspar duly prescribed a course in boxing, at this period considered a gentlemanly sport in public schools.[27] Commander Parsons was informed and supported the Doctor's 'prescription'. He arranged for Lionel to have a boxing course during the holidays.[28]

Lionel's difficulties 'did not come as a great surprise' to his uncle, who 'knowing the boy's temperament . . . was sure he would have a difficult period to go through'. He 'had hoped Lionel might be able to overcome it by himself', but his lack of self-confidence was even greater than his guardian had suspected.[29] We do not know what action Evans Prosser took in appraising his housemaster of Lionel's distress nor if any measures were taken to dissuade Lionel's tormentors from their destructive banter. Meynell's housemaster's concern with his house's performance in sport was keen but not obsessional. He cared for his house and the younger boys in it through the friendly guidance of his prefects. Younger boys had after all to find their feet and he did not generally interfere in this quite normal, if sometimes painful, process, which he had seen hundreds of boys survive. Survival was considered an essential hardening process, one of the benefits of a public school education.

Later in 1941 Commander Parsons sailed for an unrevealed destination and Mrs Parsons was left in sole charge of her ward and her own new baby. In the four years he was away, Lionel Mason changed to such an extent that when he returned his guardian told the Headmaster that he was 'impressed by the remarkable increase in Lionel's self confidence'. He went to see the Headmaster in October 1945 about

127

Lionel's career. Lionel was 'keen to take up medicine', but his guardian was 'rather at a loss how to go about it' especially in view of his ward's 'restricted income'.[30]

Evans Prosser wrote to Lord Moran at St Mary's Hospital in Paddington, where he had established contacts in the past and Lionel was interviewed in January 1946. In the months after his interview the new Labour government issued a spate of directives to the universities regulating applications from the huge influx of demobbed servicemen returning to civilian life and the luckless schoolboys also attempting to begin their professional training. Evans Prosser, increasingly concerned about the deteriorating position facing his sixth formers, enquired about Lionel's application at the end of May and received a most depressing reply from a very frustrated Dean, clearly unused to this degree of interference in the hospital's recruitment.[31] Having failed to enter medical school, Lionel stayed at school to complete his Higher School Certificate and hoped to begin his training after his military service, which he began in September 1947. He had been passed as fit by two medical boards but was discharged from the army after only three weeks, because of defective vision. It was a bitter blow and his uncle immediately wrote to several medical schools attempting to gain Lionel's admission in the new circumstances. He was unsuccessful and Lionel moved to Canterbury with his uncle, who was studying for the priesthood. There he worked for his first M.B. externally, but had to abandon his ambitions and settle for an alternative career.[32]

Lionel Mason had come to Ellesmere a fainthearted boy who, because of the lack of a father as a masculine model or the company of other boys in which to learn to assert himself, had to learn all these lessons at Ellesmere. The nervous little boy was indeed transformed, to his guardian's great satisfaction, into a self-confident young man, ready to embark on a career, a process suddenly made fiercely competitive at the end of the war.

4 THE LEES FAMILY

Malcolm Lees came, as we have already seen, from a very different background. He was the only child in an affectionate tightly knit family, whose parents believed that to break these bonds and send him away to a public boarding school was the very best start they could give him in life. Malcolm went to Ellesmere on 1 May 1945, shortly before his twelfth birthday, to become the youngest member of Talbot House. His housemaster was 'Oosh' Howard, the long-serving Deputy Headmaster, who taught English and history. Like Lionel Mason, Malcolm Lees was sensitive, but was saved the same depredations on his self-confidence because it had been decided that Colin West, who had been his classmate at prep school, should also enter Ellesmere in May 1945. The two boys made the journey to Ellesmere together and at the request of both sets of parents were placed in the same house and class.

Both Herbert and Lilian Lees were born in 1895. Family ties and loyalties were important to them, and throughout the five years their only son was at Ellesmere they carried on an affectionate correspondence. Every week Malcolm received a letter from each of his parents and occasional parcels from his mother containing homemade cakes, sweets, fruit, a comic and any items he requested and was unable to obtain for himself like torch batteries and stamps. Malcolm wrote a letter home every Sunday afternoon in the house dayroom. The letters were often illustrated with pin men showing recent happenings at school, family jokes and eagerly anticipated holidays together.[33]

His mother always gave him a stamped postcard as he was leaving home to send back immediately and inform them of his safe arrival at school. Malcolm sent it from the college or from Gobowen and described the journey on it. Sometimes Mr West took the two boys to Banbury in the earlier years. If they made the whole journey by train it could be very long and entailed four or five changes. When he went home at the end of term Malcolm's parents usually met him at Winchester station with the pet dog Taffy, and the whole family travelled together to Eastleigh. His homecoming to 'food and freedom', as it was known, was always eagerly anticipated. Like other public schoolboys Malcolm marked off each day on the school calendar and many of his letters mention how many weeks and days it would be before he would be home again in the cosiness and security of his family.[34] The prospect of tea and toast round the fire in the winter and games of cricket with his father on the beach in the summer holidays particularly excited him. His correspondence shows how the deep affection and security which characterised the Lees family was main-tained with the only son 250 miles away at boarding school. Travel was difficult and telephones rare, but the Post Office was cheap and highly efficient and the Lees family, all well used to literate com-munication, made full use of it to sustain the family ties they valued so highly. For Malcolm the smell of his mothers' buns in her parcels immediately evoked the little kitchen at home in Oak Mount Avenue, Chandler's Ford.

The correspondence also shows the most important aspects of Malcolm Lees's experience at Ellesmere which he communicated to his parents. He was a dutiful son, telling his parents the version of school life which he hoped would please them and show that he was attempting to fulfil their expectations. The letters therefore demonstrate the most important aspects of the school's educational regime, as it was experienced by the son of professional parents and his interpretation of that experience to his parents.

His first letter, written on 4 May 1945, was a model of affectionate concern for his parents and reassurance that he was coping well with his new surroundings and above all the academic work of the school. Not until 13 May did he admit, 'I sometimes feel a bit homesick'. In his next letter he drew a picture of himself coming home and told Taffy it would not be long. By 10 June he was counting the days – only 47. These feelings of homesickness, especially in the first few weeks at school, stayed with Malcolm for a number of years, but they were 'always contained'.[35] While many younger boys were homesick, to judge from the oral evidence, admissions of such feelings were rare. It broke the code of behaviour among the boys which stressed 'busy-ness', cheerful activities among friends, and manliness. 'Miseries' and 'cissies' were frowned upon. School life for Malcolm was always busy, a judicious blend of school work, games, choir practices, house activities, in which the all-important group of friends, 'my pals' as Malcolm called them, sustained each other.

The difficulties of Malcolm's early days in the school were shared and consequently eased by the presence of his longstanding friend Colin West and by the part he was able to play in the school's exuberant VE day celebrations, just a week after he had arrived. His mother had lived through two world wars and her very first parcel reflected her relief and national pride at the long-awaited peace celebrations. Although the tide of the war had turned in 1943, the German defence of the Fatherland became increasingly bitter and desperate, culminating in the dogged Ardennes offensive in the snows of January 1945. In her first parcel Mrs Lees sent Malcolm and Colin red, white and blue peace ribbons to wear and a small Union Jack for Malcolm to wave. This flag became part of the house celebrations. It was thrown 'out of the Dorm window and put up on the big flagstaff.' Malcolm was 'very proud of it' and can still recall his feelings as one of the youngest and most insignificant boys in the school with his flag right at the top of the flagpole cheered by the house and most of the school. Later it was put on the blackboard in Talbot dayroom. VE day was one of general licence throughout the school. The Talbot juniors 'ragged the prefects, pulling their beds to pieces' and scattering them everywhere. When peace was declared over the radio the boys cheered so loudly 'you could hear us miles away'. There was a picnic at Whittington and Beans and Bonfire in the evening. According to Malcolm, the bonfire was 'tremendous, they put about forty fireworks and as many dud cartridges in and didn't it go off with a bang. We made a figure of Hitler and we all threw spuds at it. I got him right in the eye.'[36] The boys thoroughly enjoyed VE day but authority felt that things had got rather out of hand.

Lees and West were put into Upper Remove, where Malcolm found the Latin in particular very difficult and he came bottom of the form, but he 'did not let it worry' him 'because the average age was about 12 years 9 months'. After three weeks the two new boys were put down into 3A where the work was similar to that at their previous school.[37]

An important landmark in every summer term at Ellesmere for Malcolm was his birthday on 25 June. His parents sent him a cake to have on the actual day on his table and arranged for him to take his friends to a tea shop called the 'Bon Ton' in Ellesmere the Saturday before the big day. The 'Bon Ton' was run by the mother of a dayboy at the school and it was the venue of all the boys' treats and celebrations at this time. These gradually increased in the years after the war, as travelling became easier and parents were able to visit their sons at the school.[38] Malcolm's letter of 24 June 1945 reported fully on his plans for the outing, gave accounts of his own games and the school teams' performances. He enquired about his family and gave them the latest news of his own health. He had been inoculated against scarlet fever which had caused a reaction.

His father was a keen cricketer, who followed the fortunes of MCC and Hampshire and captained a local team. Both Malcolm's parents watched their son's school career attentively. His father sent him some rules of cricket and of life during his second week in the school (see figure 1) and his mother subsequently sent him a short questionnaire to clear up some of their questions about his doings at school. Mr Lees exalted the virtues of 'playing the game' as a democratic English virtue, in which toughness exemplified by rugger had no particularly outstanding value. The rules of the game he sent to Malcolm represented much more faithfully the view of games of many middle-class fathers of this period who followed the MCC, county cricket and their home soccer teams fervently and for whom Rugby football was of little interest. For him sportsmanship was playing the game well as one of a team, win or lose it made no difference, it was only a game.

Malcolm's deep respect for his parents is shown in all his letters, which always began with expressions of very sincere gratitude for their weekly letters and especially the parcels, which contained welcome little luxuries in 1945. During the war many foods including sweets were strictly rationed. Luxury goods, like tinned salmon, were distributed by means of 'points'. Imported fruit, oranges and bananas had become unobtainable during the war because the main shipping lanes were mined. Only raw materials essential to the war effort were imported in convoys of merchant ships escorted by the Royal Navy. It was therefore taken for granted that school food was meagre and plain, requiring additional supplies from home. Families had become masters of the art of supplementing their 'rations' in any way they could. Allotments had become popular, urged on by the 'Dig for Victory' campaign begun in the darkest days of 1940 and the Leeses cultivated their plot avidly. The strawberry crop was particularly eagerly awaited and Malcolm was disappointed when a late frost ruined the crop during his first summer at Ellesmere.[39] In other years his parents always managed to send him some strawberries in time for his birthday. In the years immediately after the war, when Malcolm Lees was at Ellesmere, austerity continued, amid mounting resentment.[40] His mother pursued the fitful supplies of oranges and bananas which began to reappear and sent these to her son, for whom they were a novelty.

Figure 1   *Rules of Cricket and of Life*

CRICKET

ALWAYS

1. PLAY. FOR YOUR SIDE AND NOT FOR YOURSELF
2. PLAY THE GAME FOR THE GAMES SAKE
3. BE MODEST IN VICTORY, GENEROUS IN DEFEAT.
4. REMEMBER. THERE ARE 10 OTHERS WITH YOU
5. IF THEY FAIL ITS UP TO YOU TO SEE THE SIDE THROUGH
6. REGULATE YOUR INNINGS AS THE STATE OF THE GAME DEMANDS.
7. KEEP YOUR EYE ON THE BALL
8. REMEMBER YOU MAY BECOME THE BEST BAT IN THE WORLD. AND STILL <u>NOT BE A SPORTSMAN</u>
9. DO YOUR BEST TO HELP OTHERS
10. FACE THE FAST STUFF WITH COURAGE AND BE HAPPY IN THE THOUGHT THAT YOU HAVE NOT FUNKED IT
11. REMEMBER THE BEST BATSMEN HAVE BEEN BOWLED FOR A DUCK
12. TURN OUT CLEAN. IN MIND AND BODY
13. REMEMBER A GAME IS NEVER LOST UNTIL IT IS WON
14. OBEY YOUR CAPTAIN WITHOUT. QUESTION.
15. REMEMBER YOUR. CHARACTER IS REFLECTED IN YOUR GAME
16. PLAY A STRAIGHT BAT
17. SMILE IN ALL CIRCUMSTANCES

NEVER.

1. DISPUTE AN UMPIRES DECISION
2. BLAME BAD LUCK BE A MAN AND ADMIT THAT IT WAS A BAD STROKE
3. SLACK
4. GIVE UP HOPE
5. RESORT TO DOUBTFUL TACTICS
6. FORGET THAT A RUN SAVED IS WORTH AS MUCH AS A RUN SCORED
7. GRUMBLE NOR PUT THE CAUSE OF DEFEAT ON ANY OF YOUR SIDE
8. LET A MISTAKE WORRY YOU UNDULY. BUT RESOLVE NOT TO MAKE A SIMILAR ONE.
9. FORGET THAT YOU MAY PLAY THE GAME FOR 30 YEARS AND STILL HAVE SOMETHING TO LEARN.
10. FORGET THAT YOU <u>GET OUT OF THE GAME</u> EXACTLY WHAT YOU "<u>PUT INTO IT.</u>"

. . WHATEVER YOU DO DO IT WITH ALL YOUR. MIGHT

Best of Luck Daddy.

The contents of parcels were always shared among friends on a reciprocal basis. Four boys with large appetites made short work of Mrs Lees's cakes and they disappeared very rapidly, a point Malcolm felt his mother did not fully appreciate.[41] The sharing of delicacies sent from home cemented the network of friendships which were such an important and lasting feature of life at Ellesmere at this period.

The letters also reveal how Malcolm perceived his parents' wish for him to do well at work and games and all his letters contain some information about his performance in either or both fields. The evidence from the Leeses correspondence shows that Herbert and Lilian Lees undertook to bear the very considerable burden of the fees at Ellesmere to give their only son the most settled and best preparation available for a professional career. Malcolm's letters to them demonstrate that during his years in the school he did indeed successfully pursue his academic goals, enjoyed a variety of sports, participated in choral and dramatic performances, and became 'a veritable pooh bah' in the organisation of Talbot House.[42]

In his second term Malcolm's voice was tested. He was judged 'a very good treble' and he became a member of the 'carol singers chorus' (commonly known as the cat's chorus).[43] This caused great amusement at home and inspired one of the many cartoons with which the Lees family illustrated their letters, stressing their shared family meanings and sentiments. The following year Malcolm became a member of the school choir, singing in the chapel twice every Sunday and practising three times a week. From the outset he enjoyed 'being in the choir very much'[44] and, like his contemporary M. C. Cockin, particularly enjoyed the Christmas Carol Service and the annual visits to Shrewsbury Parish Church and Lichfield Cathedral when they sang Evensong. Lichfield was their favourite, where they had a 'super time . . . lots of good grub, which was the main thing'.[45] The previous year at Shrewsbury 'They did not give us very much' for tea at the Raven.[46]

The highlights of every Michaelmas term were the Bonfire Night, the Carol Service and the Play. The fireworks on Bonfire Night were cancelled in 1949 by the curmudgeonly 'Beef' because of a purported national crisis, ribaldly dismissed by the boys as an excuse, 'we all think it is a lot of nonsense,' Malcolm commented.[47] Soon after its foundation in 1884, the annual production of a Shakespeare play on a lavish scale to which the local gentry and school's supporters were all invited became a tradition of the school. Photographs in the early school magazines show the splendour of the costumes and staging for these productions. In 1938 Oosh Howard, the housemaster of Talbot, took charge of the productions. Casting the women's parts always posed a problem, as many of Shakespeare's female characters are demanding roles of women of intellect and integrity. In this all-male community, with its heavy emphasis on masculinity, the boys were rarely enthusiastic about playing women's roles and convincing performances were hard to come by. Malcolm, a slightly built treble, attracted his housemaster's eye as a likely performer. He made his stage debut as a lady in waiting in *As You Like It*. At the end of the play he 'had to dance with seven other chaps. We gallivant about the stage like a lot of drunk elephants'.[48]

He was also practising for the Christmas Carol Service and life became so busy that he wrote to his parents about the difficulty of finding time to write them letters. 'I am flooded out with practices of every description'.[49] The next year, 1948, he told his parents he didn't 'fancy the idea much' when Mr Howard had hinted he should play 'a young Jew and have to make love in the silvery rays of the moon'.[50] Despite the coy response, he did play Jessica in *The Merchant of Venice*, entailing practices from 2 p.m. to 4.30 p.m. and 7 p.m. to 10 p.m. every Sunday. In the same term he was also 2nd treble in the choir and was practising hard for a solo in the Carol Service.

Malcolm Lees enjoyed sport and games and it is rare for his letters not to mention some sports activity. The summer term was particularly enjoyable for the cricket and he always looked forward to the swimming pool being ready for use. In 1948 he attained the distinction of captaining the Talbot Junior XI and playing for the School Colts, visiting Sandbach Grammar School, Wrekin College and Merchant Taylors' School at Crosby which was marked by a memorable trip through the Mersey Tunnel.[51] In 1950 he played for the School 2nd XI, which he enjoyed. Interhouse sports competitions were also eagerly anticipated and Malcolm's letters contain many references to the rugger competition in the Michaelmas Term, steeplechase and sports in the Lent Term and cricket and tennis in the summer.

In his last summer at Ellesmere he played a leading part in the struggle for the Senior House Cricket cup. Swimming was the other great joy of the Summer Term for Malcolm. He learnt to swim at Ellesmere and in June 1948 he and Colin West 'passed their seven lengths test, permitting them to swim before breakfast if it wasn't too cold'.[52] The following year he was confident of swimming the channel in the holidays. The pool was a great joy to many boys at Ellesmere. A. E. Carver still recalls the exhilaration of the cold water before breakfast.

Malcolm did not enjoy the winter games of rugger in the Michaelmas term or hockey and athletics in the Lent Term as much as cricket, nor was he so successful. The weather often prevented play. In the severe winter of 1947 deep snow blanketed the Shropshire plain, and indeed the whole country, from late January until April. Almost the whole term's sports programme was cancelled and the steeplechase was finally run in extremely difficult conditions. Indoor games were popular in the winter and Malcolm's favourite was table tennis, the cause of frequent requests for new balls to be sent from home. House and interhouse tournaments were popular. They were organised by the boys themselves and were less formal than the official school sports and games.[53]

5 'MY PALS'

As National Service was compulsory, the school Corps provided useful preliminary training and Malcolm and his pals joined in 1947. His first field day in November 1947 was spent in Bagley where the boys had lessons in 'field craft and camouflage'. Malcolm 'revelled in this as we had to make our faces as dirty as possible. It was super though very tiring and I soon got to sleep when we came back. We made our own tea and had sandwiches and rolls and dates for dinner. We were out from 9.30 a.m. – 5.30 p.m.'[54] Later in his Corps career he learnt signalling which he enjoyed and thought might be useful when he did his National Service. Malcolm and his friends Colin West and John Savage sat Certificate A together in December 1948. They all passed and were promoted to the Certificate A Platoon. 'Colin, John and I will soon be generals at the rate we are going on', Malcolm jubilantly told his parents in his weekly letter home.[55] In the Easter holidays of 1950 the Corps visited the British Army on the Rhine travelling from

Liverpool Street by Harwich and the Hook of Holland. Foreign travel at this time was confined to the few. In the years after the war the British economy was foundering beneath the high waves of interest washed up from massive American loans negotiated after the war to rebuild the economy. One of the many unpopular measures of the post-war Labour government was the miserly limit of £5 placed on currency for foreign travel. A trip through Holland to Germany at a cost of £10 was therefore not to be missed and Malcolm did his best to describe it as graphically as possible.

Academically Malcolm Lees's progress was steady but unimpressive. In his earlier years at the school he reported his fortnightly form position in all his subjects to his parents. He was placed in the B form which did German under Colonel Hunter Watts, an irascible First World War veteran, whose daughter always attracted much attention in chapel.[56] There were about thirty boys in the form and Malcolm was happy if he came in the first ten. If he was near the bottom he always promised to try to do better next time. In his School Certificate year form placings were not mentioned but the nearness of the examinations and his chances of success were discussed. While he got School Certificate he failed maths and physics. In the term after the School Certificate, his last at the school, Malcolm specialised in subjects he was good at and thoroughly enjoyed the work. He was preparing for the Civil Service examinations and had decided to try to enter the Customs and Excise Division of the Civil Service. The problems involved in preparing him for these examinations had been discussed by his parents with the Headmaster, when Malcolm decided upon this career a year previously, and it had been decided that he should leave Ellesmere to attend a crammer, which specialised in this particular examination.

Mr Lees was glad that his son had decided on this particular career, but very much regretted that he would have to leave Ellesmere, for he found 'the boy so greatly improved in every way during the past year that I am sure a further year with you would have been ideal' but it was essential that Malcolm passed the Civil Service exam before his National Service.[57] The Leeses had found the school fees an enormous strain. In April 1947 they applied to Hampshire Education Committee for assistance but were told to move their son into a county school. On all three occasions when the fees were raised they received very sympathetic treatment from the School Governors and the rise was remitted. The Leeses were not the only Civil Servants in this position. At least two other families found the steep rise in income tax and school fees upset their original budget strategies.[58]

For the Leeses, sending their only son to Ellesmere was an investment in is future success. His father had wished him to become a 'good citizen in post war Britain and a sportsman in the true sense of the word'. While Malcolm Lees never excelled in work or games, he gained his School Certificate, participated in a very wide range of activities, enjoyed what he did and made lifelong friendships. His father's last letter to the Headmaster shows that he was well satisfied with his investment.

During his time at Ellesmere Malcolm Lees formed close and lasting relationships with 'his pals', Colin West and John Savage. The three travelled to and from school together, were in the same house and often the same class, although Lees, the youngest, took School Certificate a year later than West and Savage. They shared their parcels of food, always blancoed their Corps kit together and West and Lees scored some notable table tennis victories in doubles matches. In the later years of their sons' schooldays, when travelling became easier, the Leeses and Savages became friendly and travelled to school events together in the Savages' car. Later John Savage was best man at Malcolm Lees's marriage in 1960.[59]

For many Old Ellesmerians it is the friendships made at school which have been the school's most enduring legacy. The emotional loss of which John Wakeford and the Public School Commission of 1968 speak was mitigated by the support of pals, cemented by their constant and extreme proximity and the rigid code of schoolboy honour. Nearly all the men interviewed had made lasting friendships at school which were later formalised in reciprocal relations of best man and godfather and for those still living within reach of the school, in the Old Ellesmerian Masonic Lodge. In a letter to the school in 1980, M.F.H. Ellerton wrote with feeling of the 'immense pleasure the comradeship and commitment that the years 1938 to 1944 had meant to him.'[60] Once established at a deep level, these relationships could provide a well of emotional support to older boys in need. Mike Smith left Ellesmere in 1951 destined for a military career. In the summer holidays he was the passenger on the back of a motor bike when the driver went to sleep. Smith lost a leg and it was the support from his old friends and masters at Ellesmere and the school's emphasis on never giving up which sustained him in the long painful months in hospital and rehabilitation afterwards.[61]

6 REBELS AND PRANKSTERS

The cases of Lionel Mason and Malcolm Lees illustrate two somewhat different models of conformity, the self-confident competitor and the busy polymath. The oral evidence suggests that there was a large variety of reactions to the pressure for conformity. Almost all the informants mentioned aspects of the school's regime they had found unacceptable. Mild and usually undetected rebellion combined with working the system was a common reaction pattern. Smoking and ragging the weaker masters were the most frequently mentioned forms of protest. During the war the school kept pigs and the vicinity of the pigsties provided a secluded resort for illicit smokers where their activities were camouflaged by even more intrusive sounds and smells.[62]

D. J. Latham's favourite spot behind the squash courts was not so well disguised and he was very nearly caught one dark night. He saw the approaching prefect's purple gown flowing in the breeze and, knowing the boy concerned had broken his leg playing rugger, he 'ran like hell' to safety. His brother was also a smoker, but his cover was more ingenious. He smoked in his housemaster Oosh Howard's sitting room after Howard had retired to bed. Since Howard was a smoker, Latham senior's activity went undetected.[63] Devising opportunities for obtaining drink and illicit feeds in Ellesmere also occupied the pranksters and wits who tried to mark their last days at the school by particularly audacious exploits. Major Thornton and his four friends ordered a barrel of cider from the Black Lion. They kept watch and got it from the back of the school when it arrived on the horse and cart. Although very ill the next day, they 'somehow didn't get caught'.[64]

Masters whose discipline was weak were also fair game for the rebels and pranksters. David Bradley remembers an Irish master called Mullane in 1946, who was ragged by putting inkwells and books on

139

top of his door. 'The boys drove him out' and he left after a year.[65] Charlie Paxton, the history master in the 1940s, was also a poor disciplinarian who was ragged by the boys.[66] Lush, the science master, was extremely short sighted, and his control was 'hopeless'. The boys at the back of the class amused themselves by cooking boiled eggs on the Bunsen burners.[67] Such exploits occurred more often in C forms than A and B forms, confirming the findings of later observational studies of comprehensive and grammar schools.[68] At Ellesmere in the period under review the frustrations of the C forms may have been somewhat mitigated by the humane and kindly interest of J. W. Nankivell, the English master. Nanki was outside the ruling triumvirate of 'Beef', Sumsion and Howard and, after relinquishing control of the junior House, he moved into a house in the town. He taught geography but it was as the English teacher of recalcitrant 5C forms and the founder of the intellectual group, the Seven Club, that he is best remembered. His laconic humour never failed; he never beat a boy. Despite each succeeding 5C being 'delightful chaps but the most appalling I can remember', the percentage of passes was always surprisingly high.[69] The mutual regard between Nanki and so many boys is commemorated in a new sixth-form block, the Nankivell block, opened in 1981.

Nigel Dale, now a respected businessman and local politician, considered the school had too narrow an academic emphasis, failing to encourage boys of spirit and enterprise who were not going to university or into the professions. Entrepreneurial enterprises were frowned upon, presumably tinged with 'trade'. A thriving stamp-dealing business of Dale's was summarily closed down.[70] David Parton also remarked on the lack of careers guidance, apart from the standard advice to stay on at school, gain more qualifications and aim for higher education.[71] David Bradley suggested, as studies of other schools show, that C classes were more friendly and that they have kept in contact with the school and still support it through the Masonic Lodge.[72] It is interesting to speculate how far the business success of several former C boys reflects their conformity to the emphasis in the middle-class masculine role on success and financial independence and how far their 'failure' in the school's academic definition of a successful career contributed to their determination to succeed in business or industry.

7 SUMMARY

Character training and discipline were as important as academic prowess in preparing boys for successful careers in the professions. Like other public schools of the period, Ellesmere attempted to mould boys' characters by an all-embracing regime of rules and activities completely insulated from outside influences. Boys' reactions to the school's regime and the models presented were mediated by home and peer group experiences. Young boys who lacked the emotional support of family and friends and previous experience of emotional and physical hardening sometimes suffered great anguish in their early days at the school, if they failed to make friends, were ragged, bullied or beaten. The emotional support of a group of pals and an affectionate family sustained and mediated boys' reactions to the regime. While the public schools were criticised at this period for producing a 'type', the effects of Ellesmere's apparently monolithic regime were far from uniform. Boys' reactions were active, mediated by the cultural forms and models of their homes and peer groups. Among the possible models for reactions within the school were tough self-confident young gentleman, busy polymath and rebellious prankster. Disaffection was most common in C forms, which nurtured a model of manliness in which smoking, ragging weak masters and daring end-of-term pranks indicated their opposition to the school's regime and its failure to provide intrinsic rewards.

7

BEING A FARMER'S BOY

1 AGRICULTURE AND THE WAR

The largest single group among the seventy 'Aborigines', who entered Ellesmere College when it opened in 1884, were farmers' sons. As Canon Woodard had originally intended, Ellesmere was a second-grade school serving the lower middle classes from Shropshire, Cheshire and the Welsh Borders, which were primarily rural counties. By the inter-war period, the premiere position of farmers' sons had been overtaken by the sons of business and professional men.

Farmers, unlike clergymen and widows, were somewhat unenthusiastic correspondents. In 1942 Evans Prosser received an enquiry from a farmer in the east of the county:

> 'Dear Sir,
>   I have a son age 10 next month and should very much like to send him to your school. Please let me know how soon you can do with him.
> Yours truly,
> J. Gregory.'[1]

The sparse evidence which farmers left of their intentions for their son's upbringing and education suggests that they sent their sons to Ellesmere for three main reasons. The emphasis upon mechanisation and increased production, especially during the war, focused attention upon suitable 'scientific' training for agriculture and a number of farmers wanted to send their sons to agricultural college to learn the most up-to-date and efficient farming methods. Secondly, the farm could provide a future for only one or at most two sons. In families with several sons it was important to find alternative careers and training for sons who would not inherit the farm, and an academic education at

Ellesmere College provided a means of diverting them into the church and other professions, as the example of Prebendary Taylor has already shown.

Thirdly, like the other groups of parents, farmers were keen to do their best for their sons. Many lived in isolated communities served only by village all-age elementary schools until the implementation of the 1944 Education Act in the years after the Second World War. Local grammar schools might be a long distance away, with poor road and rail access from remote farms. To those who could afford it boarding school was often the only viable alternative to a local elementary school. 'Doing their best' for their sons may well have meant giving their sons a better education than they had enjoyed or endured. Judged by their letters, the standard of education among the farmers was lower than that of other groups of parents. Ellesmere promised a greater facility with the written word than they themselves had gained at a rural elementary school.

One farmer's wife, acutely aware of all these pressures and of that from other farmers' sons in the school, wrote to the Headmaster in 1947,

> my boy . . . seems rather distressed at not being put upp. . . .
> He tried very hard. . . . He is a very sensitive boy and I think
> it is having an affect on him with his cousins who are younger
> in a higher form. . . . I know he is backward but I feel he
> could do better if he was moved a step higher, and he is very
> keen to learn German. . . . If you feel he is not up to it, it is
> no use but I don't want him to lose heart as I feel I must do
> my best for him and I think if he put his mind to a thing he
> would get through.[2]

The experience of farmers' sons at Ellesmere in the years between 1929 and 1950 contrasted very sharply with other groups. In the inter-war years there was a severe depression in agriculture. Acreage under the plough declined and less profitable arable land was turned over to pasture. Investment was low and innovation and mechanisation slow despite the sharp decline in the agricultural workforce following the First World War.[3] In the Second World War agricultural production escaped from the doldrums in short order. The danger inherent in the country's growing reliance on imported food was realised before the war and planning initiated early in 1939. During the war the Merchant Navy was fully occupied carrying raw materials for war production and the Royal Navy had more urgent tasks than escorting imported grain and bananas. Agricultural production, therefore, became the focus of official policy, propaganda and regulation and a system of generous subsidies was introduced. Greater efficiency and increased production was organised by local agricultural committees consisting of farmers, landowners and officials of the local Ministry of Agriculture. Through careful direction of the management of farms in their areas the committees were responsible for an immediate large increase in the acreage of land under the plough and in the size of the grain and potato crops. In 1940, 1941 and 1942 between one and two million extra acres were ploughed up each year.

The response by farmers to government demands, promoted by subsidies, 'was magnificent'.[4] This very rapid increase in output brought the supply of agricultural labour to crisis point and farmers' newfound prosperity was often threatened by the shortage of labour which remained their most serious problem. One solution was to increase mechanisation and indeed many farmers acquired their first tractor through loans from the wartime county agricultural committees.[5] But the manufacture of tractors was never as important as tanks and aeroplanes and consequently their supply was erratic. To most farmers, the labour of fit, young men from farming stock remained the key to the situation. Farming was a reserved occupation and farmers' sons gained deferment from conscription, but not all had sons willing and able to help them. 'Land girls' were another possible solution to the problem of shortage of farm labour. In order to create a more efficient war economy than Germany, Britain attempted to maximise its use of labour and from 1941 women were conscripted for the first time in any of the combatant nations. The labour of those who were not deferred and did not join the armed services was directed into different areas of necessary war work, including the Land Army. Yet there were difficulties in this particular solution. Farm work had a gender division of labour hallowed by centuries of tradition and a wealth of beliefs and superstitions. The Land Army was not very popular with young women. Mucking out pigs was not as glamorous and well paid as the services and aircraft factories. Many young women were unwilling to live in isolated farms, where living conditions were Dickensian and local society appeared somewhere between the primeval and mediaeval depending on the sophistication of the observer.[6]

2 THE SUMMER HARVEST CAMPS

Farmers desperately wanted young men and they took whatever help they could get. One contribution to this chronic shortage of strong young men was the Summer Harvest Camp. In their summer holidays boys' schools, camping under canvas, helped local farmers with the cereal harvest, a time when they often felt the labour shortage most severely. In 1943, as a result of the government's strenuous campaign, the farmers' vigorous response and the very clement weather a record harvest was garnered. The Ellesmere Harvest Camps were held in Herefordshire. Most days were spent on farm work 'often till late at night'[7] mostly harvesting the corn crop, 100 acres being completed by the 1942 Camp. The boys also helped with the fruit harvest, root hoeing, potato picking and threshing.

They found the practical outdoor work exhilarating and took great pride in their ability to work stripped to the waist and in keeping their rows of stooks straight, especially those next to the road. The plentiful supply of rabbits, fruit and vegetables provided by the farmers was greatly appreciated by the boys' healthy appetites which had become used to life on 'the rations'. In 1942 the camp site was next to the Wye and river bathing was popular especially after the 'taking off facilities' were improved to reduce 'the torture of the pebbly bottom on tender soles'. Hereford provided opportunities for shopping and cinema sampling by the younger members, the 'Dead End Kids', mainly occupied with kitchen duties.[8] In 1941 the Harvest Camp also gave a rare opportunity in wartime for meeting and competing with boys from other schools. Twelve Aldenham boys were camped on the same site and a shooting match was arranged, which Ellesmere won. In the absence of away matches Harvest Camps were a means of maintaining such contests. Three boys from Ellesmere went to the Bryanston Harvest Camp near Blandford in 1941, attended by boys from thirty different schools where in addition to six hours of farm work a day a programme of outside speakers, play readings, discussions, games and a concert was organised.[9]

The Harvest Camps provided an enjoyable holiday and a 'very much worthwhile war effort' for the boys[10] who were fortunate to be able to make such an enjoyable contribution to the nation's wartime survival. To the older boys their spell working on the harvest may have come as a welcome relief from the consciousness of the increasing proximity of conscription and active service.

3 WARTIME HEROES

During the war understandings of masculinity and schoolboy heroes changed. Away matches were cancelled. The Captains of the Eleven and Fifteen lost some of their potency as heroes. Servicemen and women in uniform became the glamorous images of masculinity and femininity which adorned the advertisements in popular weeklies like *Picture Post*. Public schoolboys and their families dreamt of their becoming officers and were bitterly disappointed if they failed the medical, like Lionel Mason, or had to go down the mines as Bevin boys in the mid 1940s, when the labour shortage there became critical.[11] Reports of Old Ellesmerians on active service were prominent in the school and the Corps became much more important. There was a daily emphasis in radio news bulletins and newspapers upon fighting men and their achievements. It was their heroism which was saving the country. One Old Ellesmerian, John Brunt, was awarded the VC after the Italian Campaign in 1943 and it became every boy's ambition to bring similar honour to his school.

Many boys at this time acquired their heroes from the cinema and films like *One of our Aircraft is Missing*, *Target for Tonight* and *A Yank in the Royal Air Force*, in which soldiers, sailors, airmen and resistance workers outwitted the Jerries, Wops and Japs as regularly as cowboys had always outwitted Red Indians. The cinema, a staple of popular culture in this period, was restricted to the holidays for public schoolboys, whose hero was Leslie Banks, the paternalistic and monosyllabic CO.[12]

The greatly increased significance of militarism and nationalism in conceptions of masculinity was also reflected in comics, story papers and boys' magazines. Comics like *Beano* were proscribed at Ellesmere, but weekly story papers like *Hotspur* and *Champion* and the superior

146

Boys' Own Paper were encouraged. Indeed a Boys' Own Paper Club flourished for several years during the period under review.

Like the working-class weeklies, so chillingly analysed by George Orwell in 1940, these papers presented a xenophobic world of English heroes and foreign villians, from which the working classes, women and political developments were excluded.[13] Their purposes and tone were wholly different from the 'penny dreadfuls'. They aimed at a more realistic kind of identification from their readers and the tone in the features and stories in *Boys' Own Paper* was often didactic, emphasising scientific and technological developments and careers as well as heroism. Typical of the 1930s stories was the 'Red Caterpillar' in which two boys take a caterpillar truck one has invented across the desert with a cargo of salt. They become embroiled in a plot to inflame an uprising among the Tuaregs. Their success in foiling the rising involves disguising themselves as Arabs, negotiating an underground city, a chase on horseback through the desert and finally a daring aeroplane rescue. By 1941 the scene for the themes of adventure, heroism and treachery had become the Royal Air Force and pride of place in the *Boys' Own Paper Annual* was given to Ercoll Collins's *The Sea Falcon*. The villains had changed and Arabs, Indians and black men had been replaced by Germans or Japanese. In the first chapter of *The Sea Falcon*, 'By order of the Fuehrer', the Germans are seen as mindlessly obedient, strutting about shouting 'Achtung' and 'Donner wetter' while the hero Barry Falconer is a daredevil air ace, who gets up in his kite and is sufficiently maverick to drop the odd googlie. Despite leading a successful bombing raid, he is wrongly accused of espionage, court martialled and sentenced to be shot at dawn. He escapes to an island in the North Sea, which is a German U boat station, and sends a radio message so that the island is attacked and finally wins the VC for a single-handed attack on a whole squadron of bombing aircraft.[14] In the years after the war Captain W. E. Johns's heroes Biggles and Gimlet became very popular. Part-air ace, part-detective, they succeeded in such missions as Gimlet's to recover the seeds of a special type of rubber plant from seizure by the Japanese.

While parents, too, were influenced by changing popular culture, some still found it difficult to come to terms with their sons' desire for battle honours, especially after such devastating losses as the *Hood*, sunk in May 1941 by the *Bismarck* with the loss of all but three of the full complement of 1,324 men and 95 officers. 'Why he wants the Navy after the Hood I do not know, but he does and there are thousands like him,' one mother told the Headmaster sadly.[15] Another mother, whose eldest son was killed on active service in India, understood only too clearly her younger son's desire to be 'up and doing' to avenge the family's sense of loss and grief.[16]

These intense pressures upon young men during the war were particularly painful for farmers' sons. While the country honoured 'the few' and their peers were encouraged to seek honour and adventure, they were needed at home to work on the farm, ploughing up more acres to help the nation's food supply and their family's new-found prosperity. Some farmers' sons had to make agonising choices between conflicting loyalties.

4 FARMERS' BOYS

Anthony Hannay's father farmed 240 acres in Cheshire. He entered Meynell House, the reds, in September 1937 when he was 13, from a prep school in Buxton in Derbyshire. The file of correspondence contains interesting letters from all three members of the Hannay family. As in other farming families, communication with the school was generally by Mrs Hannay, who arranged a visit to the school and her son's subsequent entry.

At Christmas 1941 Tony Hannay was preparing for Higher School Certificate with the intention of going up to Oxford and entering Holy Orders, but his father was struggling to plough up more land and found Tony's help driving the tractor so invaluable that he wrote to the Headmaster in January 1942 just before the start of the Lent Term asking if he would allow Tony to leave without notice to 'help in the production of food which is of such vital importance at the present time' . . . 'his help at home would be more in the national interest than being at school'.[17] Both Mrs Hannay and Tony wrote to the Headmaster about their regrets at the abrupt termination of his education but in Tony's words, 'it is my duty to assist on the farm now that the shortage of labour is so acute'. At the same time he hoped his 'entry to Oxford will not be long delayed'.[18] His hasty departure did, however, cause subsequent problems and he wrote to his old Headmaster from

Oxford the following October, where he had begun his preparation for Holy Orders and was reading theology. He wished to stay at Oxford a year, which would enable him to remain a member of the university during his military service and return there at the end of the war. He would also be able to take his Army Certificate B, greatly enhancing his chances of a commission. However, the new regulations, making 17½ the age of conscription, stipulated that he had to have Higher School Certificate to get sufficient deferment to stay for three terms. Tony Hannay therefore laid the whole story before his former Headmaster, asking him to assure the Recruiting Board that he was capable of the appropriate standard. 'Please do not think I am begging you to distort the facts in order to grant me what I do not deserve,' he assured Evans Prosser.[19] He completed three terms at Oxford before being commissioned in the Guards and was wounded in France in 1944.[20] Tony Hannay returned to Oxford after the war, but did not enter the Church. His brother, who followed him to Ellesmere, also sought a professional career and entered Cambridge University. Their education therefore provided them with an alternative future to farming and the family viewed the interruption of Tony's education with a period of tractor-driving as a patriotic duty. For the Hannays the pursuit of qualifications and a professional career were of cardinal importance, but they were atypical of the farming families with sons at Ellesmere at this time. Others came home to help with the farm, their education curtailed and their hopes of adventure and heroism completely dashed.

Hugh Wood entered the Junior House at Ellesmere College in 1942 when he was 11. His father was a farmer near Shrewsbury and he had begun his education at the local Church of England Elementary School. He did not settle down at Ellesmere very well and his mother asked that he should be allowed to come home on Sundays because 'he does fret about not being able to come home more often'.[21] A period as a day boy was also tried and in 1945 the Woods decided to move their son to another school further away because Mr Wood felt his son had arrived at an age when 'he must settle down to school life'.[22]

This plan came to nothing, probably due to Evans Prosser's customary forceful intervention to retain pupils at Ellesmere whenever possible. His father finally withdrew him at Christmas 1946 when he was almost 16 because, 'He appears to be interested in the

Farm and I feel he will be very useful to me on the farm and I feel sure that he will be interested in farming.'[23] The Headmaster pointed out that Hugh had not yet gained his School Certificate, which would be useful in almost any career in adult life, but Mr Wood had other plans for his son. He was, he wrote 'very anxious that Hugh makes Agriculture his career and I am afraid his mind is always with the farm. I have decided to take him away from school at Xmas. He will be very useful to me on the Farm.'[24]

Mr Wood made a final goodwill gesture to the Headmaster, magnanimously commanded from his wife's domain, 'Mrs Wood will let you have a Turkey for Xmas'. This must have been a welcome gift indeed to the Evans Prossers. Throughout the war families had endured a healthy diet devoid in great measure of variety and luxuries. Christmas 1946 was a particularly significant festive season. To pay off Britain's huge wartime debt to the United States the Labour government, elected in 1945 with such *éclat*, had embarked upon an austerity programme, if anything more astringent than that of the war years. The ensuing mood of deep resentment this caused reached a nadir in the fuel crisis of 1946 and the bitter winter of early 1947.[25] After such a long and hard-fought war, the country was thoroughly tired of short commons. The feeling of the entire nation that it deserved a suitably festive Christmas with warm fires, turkey and plum pud was an irresistible one which only the minority could gratify. As 1946 drew to a close the Evans Prossers and the Woods both enjoyed the traditional fare.

How far it fortified them against the snow which fell remorselessly from late January until March is impossible to say. Temperatures in the school were arctic and the view from the windows polar. Lees nursed his chilblains with homely remedies from his mother's parcels.[26] Outside activities were impossible until March, and Cockin regarded the smooth contours of the vast glistening landscape with dismay. 'It seemed to last for ever.'[27] The school buildings stood out starkly and the sense of confinement in a desolate waste grew.

Not so far away Hugh Wood brooded on his schooldays and increasingly longed to return to Ellesmere to attempt to realise his own ambitions rather than his father's. After nearly a year at home he finally resolved to try to change the direction of his life and wrote a wretchedly contrite letter to his old Headmaster saying he would 'never make a farmer', he felt frustrated and had been 'a confounded fool'. He begged the Headmaster to take him back so that he could get his School Certificate and join the Royal Air Force.[28] Unfortunately for Hugh, his father proved unyielding in the face of his entreaties and polite encouragement from the school.[29] He abandoned his strong desire for a career in the RAF with the greatest reluctance and wrote again in 1949 to his mentor asking for information about entry to Agricultural Colleges. The mood of self-deprecation and frustration had not left him. He continued to be despondent, gloomily blaming his 'foolishness' which had left him without the necessary entry qualifications into a university course.[30] Hugh Wood was caught in a trap of conflicts between his overbearing father's plans for his career and those of the immediate post-war boy culture when every boy dreamt of enjoying the excitement and adventure of the heroes of the Second World War, the Royal Air Force.

5 LEARNING TO BE FEARLESS

This trap left Hugh with deep and lasting wounds – several years of self-recrimination and regret after he had left school prematurely. Hugh Wood's problems were caused by conflict with his father, loneliness and suppression of emotion. Learning to endure misery and fear silently without expression was a fundamental aspect of growing up from a boy into a man. As we have already noted, Lionel Mason's early days at Ellesmere caused such emotional pain he went to the school doctor. To become men, boys had to learn to be brave and never to cry. Such displays of emotion were defined as the antithesis of manliness. To cry was to behave like a baby or a girl. If emotions could not be suppressed or 'contained' in Malcolm Lees's words, then they had to be hidden. The need for boys to keep their anguish private was well recognised. Mike Smith's mother advised him that the best place to secrete any misery and homesickness was in bed after lights out.[31] Mothers, the only repositories of emotion, clearly sanctioned by child-rearing theories, often worried about the consequences of the withdrawal of their emotional support, considered so essential in infancy and then suddenly and equally deemed inimical to their sons' development. One way of learning to be plucky and fearless was by learning to take a beating without flinching.

It was the role of such discipline in the development of manliness which caused some of the most severe problems for parents and boys during this period. Discipline remains one of the most contentious issues in education, no more so than in the public schools. For more than a century the issue of corporal punishment dominated this debate. The flogging Headmasters, like Keate in the early nineteenth century, had receded with time into mythical monsters.[32] Corporal punishment, however, was a very potent issue in the 1930s and 1940s. As we have seen, Evans Prosser believed that learning to obey the orders of those in authority without question was a most important lesson of school life. Parents, too wanted discipline, but they were concerned about the extent to which the stick was used on their children and its consequences. One prominent Headmaster who believed that corporal punishment induced only fear rather than fearlessness and as such was an unsound basis for order and obedience was Guy Kendall, Headmaster of University College School in London. For him the most powerful reason for its abolition was the danger of sadistic enjoyment. The abolition of corporal punishment at University College School, with its agnosticism, was sufficiently unorthodox for it to acquire the sobriquet — the 'no God, no rod' school.[33]

For younger boys learning to be plucky and overcome fear could be a miserable and humiliating experience. Threatened by an unpopular prefect with a beating for fooling on the stairs, a charge he vehemently denied, Dennis Barnes wrote to his parents begging them to 'Please, please write to the Headmaster that I must *not* be beaten. I WILL RUN AWAY AND COME HOME'. he promised in a large childish hand. It was a deeply affectionate letter, written in fear and desperation, motivated by the belief that his parents would understand and help him by intervening. His fear of beating was exceeded only by that of ridicule. Thus paralysed, bereft of his former secure emotional support, he attempted to recall it. Painfully aware that he had crossed the Rubicon from childhood to boyhood he added plaintively, 'I also realise you may think me a baby, but I am not.'[34] Concerned though the Barnes family were at their son's distress, they were conscious of the need to minimise their own interference in the school's affairs and their son's shortcomings. The letter was sent to the Headmaster accompanied by a brief note from Mr Barnes saying that he did not take the matter seriously but thought there might be 'some little matter that needed straightening out'.[35]

The justification for this early obedience was 'that you must obey loyally in order that you may be fit to rule wisely'.[36] The common life of a public school community was made possible by it being 'the business of everybody to obey orders' and a number of senior boys were 'given definite responsibilities, small or great'. In Cyril Norwood's view, it was this experience of climbing 'to a Triton among the minnows' which was the most unique and valuable aspect of public school training.[37] While parents in general agreed with these principles, the practices of discipline and control in the school could cause distress to boys and parents. The new psychological ideas of the inter-war period were strongly critical of the 'spare the rod' philosophy of child-rearing, popular in the Victorian and Edwardian periods. They pointed to the dangers of psychological repression associated with affectionless families, severe patriarchal rule and excessively punitive school discipline associated with the earlier era. Many among this group of parents were the products of the earlier coercive philosophy 'You were told once and had your ears boxed after,' in one father's experience.[38] They wished to save their sons from the worst excesses of 'traditional' views, but equally feared the consequences of laxity and indulgence implied by excessive 'modernism'. Mrs Stevens was one such mother, who, while believing that 'the modern child is a menace if not controlled',[39] continued to raise innumerable problems about the disciplining of her son Paddy.

Somewhat unusually at Ellesmere, Mrs Stevens was a divorcée and, she claimed in her first letter to the Headmaster, a member of the peerage.[40] When Paddy entered the Junior House just before the war, she immediately entered into an enthusiastic and garrulous correspondence with his housemaster. Her letters were written in a large hand in green ink on thick vellum until her supply was exhausted and could not be replaced in 1941. After two terms she complained about the way the Junior House monitor had disciplined her son in the dormitory.[41] Two terms later she found evidence of more serious discipline problems and she wrote a sixteen-page letter again in green ink, marked Confidential, to the Headmaster. She had found her son's remarks about school life so 'arresting' that she had 'opened the subject of Paddy's life in Junior House pretty thoroughly'. It was, she said, 'no easy matter' as he had 'definite ideas of loyalty'. 'Be assured' she wrote 'that we are not "pushy parents"!!' but the master had 'failed to command respect from his boys and has to use other methods to keep order'. He was by turns affectionate and irritable. In affectionate mood he 'kisses them and cuddles them and puts his arm round them', when querulous 'he appears in the dormitories complete with slipper and cane and threatens and slashes about the entire time the boys are going to bed', 'Caning seems to be his chief idea of amusement,' she charged. She particularly objected to her son being hit on the head. 'Paddy can "take it" with the rest,' she believed, but only because he 'could take no more' had he broken the most sacred of all the tenets in the public school code – that of loyalty – when, in a heinous act of perfidy, he had gone to the Headmaster and laid bare his house-master's inadequacies.

Mrs Stevens saw only two ways out of the dilemma; that her son should leave the school altogether or that he should leave the Junior House. She preferred the second course but regretted that he would lose the chance to become a Junior House monitor and possible house captain of the juniors, a goal upon which he had set his heart, and into which he had put 'a lot of spade work' according to his mother. She found it 'a bit hard' that he would be plunged into the senior school as a 'grub' without gaining his objective.[42]

Stella Stevens may well have been viewed by the Headmaster as an indulgent mother who never failed to make a fuss about any issue which involved her son. Her concern about the effects of corporal punishment on her son in his earlier years and her view that masters should command respect as the basis of discipline rather than impose it through the rod, were shared by other parents. The Headmaster moved her son to the seniors. Views of the severity and effects of the school's discipline among Old Ellesmerians interviewed for this study varied widely from pranksters, who had taken their beatings in their stride, and believed it did them no harm, to others who maintained quite categorically that there was too much beating. One of the most revealing pieces of evidence is the enduring affection for 'Nanki', who never beat a boy.

While boys feared and jibbed against the school rules and their more ruthless enforcement, the strict order of schoolboy loyalty served to shelter miscreants and created a sense of camaraderie among any who were caught. This code of loyalty embraced firstly one's pals and then one's house and school. It was already sufficiently well developed in young Stevens after four terms in the juniors that he concealed the inadequacies of his housemaster, however much disliked. At Ellesmere 'shopping' your fellows was referred to as 'chizzing',[43] Mrs Stevens, unschooled in this iron code of honour, appears to have found it somewhat mystifying that her son was inhibited by loyalty to a man who caused him so much distress.

It was the audacious pranks at the end of term among the leavers which caused the greatest stress on school discipline. On one occasion the code of schoolboy loyalty led to the questioning of Evans Prosser's judgment by parents. In July 1944 the Headmaster expelled Alan King on the last day of his school career for being one of a party of pranksters who perpetrated a series of crimes, tolling the school bell, moving furniture about and writing obscene slogans on the school walls. Evans Prosser asked those responsible to own up and promptly expelled the only two who admitted to tolling the school bell, leaving the author of the obscenities unpunished. King's father was dumbfounded at the injustice of depriving his son of the reputation gained from a good school career for doing what the Headmaster asked and owning up. Fortunately the Headmaster saw the force of this argument and relented.[44]

6 SEXUALITY AT ELLESMERE

Even more suppressed and problematic than emotion in making boys into men is the development of sexuality.[45] Unfortunately, it is the area on which there is least evidence in the study. Manliness at Ellesmere required the emotions of fear and grief to be hidden, while sexuality and its associated emotions were buried completely. An all-male community, in which the tough and aggressive captain of the Rugby XV was the premier model of manhood, idolised by the younger boys, solved the problem of unsuitable female attachments being formed by the boys, but raised the equally unacceptable possibility of homosexual relationships developing. Men who were boys at the school at this time were adamant they were unaware of any such relationships. Beside their close relationships with their pals, friendships with masters were mentioned quite unselfconsciously by a number of informants as a particular source of pleasure in their older years. Nigel Dale and his friends were often invited by Jimmy Feist, the English master, for cocoa and he thought Feist 'fond' of him. Feist later married Ruth Collins, a maths mistress who joined the staff during the war. Nigel Dale recalled an attempt at sex education: talks by a bachelor chaplain. It was a flop from which he and other boys absented themselves.[46] If homosexual relationships between boys or boys and masters did develop they were apparently very rare and must therefore have been shrouded in extreme secrecy and shame. One master was injudicious enough to make passes at a boy, who promptly told his parents in the kind of outraged disgust which supports the view that most boys were quite naive about such matters. 'Mr Carpenter has gone nuts over me, I went to his room last week and he kept going up and down my forehead with his hog like nose. After my conversation, he kissed me, just like you see men kissing women, I thought he needed running in,' he confided miserably.[47]

His fathers' views were equally definite, ' . . . both Mrs Rivers and myself are determined that our son is not allowed to come into contact with anyone who may show the slightest inclination to unmanliness', he wrote.[48] At this period the school staff were almost without exception bachelors with rooms in the school and Evans Prosser was unusual in having his wife and children in a separate house. For part of his Headmastership he was the only married member of the teaching staff and he may well have been conscious that parents found this somewhat reassuring. The Anglo-Catholic faction of the Church of England was associated with celibacy and almost inevitably therefore with homosexuality.[49] While male homosexual love had been tolerated or even admired in other societies at other historical periods, it was illegal in England at this time and sexual intercourse with minors attracted heavy penalties. Headmaster, father and son had no place for homosexuals in their view of masculinity. Accounts of sexuality in public schools vary from that of Gathorne Hardy who claims that they 'were and are the most sexual places in the world' where 'at night, in the crowded dormitories, fantasies hovered thick in the darkness above the creaking beds while their physical release poured out in masturbation',[50] to W. D. Gallie who believed boys' overt heterosexual relationships displayed in photographs of girl friends at home in the holidays and luscious pin-ups hid extreme sexual naivety.[51] Emotional needs were satisfied harmlessly for many boys by romantic protective attachments between older and younger boys. They were 'extremely chaste', having 'a special quality' which 'could have existed only within the framework of a rigorously restrictive social code', and they were 'in most cases . . . beneficial'.[52]

At the outset of our period Robert Graves published a devastating attack on public school sexuality in which he argued that Headmasters were wont to point out the similarity of such romantic attachments between older and younger boys to the protective male in heterosexual relationships, but it was the exploitative relationships between peers seeking sexual relief which left a more lasting and destructive legacy in Graves's view.[53]

Recent writers on this subject suggest that schools and periods vary widely and that moral and sexual norms in schools could change dramatically.[54] There are a number of possible explanations for the evidence from Ellesmere or lack of it at this period. It is possible that both the atmosphere and activities were as fetid as Gathorne Hardy suggests, but for our oral informants to admit this to strange women researchers was to breach the strict code of loyalty learned at school. The evidence points more strongly towards the conclusion that Gallie's picture is a more accurate reflection of the situation at Ellesmere between 1929 and 1950 and that, despite its Anglo-Catholic affiliations, there was a similar all-prevailing ethic of puritanism there to Gallie's northern public school.[55]

However suggestive and mystifying the evidence about homosexuality, that on heterosexuality and women is even more tantalising. Gender was a fundamental ordering principle within the school, as we have seen, excluding women from all but the most marginal and servile positions in which they made fleeting appearances to perform necessary domestic services.

The school very strongly reinforced the implicit messages of home, family and the labour market; men and masculinity were important and in charge, women were insignificant, subordinate, their purpose to enable men to realise their aims and ambitions, through docile, domestic service. The school, as we have already noted, believed like Warwick Deeping's Sorrell that women's influence could endanger men's true purpose.[56] As Rupert Wilkinson suggested in his analysis of the great schools at the turn of the century, public school men were socialised away from the warmth of feminine emotion. Women had to be kept in their place, 'on the mat' in the case of native mistresses, and Graves, although advocating equality, maintained an equally condescending attitude.[57]

7 SUMMARY

Farmers' sons were similar to other boys in that their fathers took charge of and planned their careers. Farmers' wives, somewhat unusually, acted as the family scribe. Our first case study, the Hannays, were typical of many farming families in that their elder son's education was abruptly curtailed and he returned to the farm to solve the wartime labour shortage. Both sons later went to university, seeking careers in the professions. They were also typical of a very long tradition in the school of farmers' sons being diverted into other occupations as the number of men employed on the land shrank steadily from the time the school was founded.

During and after the war the experience of farmers' sons diverged from that of other boys. They were the only group who were not conscripted. The wartime need for Britain to become self-sufficient in food reversed the previous trends in agriculture, returning thousands of acres to arable and making agriculture prosperous for the first time since the Great War. The consequent demand for scarce male labour shortened the education of many of the farmers' sons in the group under discussion and deprived them of the opportunity for heroism and adventure in the defence of their country. This experience led at least one boy into severe conflicts with his father, which left him with intense feelings of frustration and self-recrimination.

Suppression of all emotion, especially fear, was an essential part of growing up to be a man. In the school the discipline system was a powerful means of socialising boys to conceal emotions like fear. It was a frequent source of concern among parents. The very slight evidence suggests that sexuality was even more strongly and possibly 'successfully' repressed than emotion. There was no place for the warmth of feminine emotion and sexuality. The subordination of women in the domestic service of men, learned at home, was strongly reinforced by the school.

8

SCHOLARSHIP BOYS

1 THE GROWTH OF THE SCHOLARSHIP LADDER

The high cost of education in the grammar and public schools and universities has always been one of the principal problems limiting access to them to the more prosperous groups in society. The provision of free education for children whose parents could not afford to educate them has a long tradition as a worthy object of charitable endowment, and a number of public schools originated in this way.[1] The oldest and most illustrious public school foundations, Eton and Winchester, both made ample provision for poor scholars. In 1613 Charterhouse debarred children 'whose parents have any estate of land' and admitted 'onlie the children of poor men that want means to bring them up'. In 1561 Merchant Taylors' in its original statutes required 100 out of the 250 scholars to be 'poore men's sonnes' paying no fee.[2] How far the handful of such places, spread unevenly about the country and largely confined to boys, was open to poor children is arguable. Many were awarded on the nomination of a clergyman, often a Church of England incumbent, which with the classical curriculum effectively restricted such free places to the social classes above the majority of the population. There was also evidence in the Clarendon and Taunton Commissions of diversion of endowments for poor scholars to other destinations, most commonly the pockets of school masters. At Eton and Winchester the Provost and Fellows were the main beneficiaries.[3]

In the nineteenth century, as we have seen, the public schools began preparing boys for examinations and careers.[4] By the late nineteenth century they formed a complex hierarchical network, cemented by a variety of institutions including the Head Masters' Conference and most powerfully by games.[5] Their clienteles were differentiated according to their prestige and those lower down the hierarchy drew some of their pupils from among the lower middle classes. They enabled a small number of pupils from lower middle class backgrounds to enter Oxford and Cambridge, some of whom enjoyed spectacularly successful careers as a result.[6] In England the introduction and enforcement of universal compulsory elementary education after 1870, and the expansion of occupations like school teaching requiring post-elementary education, made the issue of access of ambitious children from among the working classes to such education more pressing.[7] Critics of the social and educational exclusivity of the English public schools and universities saw a much more democratic model in Scotland where a system of parish and burgh schools had been established after the Reformation. Numerous bursaries enabled the 'lad o' pairts' or clever boy to proceed to the universities.[8] Following the Taunton reforms and introduction of scholarship pupils from the elementary schools into the grammar schools, the idea of a 'scholarship ladder' developed which would take able elementary school pupils via the grammar schools to the newly founded university colleges.[9] In Birmingham, for example, J. S. Wright, a Quaker button manufacturer, endowed a scholarship in 1877 which enabled elementary school pupils to enter firstly King Edward's Grammar School and subsequently Mason's Science College, later Birmingham University.[10]

The principle of open competition for scholarships bestowed by merit gained ground rapidly in the late nineteenth century. The Royal Commission on Secondary Education in 1895 considered that open competition would select the ablest pupils from elementary schools for grammar schools.[11] One of the most vocal protagonists of scholarships in the bitter debates which preceded the 1902 Education Act was Sidney Webb, a leading member of the Fabian Society, active in educational politics initially in London and later nationally. He popularised the scholarship ladder as a capacity-capturing machine in a polemical pamphlet about the nation's educational needs in the new century, *The Educational Muddle and Way Out*, published in 1901.[12] He believed that national efficiency required a single educational administration over all state-funded education and a scholarship system designed to capture and draw upon the capacities of the most able children.[13]

Both these requirements were fulfilled in the implementation of the 1902 Education Act which extended the control of the local authorities created in 1888, over education. Under them existing grammar schools were further expanded and new ones built. The scholarship system also became firmly established after the Scholarship Regulations of 1906 provided that 25 per cent of all grammar school places were available to elementary school pupils through an annual examination contest.[14] Changes in the regulations in 1924 and 1930 expanded free places firstly to 40 per cent and then 50 per cent and from 1933 it became possible for local authorities to introduce 100 per cent special places, which were either wholly or partially exempt from fees and the number of pupils paying full fees at grammar schools was reduced from 54 per cent in 1932 to 44 per cent in 1937.[15] Despite this expansion, Sidney Webb's capacity-catching machine netted only the brightest few. Research by J. L. Gray and Pearl Moshinsky, two sociologists, in 1936 showed that 96 per cent of those deemed sufficiently able for secondary education among the children of manual workers escaped the trawl.[16] Until the implementation of the 1944 Education Act in the late 1940s and early 1950s the majority of the nation's children, especially those from the manual working classes, left school at 14 with only elementary education.[17]

2 THE PUBLIC SCHOOLS AND SCHOLARSHIP BOYS

The public schools had no Free and Special Place system similar to the grammar schools. Most had scholarships and exhibitions, but only a very small number had the entire fee remitted. Although, as we have seen, Evans Prosser admitted boys from elementary schools into the Junior House with reduced fees for those committed to stay until the School Certficate, scholarships as in other public schools were awarded on the result of the Common Entrance examination which required Latin. Parents of public school 'scholarship boys' had to provide uniform, games kit, journey money and other 'extras'. They, therefore, came from backgrounds with stable incomes with sufficient 'surplus' to afford such an outlay. The typical domestic budgets of manual workers in the 1930s did not allow for any such surplus.[18]

While the free places in grammar schools expanded in the inter-war period, the public schools were paralysed by the economic depression, the torrent of criticism which assailed them and abortive debates about the relative merits of schemes for admitting pupils from elementary schools.[19] Their consciences were initially awakened by a radical critique published in 1909 by Anthony Hope and Cyril Norwood and then more deeply by the inordinate and unequal sacrifices of the Great War. In 1919 the Head Masters' Conference debated a motion about the admission of able boys from elementary schools who would benefit from public school education.[20] The issue was continuously raised thereafter, accompanied by the tide of criticism of the public schools in the inter-war period. In 1935 Cyril Norwood proposed a scheme, involving a period of classical education at a preparatory school from 11 to 13 for boys selected from elementary schools to enter public schools. Critics charged that the admission of elementary school pupils would put some of the most treasured values of the public school, like service to the community without reward, at risk.[21] The scheme remained stillborn for, though it solved the difficulty of preparation in the classics, it offered nothing on the much more intransigent problem of cost. The debate continued and criticism of the public schools intensified in the early years of the Second World War. The public schools, however, continued to draw their scholarship boys from the less secure groups among the middle classes. One of the most famous such cases was Eric Blair, son of a sub-deputy opium agent in the Indian Civil Service, educated at Eton from 1908 to 1912. As George Orwell, he saw himself as the product of a 'lower upper middle class' family, anxious to use their son's intelligence to secure or improve their social position. He was sent to 'St Cyprians' preparatory school, where it was impressed upon him that the consequences of failure to get a scholarship was life as a 'little office boy at forty pounds a year'.[22]

Apart from the few scholarships for clever boys like Orwell, musical boys could also gain privileged entry. Musical scholarships were given to boys who could sing or play the organ. The Church of England has a long choral tradition in which boy trebles play a leading part. In the period of the study parish churches aspired to a choir of men and boys. It was here through the good offices of local choirmasters and vicars that boys were recommended and recruited for the cathedral choir of their diocese. Vicars often knew about their choir boys' academic abilities and behaviour in school. Cathedrals maintained choir schools which were also preparatory schools attracting non-choristers as full fee-paying pupils. In many cases choirboys had full or part fee remissions. As a Woodard School, Ellesmere maintained this Anglican choral tradition. The choir and organ were essential to the religious life of the school and musical talent was assiduously sought from both parish churches and cathedral choir schools.

In October 1935, just after he had become Headmaster, Evans Prosser's attention was drawn, by a clergyman friend, to the case of a musical boy, Elwyn Roberts, at Cardiff Choir School. His parents

> are not very well off: the father is a Bank Clerk, but are anxious to make sacrifices for their only son (aged 11). I have suggested a Choral Scholarship might help matters. The boy sings in the choir of Cardiff Parish Church and has a good voice and plays the pianoforte, having passed some Associated Board Examinations. The boy has been well grounded in a private school of which I can speak well. He has no Latin as yet. Mrs Roberts' sister's husband is a vicar near Wrexham.[23]

Elwyn Roberts was indeed a talented boy. He passed the scholarship examination into Cardiff High School, gaining a special place and passed his music examinations. Evans Prosser awarded him a Choral Scholarship and he entered Talbot House in September 1936. He had an outstanding career in the school, scholastically and musically, and in 1942 Evans Prosser wrote to the Dean of a Cambridge College, suggesting Roberts as a candidate for the college's choral exhibition. The Dean replied that Roberts seemed

> well qualified . . . provided that he would be interested in helping run the chapel choir, if elected, particularly in looking after the small boys whom we pay as choristers. The amount of work is not heavy but it does need to be done with a good will.[24]

Elwyn Roberts was, by this time, senior chorister and a house prefect, accustomed to such responsibilities as holding the ring in the struggle for control of the ablution facilities of New Dorm. He was not intimidated by the contest, which was a cosy affair with six 'picked' candidates. The war, however, cast its shadow over the proceedings.

> There were three organ candidates and three choral, tenor, bass and myself. We were heard yesterday morning in the Chapel by Dr Middleton, who, I believe, directs the music at Trinity. He was most charming and soon put me at ease. I have had several interviews with the Dean and one with the Master, and they are both just a little timorous over the military service question. So the Dean requested me to ask if you might kindly write to the Joint Recruiting Board, explaining that I hold an Exhibition and applying for exemption for the next academic year.[25]

The Headmaster complied but in August a disconsolate letter arrived from Elwyn Roberts:

> My Dear Mr Prosser,
> I am enclosing a letter from the Master, from which you will gather that Mr Bevin has not been placated yet. Raymond Wilson (holder of an Academic Exhibition) registered the other week, showed his certificate and no questions were asked . . . I am feeling rather worried. I was born on the second half of the year and will register in October. It seems to me that, after all, any Open Exhibition is an Open Exhibition and I fail to see why the Ministry should make any exception on account of the fact that it is choral and not academic.
> I don't really think that the Ministry of Labour will deny me exemption to go up in October, if they do then presumably nothing can be done, unless we apply again through different channels in the hope of getting different answers. At any rate I should be very glad of any help or advice you can give; meanwhile we will wait and hope that it is a false alarm.[26]

After months of uncertainty Elwyn Roberts became a Choral Scholar at a Cambridge college.

After 1941, one of the most useful sources of suitable scholarship boys was the former school chaplain Rev. E.E.F. Walters, headmaster of Lichfield Cathedral School, who wrote regularly to his great friend and former colleague, Evans Prosser. The letters discuss the abilities and financial circumstances of the boys Walters intended for Ellesmere and give news of the progress of Walters's newly founded school at Lichfield and of the growing Walters family. There was a deep bond between the two men. Their iconography was identical: as clergy, headmasters. Freemasons and family men, they strove for similar ends. Walters admired Evans Prosser's enormous energy and, like headmasters of other preparatory schools at that time, was much impressed by the effect of his zeal and drive upon the school. 'What a pace you move at,' he commented on one occasion.[27]

Undoubtedly one of the most notable of all the boys whom Walters sent to his friend was Freddie Farrow, whose father was a police sergeant in Birmingham and would therefore 'need help' if his son was to go to Ellesmere. Walters judged young Farrow an eminently suitable scholarship boy. His music showed promise. He had a good voice, which was expected to break in a year or so. He had also made progress with the piano and organ. Walters recommended Farrow to Evans Prosser as an eminently suitable recipient for a choral scholarship, found a charity to pay for his music lessons and a further 'private source'.[28] Like the Leeses, the Farrows received sympathetic treatment from the school when the fees were raised in 1945. In 1947, when the Farrow fortunes were at a low ebb, Freddie's old Headmaster was once more instrumental in saving the day and Freddie was able to continue his education at Ellesmere until he was 18. His father wrote to Evans Prosser and recalled the 'lad with a good voice and that's about all'. 'The endeavours of Mr Walters and yourself, Sir, have transformed a boy of humble parents into a real man, Christian and a gentleman always.'[29] Freddie entered Sandhurst and was subsequently commissioned in the Sherwood Foresters. He went to New Zealand and was later knighted.

Sir Aino Farrow, as he is now known, is one of the most outstanding examples from Ellesmere of spectacular upward social mobility. David Rubinstein has demonstrated that the public schools, except two or three very exclusive schools, drew a small number of boys from the lower middle classes, clerks, commercial travellers and shopkeepers. He has assembled biographical evidence to show that some of these boys subsequently entered Oxford and Cambridge and a number had near-meteoric careers thereafter.[30] Research on the grammar schools is now needed to examine the extent to which they also promoted outstanding upward social mobility, as the careers of Edward Heath and Margaret Thatcher suggest.

3 SOCIAL RECONSTRUCTION AND THE PUBLIC SCHOOLS

From 1941 a debate gathered momentum in Britain and among the forces abroad about the building of a new society after the war, in which the distress of the 1930s could not recur. The place of the public schools in the education system and the way in which the sometimes striking benefits of public school education could be made available to able children from the hitherto excluded working classes was in the forefront of the debate.

Opinions were deeply divided. Churchill, who became Prime Minister on the resignation of Chamberlain in February 1940, was opposed to any debate about the lineaments of post-war society, which would be divisive and weaken the nation's war effort, a view notably at odds with popular opinion.[31] In January 1941, in an ostentatious opening salvo in the debate, *Picture Post*, a bestseller in the now-defunct market of popular news weeklies, devoted its entire issue to post-war reconstruction. B. L. Coombes, a South Wales miner, contributed an eloquent attack on the wasted human resources among Welsh mining families like his own. For him the cause was the inanities of those in power, placed there by a class system in which one class was 'born to govern' and educated to believe 'only the best is good enough for them'. Among the grim pictures of silent pits and idle and frustrated young men, he asked, 'Will there be any place for the grandsons?' His own recipe was 'more sledgehammer users in our government and fewer umbrella carriers'.[32] The article on education was prefaced by a historic photograph taken outside Lords Cricket Ground of three curious working-class boys surveying two Eton boys leaning superciliously on their traditional silver topped canes, umbrellas being the favoured ostentation of Westminster boys at that period.[33] The caption read 'The two systems of education, A picture which sums up our main problem'.

The article beneath was contributed by A. D. Lindsay, Master of Balliol College, Oxford, who had an impeccable record as an educational radical and reformer. Lindsay was a Scot, a vigorous and independent tutor, supporter of the Workers' Educational Association, who in the years before the war, had been responsible for democratising entry to Oxford. Lindsay believed that the ladder between the two systems required 'such excessive preoccupation with examinations, such continuous driving that many of the successful candidates arrive undeveloped in body and warped in mind' at the universities. Lindsay thought that all children should learn the same things until 13 when it would be decided what education each should have in a varied and elastic system free from social prejudice. The public schools, because of the superiority of their all-round education, would remain the peak of the hierarchy. He hoped the public schools 'would rise to the occasion' and voluntarily form closer ties with the state-supported schools.[34]

Lindsay's ideas followed numerous previous suggestions for wider access to public school education, which were receiving popular attention for the first time in 1940 and 1941. From 1939 criticism of the public schools and proposals for their reform reached a new intensity.[35] In a particularly ferocious attack in 1940, T. C. Worsley, a former public school master, attributed the continuing British military disasters to the education of the ruling classes in the public schools. His book, *Barbarians and Philistines*, provoked much discussion and a great variety of defensive reactions and proposals for reform.[36] F. H. Spencer, a leading socialist HMI, wrote *Education for the People*, a discussion of the post-war reconstruction of education widely circulated in the Forces from 1941, in which he declared, 'Though a socialist and a radical, I still have enough sense to view the ruin and abolition of Eton and Winchester as a national disaster.'[37] Reform and closer integration with the state system was being advocated by radical public schoolmen to save the schools from financial ruin and by socialists and radicals to end their social exclusivity. By 1941 a considerable head of steam had built up behind popular demands for the reform of secondary education, into which the public schools should be integrated. In July 1941 Churchill appointed R. A. Butler President of the Board of Education. He was a young reforming conservative, who did not consider the public schools' independence inviolable. Churchill, remembering the bitter political and religious conflicts of the 1902 settlement, did not want an Education Bill. Butler, however, continued the planning work begun by his predecessor and, with varying degrees of enthusiasm and support from his officials, planned a new Education Bill as the framework for educational reform so long postponed in the years before the war. The main obstacle to getting the bill on to the statute book were the churches, who controlled a significant part of elementary education and, despite the failure to reorganise along 'Hadow' lines before the war, rigorously opposed any reduction in the extent of their bailiwick. Butler early abandoned any attempt to include the public schools in his proposals and concentrated on the protracted and delicate negotiations with the churches largely because the public school and Church of England lobbies overlapped and Butler decided to fight them on a limited front in order to minimise the threat to the more important goal of secondary education for all. Despite the otherwise very propitious circumstances, he neatly sidestepped the public school issue by appointing a committee in July 1942 under Lord Fleming to examine ways in which closer relations could be established between the public schools and the state-supported sector.[38]

Fleming's committee reported in 1944, having consulted a wide range of opinion. Many of the Committee's witnesses were agreed on the great value of boarding school life, which lay in its being a community governed and organised by the pupils themselves. In this way they learned self-reliance, confidence, give and take and how to work with people of all kinds, whether congenial or not.[39] Disagreement came especially among the Labour movement about the social exclusivity of the schools. The Committee suggested two schemes for greater cooperation between independent and state schools. In the post-war period the independent schools were full and no longer fearful for their survival, as in the 1930s when they were more receptive to ideas of state support. The Fleming plans were taken up by a few local authorities but they were very expensive and gradually local authority support fell away.[40]

Butler's Act was not radical, but it was far-reaching. It brought together the tentative and partially successful attempts at educational reform in the inter-war period. It raised the school leaving age to 15, which was to have been done on the day war was declared, abolishing elementary education and making 11 the age of transfer from primary to secondary education. This was the principle of the Hadow Report on *The Education of the Adolescent* published in 1926, which had become the basis of so-called Hadow reorganisation introduced by some local authorities during the somewhat more favourable financial climate of the 1930s. [41]

The Act itself did not specify the precise connotation of 'secondary education', which was clarified by local authorities who laid their plans before the newly created Ministry of Education. The Act did, however, contain two significant pointers to the kind of secondary education which would be developed by its implementation. It laid upon the Ministry the duty of providing education for the people of England and Wales according to their 'age, ability and aptitude.' By way of continuing the expansion of free and special places in local authority grammar schools in the period immediately before the war, the Act abolished fees in local authority grammar schools altogether. The meritocratic model of secondary education and the era of scholarship boys and girls was thus inherent in the 1944 Education Act. The meritocracy thus created depended upon the assumption that ability was a single, homogeneous, unilineal characteristic which could be assessed by tests and examinations. Pupils were then assigned to appropriate types of secondary education. [42]

Implementation of the Act was the task of the Labour government under Clem Attlee, an old Haileyburian. Labour Party and TUC policy favoured 'multilateral schools', an early conception of comprehensive education, discussed but discarded in the 1938 Spens Report on secondary education. Instead the government followed the report published in 1943 under the chairmanship of Sir Cyril Norwood, former Headmaster of Harrow, and author of *The English Tradition of Education*, with which we are already acquainted. The Norwood Report argued that there were three distinct types of mind, abstract, practical and concrete, which corresponded to three types of secondary education, grammar, technical and modern. [43] The plans of local authorities for the abolition of elementary education and introduction of universal secondary education more often followed a bipartite than a tripartite structure; few secondary technical schools were built. The abolition of grammar school fees therefore ushered in the era of scholarship boys and girls, the successful candidates in the now much widened contest, the 11+ examination. Unsuccessful candidates proceeded to a three-year course in a secondary modern school with a narrow curriculum, terminating at the minimum school leaving age of 15, with no possibility of gaining the School Certificate, or proceeding to further or higher education.[44] As A. H. Halsey's research has shown, the type of secondary education boys received became the single most important predictor of their educational careers and attainments.[45]

The protection that middle-class parents had apparently enjoyed for their children in the fee-paying places at grammar schools was thus abolished and the effect of this upon demand for places in the public schools was immediate. The disruption of state-supported grammar schools and the prosperity enjoyed by many sections of the middle classes during the war had filled the public schools. The 1944 Education Act ensured that they were packed to capacity in the ensuing years.

4 FAILURE AND ITS CONSEQUENCES

1945 and 1946 brought many hopefuls to Ellesmere, fleeing the rigours of this new, more competitive entry into the grammar schools. Some came from similar backgrounds to Freddie Farrow, but not all were so successful. In March 1945 William Tyson, a railway guard from a nearby market town, applied for a place in the junior school for his son Colin. The school was full and his name was placed on the waiting list. After nearly a year Colin entered the junior house in January 1946, but young Tyson was no 'scholarship' boy and all did not go smoothly. Colin failed to make satisfactory progress and after a series of letters and discussions his parents were informed in May 1947 that he could not enter the senior school and was being superannuated. This came as 'a bitter blow' to them.[46] They considered it 'a privilege' for their son to have been under the Headmaster's guidance at Ellesmere and had arranged individual tuition in the hope that if he benefited from it and showed substantial progress he might return to the school, 'it has always been our ideal that Colin should have the advantage of an Ellesmere College education'.[47] The school's promise that the Headmaster would reconsider Colin's case in a year 'comforted' Mr Tyson and his wife 'quite a lot'.[48]

The pressure upon boys to succeed, the fear of failure and the bitter disappointment in the event of failure were not confined to scholarship boys or those from lower middle-class backgrounds. It is a theme common to many of the case studies we have already examined. The principal source of pressure was quite clearly fathers, as we have seen outstandingly in the cases of Lawson, Laker, Heywood and Roper. The mothers in the study appear to have applied less direct pressure, but may well have been equally anxious.

As contemporary analyses of masculinity have argued, success through competition in a hierarchy is one of the most crucial elements in concepts of masculinity among the middle classes. Competitive success in a hierarchy underlies most of the life cycle of middle-class men at school and subsequently in their careers and working lives.[49] Only childhood and retirement are excluded. Manly character implied the ambition, self-confidence, energy and independence necessary to succeed in the man's world of competitive success in a hierarchy. The dominant public school ideologies of the period – team spirit and service to the community – subordinated individual success to that of the group. These values found strong official support at Ellesmere. In January 1946 the editorial of *The Ellesmerian* considered the question of why boys who shone on the games field were accorded greater honour than those who won Oxford and Cambridge exhibitions. Whereas academic honours were bestowed upon the individual, success in sport contributed to the success of the community, the editor argued.[50] The school culture supported these values by rewarding games captains and members of teams with colours, and other marks of distinction in their dress, which were constantly paraded. As we have seen, it was those boys who were successful at games who were idolised in the much more pervasive, unofficial schoolboy culture. But this seductive ideology contained two fallacies, adherence to which could prove a trap to the unwary. Firstly it was individual performance, not team achievement, that was admired.[51] Secondly the achievements were in games not academic qualifications so desired by parents and so crucial to the careers they planned for their sons. Trevor Booth was an example of a boy who suffered the consequences of this conflict between his school's and his parents' values.

Trevor Booth entered Ellesmere in 1941 when he was 11. His father was a Lancashire businessman, whose business had its ups and downs and so the family had difficulties finding the fees at times. Mr Booth had high ambitions for his son. He intended Trevor to 'stay at

Ellesmere until he has passed the School Certificate Examination and I am anxious that he should remain to take his Higher School Certificate Examination prior to undertaking a university course.'[52] Trevor took his School Certificate in July 1946 and failed. His father, incensed, told the Headmaster:

> I am satisfied that he has devoted to [sic] little time to serious study in the past and has concentrated to [sic] much on prowess at games. He left home last week with no doubt in his mind as to my own views on his failure and has given me a solemn promise to really work for success in his next effort. I am sure that he realises that the next few months are vital to his future and I am convinced that with the right guidance he will make good. We have in mind a career in Dentistry or Engineering as a possible target. . .[53]

Trevor failed again in December and his father wrote disconsolately to the Headmaster:

> It has been a disappointment to me that he has not shown any particular aptitude for scholastic learning but I feel also that he has perhaps developed to [sic] great a prowess for sport to the detriment of his lessons. I had visualised a university career but in view of his failure in examinations this must now be eliminated from our minds.[54]

The introduction of examinations into schools and colleges brought with it the fear of failure and consequent symptoms of anxiety from pupils and students. This feature of examinations was noted at Oxford and Cambridge from the late eighteenth century when examinations became established there. The evidence about the effects of examinations at Oxford and Cambridge during that period has been carefully examined by Sheldon Rothblatt, who argues that examinations induced ambition and achievement, reshaping the student subculture, and increasing the emphasis upon success and failure. Anxiety about the effects of working for examinations upon their sons' health grew among parents, as the connection between health and academic work became more established during the nineteenth century. During that period Oxford and Cambridge slowly acquired a new system of values, based on principles of competition, in which undergraduates were increasingly exposed to a pervasive success ethic, with the fear of public shame and humiliation encouraging ambition and hard work. Anxiety was heightened by the taboo against talking about failure and its consequences and in Rothblatt's view undergraduates had little alternative to withdrawal or learning to live with worries and fears.[55]

The evidence from Ellesmere supports this view. One boy, deeply sensitive to his father's and schoolmasters' ambitions for him, had periodic attacks of dizziness and fainting, which worried him in later life. He wrote to the school anxious about any possibility of epilepsy in the medical diagnosis of his previous bouts of illness.[56]

Much more serious and damaging to boys' self-image than headaches and dizziness was bedwetting. Although a relatively common problem among boys of school age, it was not well understood clinically or psychologically at this time and was in any case difficult to deal with in a boarding school. It was an unmentionable and shameful subject with powerful associations and overtones of dirtiness and lack of normal adult control of bodily functions. For the boys concerned what had been a private family matter, mainly affecting their mother's pride in the cleanliness of her home and laundry, became a source of deeply felt public humiliation and anguish. George Orwell breached the taboo and gave a graphic account of the depth of self-loathing it induced in him. 'I knew that bedwetting was (a) wicked and (b) out-side my control. The second fault I was personally aware of and the first I did not question. It was possible therefore to commit a sin without knowing and without being able to avoid it.'[57] Orwell, perhaps because of his outstanding academic ability and potential scholarship to Eton, stayed at St Cyprians and duly entered Eton College.

At Ellesmere in the 1930s and 1940s, with child guidance in its infancy and only the merest beginnings of psychological understand-ings of severe cases of stress and repression beginning to develop, knowledge and treatment of such cases was incompatible with the ideals and organisation of the school. The relevant files show that medical, psychiatric and psychological advice was sought but in a number of cases the situation could not be contained, far less ameliorated, within the rigid structures of the school and expulsion

174

was inevitable. David Gray was 10 when he entered the Junior House in 1943. His father was a shopkeeper in Wrexham. He noted on his son's health certificate, completed when he entered the school, that he had occasional incontinence during sleep.[58] He had persistent problems with bedwetting at school and was put on a rigorous course of treatment by the family doctor, being given nothing to drink from 4.30 p.m. and got up every night at about 11 p.m. He was also being given belladonna three times a day to inhibit activity in the part of the nervous system which causes the bladder to empty. High dosages were required with unpleasant side effects, including a dry mouth, increasing the desire to drink.[59] The treatment had little effect and David had to take a rubber sheet and extra cotton sheets from home. To add to his humiliation and isolation he was made responsible for stripping his bed in the morning after a mishap. There was also evidence that his shirts were wet during the day. The term before he was due to enter the seniors his housemaster went in desperation to see Dr Caspar and as a result Evans Prosser informed his parents that bedwetters were not able to enter the senior school. David's parents approached the local child guidance clinic and, after the intervention of the psychiatrist, Evans Prosser agreed to a stay of execution.[60]

The psychiatrist changed the regime to one dependent wholly on the boy himself rather than drugs or the intervention of others. He arranged for David to come with his father every Friday for psychiatric help. He believed David's difficulties were psychological in the main, to which certain physical abnormalities contributed. Like the GP earlier, he stressed the importance of sympathetic handling and the damage which could be done to the boy's fragile self-confidence by shaming him in front of his peers. He asked that 'no comment should be passed about his disorder'.[61] But great damage had already been done. The matrons and masters who dealt with David had complained to the Headmaster that he was 'most elusive and recalcitrant' when told to change his bed and his dormitory mates had also made it clear to his housemaster that they found his presence objectionable.[62] The effects of three years of anguish could not be reversed in a term and one boy's miserable and failing efforts to demonstrate control of his bodily functions to his schoolmates were abandoned. Bladder control, like crying, was assumed to be associated with infants. Older boys in the seniors had to look after themselves was the assumption. One can only imagine the desperation of this boy surrounded by others, who considered him a childish and dirty pariah.

5 SUMMARY

Scholarships for poor scholars had a long tradition in the English public and grammar schools and universities. From the nineteenth century they were increasingly open to free competition by examination rather than nomination by a patron. In the late nineteenth century a scholarship ladder began to be established linking the elementary schools, grammar schools, colleges and universities, which was expanded in the period under review, especially after the implementation of the 1944 Education Act.

The public schools, with virtually no 'free places', offered scholarships for clever and musical boys. Some of the boys at Ellesmere and other public schools during this period came from lower middle-class backgrounds, shopkeepers, bank clerks, elementary school teachers and commercial travellers. Ellesmere was among the schools which enabled such pupils to have outstandingly successful careers.

The increasing emphasis upon examinations brought anxiety and the fear of failure to many boys, whose fathers, especially, exerted pressure upon them to succeed academically. While the school rewarded individual success, games were more significant than academic success, especially in the schoolboy sub-culture. As in nineteenth-century Oxford and Cambridge, the symptoms of anxiety and fear of failure, like bedwetting and headaches, had to be endured silently and alone, the school's culture and organisation making them shameful and unmentionable, and in extreme cases the cause of expulsion.

9

THE SCHOOL AS FATHER AND MOTHER

MOTHERING AND FATHERING

While most parents of boys at Ellesmere College between 1929 and 1950 were very actively involved in their sons' upbringing during their schooldays, there was also a group of boys whose parents were too far away for this, some as far as two or three weeks' sea passage and a journey up country. For these boys the school was both mother and father, sometimes for as long as ten years. There were three very different groups of boys for whom the school cared in this way, the largest being that of expatriates abroad, many in the service of the British Empire. The second was a very small group of boys from other countries whose parents wanted them to have an English public school education and the third was an equally small group of Czech and German Jewish boys who came to the school in 1939 fleeing Hitler's persecution.

The evidence presented in previous chapters has shown that among the group of parents in the study fathering and mothering were strongly differentiated; fathers were the financial providers, which legitimated their authority to dominate the family. Mothers were subordinate and domestic. This pattern of relationships is similar to that found by subsequent researchers in middle-class families in more recent times.[1] This evidence supports the judgment that relations within these families were patriarchial. Although there is controversy about the precise connotation of patriarchy, it implies those structures of social ideas, relations and institutions by which men dominate women.[2] The domination of sons by fathers differed from that of mothers and daughters because it presaged their own future position, enabling them to accept the more problematic aspects of their relations with their fathers. Although as we saw in the comparison of

Lawson, Laker and Heywood there was wide variation among fathers, three aspects of their relations with their sons may be distinguished in the evidence presented above. Chapters 3 and 4 showed that one of the most important aspects of relations between fathers and sons was that of model and imitator. A common form which this took was for sons to follow their fathers into an identical or similar career. One father, Howard Lawson, cast a long and baneful shadow upon his son after his death and another, Canon Heywood, was followed into the church by no less than three sons. A second aspect of the father–son relationships noted earlier was the way fathers provided for and directed their sons' careers. As we have seen this process was often fraught with pressure to succeed and bitter disappointment in cases of failure. The third feature of fathers' relationships with sons suggested by the evidence above is that of an authority figure. Again there was very wide variation; some, like Herbert Lees, giving friendly counsel, others, like the overbearing Victor Wood and Sam Laker, issuing orders, which they confidently expected would be obeyed.

The picture of mothers' relations with their sons which emerges from this evidence is that it was primarily about emotional support, domestic services and welfare. Mothers' concern was to provide clothes, tuck and other domestic services which make life comfortable. The difficulties of wartime rationing, to which the school clothes list made only the slightest concessions, required all their patience and humour.

Theories of mothering during this period stressed the responsibility of mothers for the emotional health of their children. Certainly the mothers in this study like Myra Roper and Stella Stevens worried about their sons' emotional welfare, although it is not clear how far they succeeded in providing adequate emotional support for their sons away at school. The only well-documented example, the Leeses, suggests they did sustain their very affectionate family ties largely by regular correspondence.

In contrast to fathers, mothers served as 'anti-models' of characteristics to be eliminated. *Punch* cartoons of the period showed public school boys' scorn for their mothers' concern for their welfare. The assumption of a public school education was that between 9 and 13 boys left home to be educated by men and other boys, in which they were not only separated from women but taught to eschew anything babyish, cissy or womanish. The idea that mothers might become a danger after carrying out their initial essential function of producing and nursing an infant was given its most powerful legitimation in the elevation of the Oedipus myth to quasi-scientific status by Sigmund Freud and his followers. These ideas were becoming more widely known and popularised in the period under review. They served not only to legitimise public school education for boys but also to support notions of parenting which eliminated fathers as primary carers, placing all the emphasis upon a mother's devotion to her children in infancy followed by her necessary rejection, firstly and most traumatically by her sons and later by her daughters. The notion that mothers could pose a threat to their sons' intellectual development was sufficiently widely held to be used by *The Listener* in an advertisement in 1944, which asked 'Is this mother dangerous?'[3]

The mothers in the study were aware of these beliefs. Stella Stevens saw herself as a threat to her sons' independence and told the Headmaster, apologetically 'I do too much for my boys', and another mother who requested a place for her younger son at the school in 1943 said, 'I feel that he will make greater headway away from me.'[4]

The other very marked difference between the mothers and fathers in the study in their relations with their sons was their authority. There are no instances in the correspondence from mothers of the kind of bombastic style redolent of Messrs Laker and Lawson. A mother's role was not to make decisions and exercise authority but to support and enable her husband's and son's decisions and actions, as that 'wise woman' the mythical Mrs Brown had done on her son's sudden departure for Rugby School. Mothers' influence upon their sons and their school was indirect and discreet, exercised by persuasion and cajoling, rather than demanding.

The boundaries between mothers' and fathers' responsibilities for their sons in the study were rigidly defined and strictly maintained. Apart from those with pressing financial worries, fathers rarely enquired about domestic or emotional matters. It was territory in which they did not wish to be detained, and they regarded it with suitable *hauteur*. Lawson was quick to push responsibility for his son's gaucheness in domestic matters back on to the school and Mr Barnes dismissed his son's fear of being beaten as 'a small matter which may

Figure 2   *Advertisement from* The Times Educational Supplement, *1944*

"The child is father of the man"

IS THIS MOTHER DANGEROUS ?

Her doting possessiveness menaces the development of her son's character and tends to alienate him from his tutors   There may be such potential mothers in your school today. Introduce them to *The Listener* so that a quiet study of the broadcast talks may widen their horizons.

need clearing up'. Mothers were equally reluctant to take on their husbands' decision-making mantle and did so only if it was unavoidable. Myra Roper agreed that Martin should enter the senior school when her husband was ill and 'could not tackle it'.

While the majority of boys looked to their mothers and fathers for different functions, boys whose parents were a great distance from the school were placed in the care of the school as entire charge pupils. For them the school acted as mother and father, arranging their holidays, travel and clothing. They were largely without the attention and affection of their parents, often for several years.

In all these cases the school was a good father, providing financially for them, planning and supervising their careers and giving models of success. Its activities as surrogate father were most conspicuous in the financial support of the refugee Jewish boys and the boys made destitute by catastrophes such as the fall of Singapore. It enabled them to stay at the school and encouraged them to continue their academic education. The total care of these boys presented many problems, which were infinitely exacerbated during the war. The school was more successful as surrogate father than surrogate mother. Its nurturing was often sadly lacking and there were persistent complaints from parents about food and health care. It is much more difficult to estimate how far the lack of nurturing and emotional support associated with mothering affected these boys, a number of whom underwent very severe emotional strains and shocks when sudden deaths and disasters befell their families.

2 JEWISH REFUGEES FROM NAZISM

One group of boys whose entry into the school was particularly traumatic was the Jewish refugees. The spread of Jewish persecution with Hitler's rise to power and his annexation of firstly Czechoslovakia and then Poland, forced millions of Jews to emigrate from central Europe. While the majority went to America, Jewish communities in Britain organised committees to enable some to come to Britain. The period of profound public relief, following the agreement of Hitler and Chamberlain at Munich on the 30 September 1938, that Germany would not go to war with Britain, was shortlived and public opinion changed as the terms of the agreement between France, Britain and Germany about Czechoslovakia and the extent to which it had been sacrificed became clear. Sympathy for the Czechs grew, fuelled by debates in the House of Commons, books, pamphlets and meetings denouncing Chamberlain's policies. Fears of increased persecution grew as Hitler extended his demands into Poland and 'incidents' in the free port of Danzig became more frequent. Chamberlain then changed his policy and pledged Britain to support Poland against German aggression.[5] In late 1938 and 1939 the feverish efforts of the Jewish community in Britain to help as many Jews as possible escape Nazi persecution received widespread sympathy and support. British honour was at stake after the betrayal of the Czechs. The bestial acts of Hitler's storm troopers were being reported and everything had to be done to save as many as possible from the anticipated pogroms. One parent who sent £1 for the War Memorial Chapel fund in October 1938 remarked that the money should more properly go to 'the wretched Czechs who have suffered so much for our so called peace'.[6]

All refugees had to have a sponsor or means of support and there were instances of Jews being sent back to Germany and Eastern Europe from Croydon Airport.[7] From the autumn of 1938, Evans Prosser received a steady stream of letters from a Mrs Rosenfeld in St John's Wood, who was constantly receiving details of needy cases of German Jews for whom she had to try to arrange transport, accommodation, jobs and schools all at a moment's notice. From her letters it seems that she found Evans Prosser more sympathetic than some other Headmasters and Headmistresses, as she hastily plied him with all the details of her most difficult cases of mixed race and religion. He had no inconvenient scruples about accepting Jews into a Church of England school, and was very generous with almost instantaneous offers of help. In the case of the Crohn family there can be little doubt that he contributed to a providential last-minute escape from Nazism. In December 1938, Mrs Rosenfeld wrote that she had received 'an S.O.S. from Berlin about a thirteen year old boy, whose father died just before they were going to Australia'. The mother now had to leave with her two children. Unsure about any financial arrangements, Mrs Rosenfeld asked if the boy could come to Ellesmere for no charge. Evans Prosser suggested 10 guineas a term and Mrs Rosenfeld found a Jewish doctor in London, Kleeburg, willing to pay the fee. Later that month Evans Prosser received two letters from Wolfgang Crohn and his mother in Berlin and an ecstatic postcard of thanks from Mrs Rosenfeld inviting him to stay in London. Wolfgang Crohn sent a photograph of himself and an account of his education and interests written in flawless English. He was clearly a very able, well-educated boy who came from a cultured background. His mother, a doctor, wrote of her gratitude to the school for their generosity. Wolfgang entered the college in January 1939 and stayed two terms. In July 1939, with Hitler poised to attack Poland and Chamberlain warning that that would mean war between Britain and Germany, Dr Crohn wrote to Evans Prosser saying that she was leaving Berlin and taking her son to Australia.[8]

In May 1939 Jan Kodicek, a Czech Jew from Prague, had entered the school. An intelligent and engaging boy, he made many friends there. With the Nazi occupation of Czechoslovakia, life for the Jews became daily more difficult and emigration increased rapidly. In early July 1939 Evans Prosser received a letter from Stanley Isaacs, a jute merchant in Mincing Lane, asking if he could offer a specially low fee to Jiri Luft, a reputedly 'healthy and intelligent' Jewish boy from 'a very good class family' in Prague, whom Isaacs and his brothers were expecting to arrive in London later that month. A fee of £45 per annum was quickly agreed and Isaacs promised to let the Headmaster know as soon as possible after Jiri Luft's arrival about whether or not, in Isaac's judgment, he would be coming to Ellesmere.[9] He was as good as his word and the day after Luft's arrival Evans Prosser received a rather perplexed letter from him:

> Jiri Luft has arrived in London today from Prague and I met him at the station and took him to my office. My brothers and I are very agreeably impressed by the lad. He . . . seems to be very intelligent . . . but there is one drawback. He can only speak Czech and does not know a word of English and we are therefore finding it very difficult to converse with him. Do you think it best that he comes to Ellesmere at the beginning of next term, hardly knowing a word of English. . . .?, or do you think it would be better that we send the lad . . . to a school in London . . . where he could learn English . . . and then come to Ellesmere in January?

asked the jute merchant, clearly out of his depth.[10] Evans Prosser, presumably relying on the Czech boys already in the school to smooth Luft's passage, advised the former course.

On 3 September war was declared and any possibility of Jiri Luft maintaining his ties with his family in Prague ceased. Stanley Isaacs assumed full responsibility for him and wrote to the Headmaster immediately before Luft's arrival at Ellesmere, informing him that Luft's English was still 'sadly lacking' and asking the Headmaster 'to see that the boy is looked after in the school'.[11] On 15 September 1939 Jiri Luft left London for Ellesmere, with Kagan, a young relative of Stanley Isaacs, who was already at the school. In just two months he had been translated from his family and the Jewish community in his native Czechoslovakia via the Jewish community in London into a Christian public school in the English Midlands. Fortunately for Jiri Luft, he had known Jan Kodicek before they left Prague. Both were quite new to boarding school life. In Kodicek's judgment the English public school's preparation for social life was superior to the continental schools and he was particularly taken with the friendliness of masters to older boys outside the classroom. Continental schools were, however, free for all to enter and the subject teaching was better, but they omitted an important part of education, social life and games.[12] Attitudes among Ellesmere boys and masters to the Jewish refugees were mixed. Some made lasting friendships: Roy Carver still corresponds with his best friend at school, Rudolf Mauther, a Czech Jew now in America who visits him in England from time to time. One parent, a Jewish refugee from Bohemia, complained of treatment 'unworthy of a pedagogue especially in front of all the boys of the form' from a master towards his son.[13]

Evans Prosser's decision to take Kodicek and Luft, two Czech boys, was rewarded: both went on to higher education and professional careers, Luft at Regent Street Polytechnic and Kodicek at Barts. Luft's entry very nearly paid a very handsome dividend. In 1940 Stanley Isaacs came very close to transferring his own son from St Paul's School to Ellesmere. Because of the Blitz St Paul's School made a very sudden and ill-arranged evacuation to Berkshire, where the billeting arrangements for such a large, unexpected influx caused problems. The threat of transfer to Ellesmere caused Isaacs's housemaster to take the boy into the house he himself was occupying, and the crisis was averted.[14]

3 THE FALL OF SINGAPORE

Another group of boys for whom the school provided total care were those boys who were cut off from their parents throughout the war. Those whose parents were in Malaya had the most gruelling time, for in the last few weeks of 1941 and early 1942 they endured the intense agony of learning about the lightning Japanese advance through Malaya and then the fall of Singapore in February 1942.

The Richardsons were one of the more fortunate families who left their children in England and returned to Malaya, fearing war and its possible outcomes. Their letters are particularly interesting because both parents were so forthcoming about the effects of the prolonged separation from their children.

In September 1938 Eric Richardson entered the Junior House. He was then 10 years old and had previously attended the preparatory department of a grammar school in Shropshire. His entrance to Ellesmere was arranged by his mother in the summer of 1938. She had found it very difficult to decide what to do because the 'dreadfully disturbing situation' looked 'very black' to her.[15] She knew that a war would close the Suez Canal and wondered if she and her children should all return to Malaya immediately. Decisions were further slowed because it took so long to get replies from her husband in Malaya. It was finally decided that the two children should be settled at school in England, spending their holidays with their grandmother and that Mrs Richardson should return to Malaya. This would entail a long separation from their children, as Mr Richardson was not due for leave until 1940. This distressed both parents and although they both felt bereft, they accepted that this was the best plan in view of the war. Jack Richardson had 'many misgivings' about his wife 'leaving the children to rejoin him' but found Evans Prosser's 'assurances about the future welfare and progress' of his son during his 'enforced absence from the old country' reassuring. Mr Richardson had already sailed when it was decided that his son should be placed in a school which would also be responsible for him during the holidays as an entire charge pupil. He had never met Evans Prosser, nor seen Ellesmere College. Although his son was only 10, his father had formed an assessment of him and had plans for his career. In his view Eric was 'by no means a genius and inclined to imagine difficulties, he is a plodder and so should make headway'. Jack Richardson hoped he would 'eventually qualify in medicine' and trusted 'Latin, Greek, Physics and chemistry would be incorporated into his curriculum'.[16]

Mrs Richardson returned to Malaya in the spring of 1939 and wrote to the Headmaster about one of her main concerns, her son's health. He had had persistent problems with his feet and a specialist had prescribed specially built-up shoes.[17] She had also heard that there was an outbreak of scarlet fever at the school and hoped it had been a mild one. As she remarked '. . . where children are, these things will happen'. Their sons' health was always a major anxiety for parents. Epidemics were the scourge of boarding schools and however mild, were dreaded for the misery they caused the sick and intolerable strains they placed upon those who were responsible for their care.[18] Mrs Richardson found the emotional strain of separation considerable and confided that she still felt 'very lost without our two darlings, and it has been a terrible wrench to part with them especially for so long a period'.[19] Her son's letters reassured her. They were 'very amusing at times' and they 'just longed for mail days to arrive'. Mrs Richardson, always open and communicative, was much distressed by the outbreak of war in September 1939 with the prospect of being 'separated from our darlings indefinitely', but like other mothers in the study she consoled herself with thoughts of the less fortunate. It was 'not a fraction as bad as for those whose sons and husbands are of eligible age to join up'. 'It has all been too unjust and it makes one wonder where it will all end. We are so helpless . . . and have to rely on our friends in England to do their best for our two children.'[20]

The expected leave in 1940 was postponed and in September 1941 Mr and Mrs Richardson wrote to Evans Prosser that all UK leave had been cancelled and that they were taking a short leave in Australia and New Zealand. They were 'not a bit interested' in it, but would 'make the best of it'. Malaya had been 'rather tense lately with the Japs trying on their rather nasty work of aggression so near us' but the country was in a state of preparedness and 'teeming with troops'.[21] 'The little yellow men are going to find it no easy going if they do venture further south.' Things were 'quite normal.'[22] Mrs Richardson had been staying at a hill station, where she encountered 'the pug marks of a rhino and her baby, who had been sleeping under one of the halting sheds, on a walk to see the delightful view at the top of the station'.[23]

News of their son was becoming more difficult to come by as the post was disrupted, but they continued to receive a brief weekly message from him telegraphed by Wrekin College from a postcard sent by Eric Richardson. With such sparse news of his development and needs, the Richardsons could only reiterate their old concerns and Mr Richardson once more enquired if his son had settled on a profession.[24] Mrs Richardson's worries about her son's feet had been somewhat allayed by his report that he did not get so tired.[25]

To the Richardsons, still in Australia, the Japanese advance culminating in the fall of Singapore on 15 February 1942 was a devastating blow. They lost their home and then in August came the news that Mr Richardson's appointment was abolished. He wired Evans Prosser that he could not maintain the fees and was returning to England immediately. Jack Richardson wrote to Evans Prosser,

> The whole business has been one of misfortune for us – we left everything we possessed in Malaya and now this! . . . We are very fortunate to have been on leave in this country at the time when the occupation occurred and were thus spared all of the horrors which only modern warfare can bring.[26]

They would return to England and discuss their future plans. The notice was provisional; the Richardsons hoped to be able to keep their son at Ellesmere and looked forward eagerly to the reunion, possibly at Christmas. Their narrow escape from the invasion and possible capture by the Japanese brought Jack Richardson's hitherto suppressed emotions for his children to the surface, and he wrote 'The past four years have been fraught with all of the aches and yearnings which parents have for their children, separated as we have been in these troublesome times.'[27]

Their return to England was slow. In November they were in Pernambuco in Brazil, and any hope of a Christmas reunion had faded. Mrs Richardson apologised for the delay, knowing that the arrangements made in Australia to pay the school fees only lasted until Christmas. As usual she was cheerful and outgoing and continued to take an interest in her surroundings. Pernambuco was 'rather hot and sticky ... Quite a little old world town with narrow streets and obsolete trams, which groan and grind on their weary way.' This letter written on 16 November 1942 was received at the school on 23 February 1943, a month after the Richardsons had arrived in England. Mr Richardson got a job with the Air Ministry and his son stayed at Ellesmere. Mrs Richardson longed 'to unpack and stay unpacked' in a house of her own, now that she had her children with her, but the chronic housing shortage and the way her husband was moved about made this difficult.[28] Eric Richardson decided to follow his father's career. In 1944 he tried to get into Oxford to read forestry but the competition was stiff and he finally went to Bangor. In 1948 he applied to the Colonial Forestry Service to follow his father to Malaya.

Public schools often refer to their 'old boys' as 'sons' of the school, especially where the school may be proud and take credit from their subsequent achievements. Ellesmere College and its magazine, *The Ellesmerian*, is no exception. James Wilkinson, a captain of school during the second decade of the century, was in the Colonial Service for nearly thirty years, mostly in Malaya, and 'suffered severely' during his three years in a Japanese prison camp. His death in the 1960s 'robbed ... the school of one of its most devoted sons'.[29] To those boys in the school who were left without parents for a prolonged period the school assumed the active role of father, supporting them financially, planning and arranging their careers. Indeed Wilkinson's two sons, Philip and Frederick, were in many ways sons of the school in this sense during the war, when they had little contact with their mother for three and a half years and none with their father for five years. Wilkinson had left England in January 1940 knowing that he would not see his two sons for a very long period, up to six years, he forecast gloomily[30] and his wife sailed later in 1940. In the event the fortunes of the Wilkinson family were catastrophically affected by the war. When they left England in 1940 Mrs Wilkinson's mother, Mrs Lamont, became her grandsons' guardian.

During the Japanese invasion of Malaya in November and December 1941 the Wilkinsons' house received a direct hit and they lost everything.[31] Mrs Wilkinson was evacuated and cabled her mother from Melbourne in February 1942, within days of the fall of Singapore, saying that she was safe in Australia but that she was penniless and she believed her husband was still in Singapore. Her mother, racked with anxiety about her son-in-law's fate and the uncertain financial intentions of the Colonial Office, then gave provisional notice of removing the boys and found Philip, the elder boy, a job on the local newspaper in Great Yarmouth. In July Mrs Wilkinson wrote to the Headmaster from Melbourne, where she was recovering from an operation. The Colonial Office had set up an office in Australia and were paying her a proportion of her husband's salary which enabled her to send sufficient money to her mother for Freddie's fees, but if her husband had not survived, a thought she 'dare not dwell on', she would receive only a small pension. She had spoken to a man who had escaped after the surrender, who had seen her husband after hostilities ceased and she was presuming he was a Prisoner-of-War. Her medical expenses in Australia had been very heavy and, although she very much wanted to work to earn money to send back to England for her son's education, the doctors had said it would be a year before she was properly fit again.[32] She arrived in England in November 1943 and went straight to Great Yarmouth. 'Exhausted after the nervous strain of weeks on the sea', she wrote and asked if Freddie could have a long weekend with her and his brother, reunited after three and a half years.[33] Mrs Wilkinson visited the school at the end of term, a month later, and discussed her younger son's future career with the Headmaster, after which she wrote to fourteen schools of architecture.[34] Acting as a surrogate father, like the widows in Chapter 5, she was anxious to prepare her son for a career in architecture within the limitations of her allowance from the Colonial Office and throughout the previous year had pressed the school through her mother to prepare Freddie for the School Certificate with all possible speed.[35]

4 THE SCHOOL AS SURROGATE MOTHER

In all matters connected with careers and financial problems the school was supportive and filled the role of surrogate father, but the evidence suggests it was much less successful at being a good mother.

Providing good food to nourish growing bodies was a fundamental aspect of good mothering, which became infinitely more difficult during the war, entailing long hours of queuing and greatly increased ingenuity. In the summer holidays of 1941 Evans Prosser received letters firstly from Mrs Lamont and a month later from the boys' paternal grandfather complaining that both boys had lost weight; Philip had lost 8 lb in a term. They had been seen by a doctor who had pronounced them run down and prescribed a regime of building up, including tonics. Both grandparents felt the fault lay in the insufficient quantity and poor quality of the school's food. In an invidious comparison, Wilkinson Senior charged, 'I learn that at Shrewsbury, Denstone, Rossall, the Wrekin and other schools any difficulties about food have been overcome and the boys are well and properly fed but it does not seem that the same can be said about Ellesmere.' If no reassurance of an improvement was forthcoming he 'must reluctantly report by cable to my son and ascertain what steps he would wish to be taken,' he told the Headmaster.[36] Mrs Lamont, however, had already informed their parents 'as otherwise I should consider myself failing in my responsibility'.[37]

1940 and 1941 had been difficult years for the school, with evacuees from the Channel Islands after their occupation, followed closely by Lancing College who left Sussex as the threat of a German invasion loomed after Dunkirk. The school had been extremely overcrowded. The immediate need to find increased food supplies and prevent the spread of infectious illness caused the greatest problems. Although parents were aware that the war had caused many difficulties for the school, their concern for their sons' welfare brought a spate of letters leaving the Headmaster in no doubt about the importance of the maternal functions of feeding, welfare and nursing to them. While the school values encouraged toughness and success, suppressing the feminine values of caring, nurturing and emotion, nonetheless health and feeding were two aspects of its own mothering it could not ignore.

In July 1944 Sam Laker threatened to withdraw his second son, Sandy, from the school because of the 'food question', complaints about which had been so persistent and longstanding that they 'could not be ignored' and 'lately matters appear to have become worse'. He added menacingly that one parent 'had suggested that a number of parents got together and approached the Governors on this same subject' and that, 'I can say that adverse comments on the food have come spontaneously from widely different sources.'[38] Men, in whom these masculine values were deeply internalised, with little regard for the tasks of mothering and no experience of their difficulties and demands, could be particularly critical of the school's failings in this direction. Mr Laker, as we have seen, prided himself on his contribution to the nation's war effort. Another father, who had been in West Africa throughout the war, was so dissatisfied with his son's condition, when he returned in 1944, that he promptly gave the school a term's fees in lieu of notice and removed the boy. Sumsion, replying to his charges, gave a detailed account of the boy's illnesses and the school's efforts to help him, especially during the time when both parents were abroad and the school had arranged the boy's holidays, a week of which had been spent in the Sumsion's home at Overton Bridge. He reminded the irate father that the boy's mother, who had returned to the miseries of England in 1940, was always satisfied with the school's substitute maternal care of their son. The school, Sumsion said, 'did its very best for your boy during the last four or five years which have probably been the most difficult, not to say anxious in our history.'[39]

Health care was another aspect of its mothering function in which the school had to exercise extreme vigilance. In 1948 a boy was withdrawn because of alleged defects in the medical care. George Hampshire was 12 when he entered the school in September 1947. In his first term he spent five days in the sick bay with tonsillitis and a day after returning to school went back to the matron with a swelling on his neck. The matron apparently treated this once and told the boy to return if there was any further trouble. When he returned home at the end of term the swelling was very pronounced and medical attention was sought immediately.[40] The swelling was infected with bovine TB and the boy was ill for several months. An acrimonious correspondence ensued, in which the parents alleged that the matron had been negligent and the school claimed that a term's fees were due because the boy had been withdrawn without a term's notice.[41] The Provost of the Midland division of the Woodard Foundation, Dr R. C. Mortimer of Christ Church, Oxford, was consulted. He received assurances from Dr Caspar, the school doctor, that boys never made decisions about the continuation or termination of treatment for their ailments, and that a swelling in the neck had not been neglected by the matrons or housemaster, whom he had always found vigilant and cooperative.[42] Despite this, Dr Mortimer judged that the school had left itself rather vulnerable and that the matter of the fees should not be pressed to the full. Accordingly a settlement of half the fee was agreed and settled by the school's solicitors.

Health was always a major concern for parents and potential problem for the school. In October 1946 there was an outbreak of infantile paralysis. As many boys as possible were sent home for three weeks. The remainder were quarantined in the school, where they found the peaceful surroundings and extra space very welcome. The main medical precaution was gargling night and morning. A special Emergency Games Organisation was devised which included a school versus staff soccer match and a grand Hare and Hounds.[43] As a result of this outbreak two boys, John Knaggs and John Stanier, contracted the disease and the work of the school was disrupted.

For boys separated for a long period from their parents, mothers' emotional support may have been the loss for which they had greatest difficulty finding an alternative. The evidence about the school's concern with the boys' emotional needs is much more fragmentary and difficult to interpret. Telling boys about the death of their nearest and dearest was one of the most difficult tasks they had to undertake. One of the most taxing cases with which the school dealt, was that of two brothers cut off from their parents by the war. Evans Prosser was informed of the father's death by his widow in a letter in which she tersely assumed the role of surrogate father and issued specific instructions for her sons' future. She sent money to the Headmaster charging him with the responsibility of carrying out her late husband's plans. Their father's death was to be kept from his sons until after their School Certificate examinations and everything was to be done to ensure both boys went up to Oxford in accordance with their father's wishes. Evans Prosser carried out her instructions to the letter and withheld the news of their father's death from the boys. Unfortunately they heard it while away from the school on holiday and their initial distress was magnified by the school's apparent insensitivity in the matter. They later fully acknowledged the sense of their mother's and Headmaster's actions.[44] Both subsequently had successful university and professional careers.

5 THE SURVIVAL OF THE FITTEST

The school's function in eliminating feminine 'weaknesses' from the boys, coupled with the low priority and poor provision for caring and nurturing, meant that the school was no place for the physically weak, intellectually backward or those with any sort of psychological or emotional problems. As we saw in the case of Tyson in chapter 8, boys who were too far below the school's intellectual standard were superannuated, with all its connotations of failure and consequent distress for the boy and his parents. Physical weakness brought the same inevitable consequence. A boy with a TB ankle was asked to leave after an impossible struggle with the school's endless staircases.[45] A diabetic also left after the diagnosis was confirmed.[46] Symptoms of psychological problems, emotional disturbance or sexual problems which posed a threat to the school's discipline led to expulsion. Apparently incurable bedwetters, as we have already seen, were asked to leave. One boy, an insatiable pugilist who took on all comers, was considered 'a thorough nuisance in every way', and expelled after two terms. There was one particularly notorious case, still recalled by his contemporaries, of a boy who took to wandering about the school at night and disturbing the female domestic staff asleep in their rooms.[47] All such problems led inevitably to removal. The reigning social principle was social Darwinism, the survival of the fittest. The weak suffered in silence and the weakest were eliminated.

6 ATTITUDES TO WOMEN

Ellesmere was about manliness and success. Not only were girls excluded and invisible and caring and nurturing given minimal attention and importance in this largely all-male world, dedicated to making men, but feminine characteristics were purposefully eliminated. It was a society which produced tough and successful men's men. Weak boys were expelled and those who remained were imbued with the tough competitive spirit of prevailing masculine values. The school's only source of emotional support was the group of pals, who were so invaluable in circumstances which demanded manly virtues like courage and determination, as Mike Smith found when he had his tragic accident. This regime had important and far-reaching limitations. Relationships with pals took time to grow and were often undeveloped when they were most needed to sustain younger boys like Lionel Mason unable to cope with the early agonies of the toughening process.

The invisibility of women, the low value placed on their caring and nurturing activities and the elimination of feminine characteristics in making boys into men was a sorry preparation for future relationships with wives, sisters or mothers. Ellesmere was an extreme example of a man's world, having no girls, few married masters or mistresses on the staff. Although the majority of boys at Ellesmere could expect to spend most of their adult lives with a marriage partner and finding her was clearly of momentous significance, their schooling proscribed relations with girls and systematically magnified the extent of the differences and the rigidity of the boundaries between the sexes. Preparatory to marriage, therefore, they were ignorant of girls, despised femininity and held caring and nurturing in low regard, a 'perversion', which few public school boys overcame in Robert Graves's view.[48]

W. B. Gallie had the advantage of masters' wives at his northern public school from which to draw models of women and marital relations. One Old Ellesmerian felt that more 'masters' wives pushing prams' would have been an improvement at Ellesmere.[49] One of the masters at Gallie's school had married 'a young girl fresh, strapping and rosy, the kind of girl who looks best in a sun-bonnet.' The master concerned was the subject of jokes by boys and masters about being 'swamped with an endless flood of children . . . and steaming nappies.' Gallie, however, regarded the jibes from a position of considerable spiritual superiority and, in his adolescent striving to purify his 'dirty and misdirected' sexual thoughts, found the image of this marriage an uplifting one.[50]

Women, even when admitted to the man's world on such condescending terms, were confined to a single narrow domestic and maternal role providing every conceivable service for men from sexual satisfaction to spiritual uplift. Ignorance of women and their needs could thus be justified as no great disadvantage in choosing a life partner. And as Rupert Wilkinson has noted, public school men remained insensitive to and untouched by the delicacies and emotional warmth characteristic of feminine relationships.[51]

Most parents were strongly socialised into the middle-class model of masculinity of toughness and individual success which was common to the school's and their own assumptions about their sons as independent family providers with a career. Its heavy costs eluded them and they believed they had made a good investment, valuing their sons' successes and minimising the psychic and social costs.

6 SUMMARY

The school was mother and father to a motley group of boys whose parents were abroad. It amply fulfilled the fatherly functions, exemplified by fathers in the study, providing financially, maintaining suitable models and managing boys' careers. It was less successful as a surrogate mother, and there were complaints about food and health care, especially during the difficult days of the war. The school's model of masculinity was about toughness and individual success, which were antithetical to feminine characteristics associated with caring and nurturing. Emotions were suppressed and women and girls were rendered invisible and servile to the man's world. One of the main means of inducing toughness and success was the survival of the fittest, the weak and unsuccessful suffering silently or rebelling and the weakest and failures being eliminated. Parents approved this model of middle-class masculinity. While complaining about the most extreme cases of inadequacies in caring and nurturing, they believed they had made a good investment in their sons' futures and minimised the importance of the psychic and social costs for their sons.

10
CONCLUSIONS

The process of making boys into men is a powerful engine of social class and gender reproduction and change. In modern British society it is their work and the income it brings which mainly differentiates men from each other and from women. Work dominates the most active fifty years of men's lives between leaving school and retirement.[1] It is the single most important factor in men's lives, enabling them to support a household in an appropriate style, legitimating their social position and value and their authority as family heads.[2] Making boys into men is therefore about preparing them firstly and most importantly for work, from which their role in the home and family as provider and authority figure follows. The preparation of boys for their adult lives as men concentrates on work and they are prepared to enter the highly differentiated and rapidly changing labour market of an advanced industrial economy.

Before the introduction and enforcement of compulsory school attendance, in industries where production was organised in domestic workshops, boys and girls were introduced to work by their family and neighbours.[3] Schools like Ellesmere developed during the nineteenth century with the increasing size and complexity of administrative, commercial and industrial organisations and the gradual introduction of examinations as a means of recruitment and promotion.[4]

From the late nineteenth century schools played an increasing part in preparing boys and a smaller number of girls for the labour market. The lives of women and girls continued to be dominated by marriage and domesticity, preceded for some by a period in the more limited and low-paid female labour market.

For the boys in this study, brought up and educated at Ellesmere College between 1929 and 1950, learning to be men began at home.

Before coming to school they had already acquired a stable identity as boys and learned the boundaries of masculinity and femininity from their fathers and mothers. The process whereby fathers become models for, and directors of, their sons' careers was already well established.

Recent feminist analyses of Freudian theory by Nancy Chodorow and Judith Arcana have emphasised the importance of mothering in the reproduction of gender differences in their sons and daughters.[5] The mothers of boys at Ellesmere between 1929 and 1950 played an equally crucial role in making their sons into men by ensuring they were surrounded by masculine models and influences and by reducing and subordinating their own role to that of neutral supporter. Mothers and sisters became 'anti-models' for their sons; domestic, dependent and subordinate, concerned with emotion and nurturing; their interests at best tolerated, at worst consigned to the despised realm of the 'cissy', while fathers' influence as directors and models become increasingly significant in their sons' upbringing.

For most of these boys their fathers were the single most important factor in their upbringing, giving them a model of successful provider and careerman to emulate. The pressure on many boys was strong and for the most part accepted. Some entered a similar occupation to their fathers and all tried to attain a similar or better social position. In learning to become men, boys become the main mechanism in the powerful engine of social class reproduction and aspirations for upward social mobility. It was through their sons that parents sought to ensure the family's future social position. Bringing up sons was about masculinity but it was much more importantly about social class. For them class reproduction encapsulated gender reproduction. Becoming a man was about having a suitable occupation, income and social position, able to support a dependent wife and accompanying household. Parents wanted their sons to be manly and successful in the competitive hierarchy of occupation and social class. Their deepest desires and hopes were invested in their sons and accordingly they devised strategies, sacrificed their means and were actively involved in gaining their objectives. Manliness was about occupation and class. Education and schooling were therefore means to that end. Parents viewed schools pragmatically, as means of social reproduction or hopefully upward social mobility, not as forms of education.[6] Schools continued the processes of socialisation begun at home, elaborating the models of masculinity and femininity encountered there and initiating processes of selection and differentiation in preparation for entry to the labour market.[7]

These models and processes are specific to particular gender, social class and ethnic groups. Paul Willis has argued that working-class lads in the Black Country in the 1970s were prepared for their future experience of the social relations of production through their alienation in the similar relations of school life and the reactions of the gang of mates to this experience.[8] Sara Delamont, in a study undertaken in a girls' public school in the 1970s, has shown that the girls' reactions to their schooling were mediated by their families' cultural and social backgrounds; those from professional families, whose mothers had careers, tended to be 'swots and weeds', whereas those from business families whose mothers were at home, were more often 'debs and dollies'.[9]

Previous analyses of the boys' public schools have assumed that they were narrowly reproductive in enabling small and insulated elites to retain their domination of the centres of power and influence such as the judiciary, foreign service, Civil Service and episcopate.[10] Only a small minority of older public schools originated in the mediaeval period. Their expansion and rise to prominence was part of the process of bureaucratisation so carefully analysed by the German social historian Max Weber. As the administration of industry, commerce and the state became larger and more complex, government by a hereditary aristocracy was gradually replaced by trained specialist officials selected by competitive examinations.[11] In Britain Harold Perkin has argued that the decline of aristocratic power was associated with the rise of the ideology of meritocratic competition and the expansion of its protagonists, the middle classes.[12] As Honey, Bamford and Rothblatt have shown, the expansion of the state and the empire and the introduction of examinations to select government officials was associated with the establishment of a hierarchy of public schools, with strong contacts in particular Oxford and Cambridge colleges.[13] In the period before the First World War the public schools were consolidated into a hierarchical network, preparing boys for successful careers, notably those in government service at home and abroad.[14]

David Rubinstein has recently demonstrated that the public schools were not only about elite reproduction but that most of the schools drew from a wide social range and by enabling boys from a variety of social origins to enter elite positions they were part of the increasing openness of recruitment to British elites.[15]

Ellesmere College, in the lower echelons of the public school hierarchy, was not about reproducing the British elite by ensuring that the sons of judges, bishops, diplomats and generals enjoy similar elite positions. Its clientele was diverse and included a railway guard, bank clerks, a police sergeant, shopkeepers and farmers. Like those interviewed by Bridgeman and Fox recently, these parents were pragmatic, they had little 'traditional' fixed allegiance to a particular form of schooling but sought the school best suited to the strategy they had devised to enable their sons to enter suitable careers.[16]

The school, like similar schools today, was sensitive to these demands of the parents for suitable careers for their sons.[17] During the period under review the most marked expansion in such careers was in the scientific, medical and technological professions. New laboratories were added to the school in 1939, enabling a steady stream of boys to enter medicine, engineering and other expanding professions. Ellesmere was also quick to channel boys into wartime university short courses.

Among those it prepared for such careers were a number of boys of average and below-average ability with indifferent reports of their intellectual powers from their previous headmasters and mistresses. As the competition for grammar school places apparently became more open in the late 1930s and particularly after the implementation of the 1944 Education Act one of the functions of the public schools was to serve as an insurance policy for those who might previously have purchased a place at the local grammar school.[18]

In addition to coaching borderline candidates towards successful School Certificates, the school was also the means of promoting a number of quite outstanding careers by boys from lower middle-class backgrounds. The school thus enabled boys to benefit from the increasing openness of recruitment to the upper echelons of the British occupational structure. A number of boys had meteoric rises, like those of Sir Aino Farrow and Sir Paul Dean, a Conservative MP since 1964 and Deputy Speaker of the House of Commons. The school was above all successful in enabling boys to enter the kind of expanding professional careers which required educational qualifications. Parents of boys at Ellesmere were generally very satisfied with their sons' education there. Mrs Cockshoot, a Cheshire publican's wife, told the Headmaster in 1942, 'You have certainly educated him well and made a man of him.'[19] The school was an effective means of making their boys into the kind of men which parents sought and on the whole they considered their investment a sound one. An *OE Chronicle* in 1982, for example, gave news of 12 men who had been at the school between 1929 and 1950, among whom were a clergyman, a farmer, an accountant, an army officer and several businessmen.

There is now very strong evidence to suggest that their choice of education was realistic and their satisfaction with their investment justified. Recent research by John Goldthorpe and associates has shown that one of the most arresting features of the male occupation structure in Britain since the 1920s has been the steady expansion of the sorts of salaried occupations for which Ellesmere prepared its pupils.[20] This expansion has also been associated with a continuing rise in the level of qualifications needed to enter an increasing range of occupations. Throughout this period the HMC schools have remained consistently the most successful type of school in keeping boys at school after the minimum school leaving age, enabling them to pass examinations and enter higher education.[21] The schools have also been successful in ensuring boys from middle-class homes retained a similar social position to their fathers, an important educational requirement for their Victorian forebears which we remarked in chapter 1.[22]

The school's effectiveness was based on the rigour of the regime, every aspect of which was harnessed towards the end of producing successful career men. Every moment of boys' time was regulated and purposefully spent. They were insulated from all harmful external influence and all aspects of the school organisation, like streaming and interhouse competitions, served similar ends. This regime produced disciplined professionals who could pass examinations and be successful in competitive hierarchies. When asked for advice about careers the school's only suggestions were staying on at school, going to university and entering the professions. To some of those in C classes, who were not academically very successful, the school left a legacy of failure and low self-esteem. Entrepreneurial enterprise was proscribed and the possibility of varied and prosperous futures in business careers ignored.

The regime at Ellesmere promoted vigorous reactions among the boys. There is no doubt that it was costly for some boys especially in their earlier years. Among the reactions and models identified in the study were busy polymath, self-confident young gentleman and rebellious prankster. The regime was essentially one of survival of the fittest in which the weak and unsuccessful suffered in silence or rebelled and the weakest, intellectually and physically, were eliminated.

The school was a good father but a poor mother, providing for boys, managing their careers and supplying models of masculinity. The low status and limited organisation of the mothering functions of caring and nurturing in the school caused parents grave concern especially during the war, when the school was very overcrowded, female domestic labour and food scarce, and the risk from the spread of infectious diseases high.

While this type of organisational regime was characteristic of the public schools at this period, the conceptions of masculinity which they sought to reproduce in their pupils through the regime did not originate there. The models of masculinity underlying public school education were variations of class-specific concepts. The schools, as parents realised, were the most effective means available of reproducing conceptions of masculinity also found in the grammar schools, the media of the labour market.

While Ellesmere and other schools like it produced many success-ful career men, they did so at a price. Many critics and analysts, among them Robert Graves, George Orwell, and Rupert Wilkinson, have discussed the possible baneful consequences of a public school edu-cation like that of the boys at Ellesmere between 1929 and 1950. The present evidence supports the view that the loneliness of possible or actual failure in a competitive hierarchy was one of the most import-ant single consequences of these conceptions of masculinity and the schools as a means of reproducing them, which affected a number of boys at some time in their careers. A second consequence may well have been even more far-reaching. It is impossible to assess the effects on their future life with a marriage partner of a preparatory experience in which the extent of the differences, the rigidity of the

201

boundaries and the political inequalities between men and women were continuously emphasised. It is, however, important to repeat that critics of the public schools, like Robert Graves and George Orwell, who drew attention to those harmful effects of public school education, were criticising not so much the public schools but class-specific gender conceptions and the public schools as highly effective reproducers of them. We now have a considerable body of knowledge about the changing processes of the making of femininity in homes, schools and work places. We also know a great deal about changing male occupational structures and education. We now urgently need a more sophisticated understanding of social class and social mobility including women and taking account of gender relations in families, schools and the labour market. In order to further our understanding of the making of masculinity and its effects, we must bring together and extend our knowlege of the public, grammar, secondary modern and comprehensive schools as class and gender reproducers and the extent to which other schools exact a similar kind and equally high price in making boys into men as public schools, like Ellesmere College between 1929 and 1950.

NOTES

CHAPTER 1 BRINGING UP SONS IN A CHANGING WORLD

1 'Little' correspondence, 18 January 1939.
2 Millerson, G. (1964), *The Qualifying Associations: A Study of Professionalisation*, London, Routledge & Kegan Paul, pp. 221–45; Carr-Saunders, A. M. and Wilson, P. A. (1933), *The Professions*, London, Frank Cass, pp. 307–18, 365–86.
3 Board of Education (1938), *Report of the Consultative Committee on Secondary Education with Special Reference to Grammar Schools and Technical High Schools* (Chairman, Mr Will Spens) London, HMSO, pp. 95–103.
4 Bernbaum, G. (1967), *Social Change and the Schools 1918–1944*, London, Routledge & Kegan Paul, pp. 70–71; Simon, Brian (1974), *The Politics of Educational Reform 1920–1940*, London, Lawrence & Wishart, pp. 116–224.
5 'Little' correspondence, 20 January 1939.
6 Banks, O. (1955), *Parity and Prestige in English Secondary Education: A Study in Educational Sociology*, London, Routledge & Kegan Paul, pp. 220–1.
7 Branson, N. and Heinemann, M. (1973), *Britain in the 1930s*, London, Granada, p. 163.
8 Heeney, B. (1969), *Mission to the Middle Classes: The Woodard Schools 1848–1891*, London, SPCK; Kirk, K. E. (1937), *The Story of the Woodard Schools*, London, Hodder.
9 Oral evidence from Mrs Nankivell, 'Evans Prosser invented Bursaries'. There were, however, widespread competitive fee reductions at this time; Simon, Brian (1944), *The Politics of Educational Reform* (op. cit.), pp. 274–5.
10 'Little' correspondence, 20 January 1939.
11 Ibid., 17 September 1945.
12 Ibid., 14 March 1946.
13 Ibid., 19 May 1946.
14 Ibid., 14 January 1972.
15 Ibid., 20 January 1939.
16 Walker, T. (1982), *The High Path*, London, Routledge & Kegan Paul, p. 1.
17 Ibid., p. 17.
18 Ibid., p. 16.
19 Ibid., p. 57.

20 Ibid., p. 79.
21 Ibid., pp. 91–3.
22 Ibid., p. 108.
23 Ibid., p. 109.
24 Ibid.
25 Ibid.
26 Steedman, Carolyn (1986), *Landscape for a Good Woman*, London, Virago.
27 Lees correspondence, 25 November 1945.
28 Malcolm Lees, oral evidence.
29 Lees correspondence, 25 November 1945.
30 Malcolm Lees, oral evidence.
31 Lees correspondence, 1 October 1944.
32 Ibid., 9 March 1947.
33 Malcolm Lees, letters passim.
34 Malcolm Lees, oral evidence.
35 Tolson, A. (1977), *The Limits of Masculinity*, London, Tavistock; Pleck, J. and Sawyer, J. (eds) (1974), *Men and Masculinity*, Englewood Cliffs, N. J., Prentice Hall.
36 Roberts, R. (1973), *The Classic Slum: Salford Life in the First Quarter of the Century*, Harmondsworth, Penguin, pp. 16–31, 144–5.
37 *Census of England and Wales, 1951* (1956), Occupation Tables, London, HMSO, pp. 651–2; Table C, Occupations of Males and Females in 1931 & 1951.
38 Marsh, D. C. (1965), *The Changing Social Structure of England and Wales, 1871–1961*, London, Routledge & Kegan Paul, pp. 130–50.
39 *Royal Commission on Equal Pay* (1946), Cmnd 6937, London, HMSO, passim.
40 Ibid., p. 108.
41 Woolf, V. (1977), *Three Guineas*, Harmondsworth, Penguin, p. 8.
42 Williams, G. (1945), *Women & Work*, London, Nicholson & Watson, p. 48.
43 Ibid., p. 55.
44 Goldthorpe, J. (with Llewellyn, C. and Payne, C.), (1980), *Social Mobility and Class Structure in Modern Britain*, Oxford, Clarendon; Halsey, A. H., Heath, A. F. and Ridge, J. M. (1980), *Origins and Destinations: Family, Class and Education in Modern Britain*, Oxford, Clarendon. These two studies are the most far-reaching examinations of changing class relations and class and educational relations in the period under review. They are, however, confined to a sample of 10,000 men in four age cohorts 1912–1922, 1923–1932, 1933–1942, 1943–1952. The relationships between class, gender and education consequently remain to be investigated empirically on this scale. For a comparison of family strategies including both class and gender differences see Holley, J. (1981), 'The two family economies of industralism', in *Journal of Family History*, 6, pp. 57–68.
45 Douglas, M. (1973), *Rules and Meanings; an anthropology of everyday knowledge*, Harmondsworth, Penguin, pp. 9–13.
46 Venables, D. R. and Clifford, R. E. (1957), Academic Dress of the University of

Oxford, private publication quoted in Douglas, Mary (1973), *Rules and Meanings* (op. cit,), pp. 209–11.

47 Douglas, M. (1973), *Natural Symbols: Explorations in Cosmology*, Harmondsworth, Penguin; Bernstein, Basil (1970), 'On the Classification and Framing of Educational Knowledge', in Young, M. F. (ed.), *Knowledge and Control, New Directions in the Sociology of Education*, London, Macmillan, pp. 47–69.

48 For discussions of the negotiation of meanings see for example: Berger, P. and Luckmann, T. (1966), *The Social Construction of Reality*, New York, Doubleday; Garfinkel, H. (1967), *Studies in Ethnomethodology*, Englewood Cliffs, N. J., Prentice Hall.

49 The literature in these areas is now vast, particularly in America. The present study owes a particular debt to Ryan, M. D. (1981), *Cradle of the Middle Class. The Family in Oneida County New York 1790–1865*, Cambridge University Press; White, J. (1980), *Rothschild's Buildings: Life in an East End Tenement Block, 1887–1920*, London, Routledge & Kegan Paul; Parsons, C. (1978), *Schools in an Urban Community; A Study of Carbrook 1870–1965*, London, Routledge & Kegan Paul; Steedman, C. (1986), *Landscape for a Good Woman*, London, Virago.

50 Graves, R. (1929), *Goodbye to All That*, London, Jonathan Cape; Greene, G. (ed.) (1934), *The Old School*, London, Jonathan Cape; Simpson, J. H. (1954), *A Schoolmaster's Harvest: Some Findings of Fifty Years*, London, Faber; Waugh, A. (1955), *The Loom of Youth*, London, Richards Press.

51 Mowat, C. L. (1955), *Britain Between the Wars*, London, Methuen; Marwick, Arthur (1963), *The Explosion of British Society 1914–62*, London, Pan.

52 Pollard, Sydney (1969) (2nd Edition), *The Development of the British Economy 1914–1967*, London, Edward Arnold, pp. 245–6.

53 Ibid., p. 290.

54 Ibid., p. 286.

55 Ibid., p. 287.

56 Stevenson, J. (1984), *British Society 1914–1945*, Harmondsworth, Penguin, pp. 129–30.

57 Quoted in Stevenson, J. (1984), *British Society 1914–1945* (op. cit.), p. 159.

58 Weeks, J. (1981), *Sex, Politics and Society, the Regulation of Sexuality since 1800*, London, Longman, pp. 201–14; Hamilton, C. 1940, *The Englishwoman*, London, Longmans, for the British Council.

59 'Owen' correspondence, 15 September 1938.

60 Gosden, P.H.J.H. (1976), *Education in the Second World War: A Study in Policy and Administration*, Methuen, pp. 13–31.

61 Calder, A. (1971) *The People's War: Britain 1939–1945*, London, Granada, pp. 40–55.

62 'Little' correspondence, 15 June 1939.

63 Marwick, A. (1971), *The Explosion of British Society 1914–1970* (2nd ed.), Macmillan, p. 99.

64 Taylor, A.J.P. (1970), *English History 1914–45*, Harmondsworth, Penguin; Pelling,

Henry (1970), *Britain and the Second World War*, London, Collins.

65 Broad, R. and Fleming, S. (eds) (1981), *Nella Last's War*, Bristol, Fallingwall Press.

66 Marwick, A. (1971), *The Explosion of British Society* (op. cit.), p. 100.

67 Calder, A. (1971), *The People's War* (op. cit.), p. 204, p. 469; Waugh, E. (1984), *The Sword of Honour Trilogy*, Harmondsworth, Penguin.

68 Pollard, S. (1969) (2nd ed.), *The Development of the British Economy* (op. cit.) pp. 339–48.

69 Addison, P. (1975), *The Road to 1945: British Politics and the Second World War*, London, Quartet, pp. 229–69; Fraser D. (1984) (2nd ed.), *The Evolution of the British Welfare State*, London, Macmillan, pp. 222–4.

70 Pollard, S. (1969) (2nd ed.), *The Development of the British Economy* (op. cit.), pp. 364–76; Fraser, D. (1984), *The Evolution of the British Welfare State* (op. cit.), pp. 224–30.

71 Marwick, A. (1982), *British Society Since 1945*, London, Allen Lane.

72 Fraser, D. (1984) (2nd ed.), *The Evolution of the British Welfare State* (op. cit.).

73 Floud, J., Halsey, A. H., and Martin, F. M. (1956), *Social Class and Educational Opportunity*, London, Heinemann; Halsey, A. H., Heath, A. Ridge, J. M. (1980), *Origins and Destinations* (op. cit.).

74 Board of Education (1944), *The Public Schools and the General Educational System*, Report of the Committee on Public Schools appointed by the President of the Board of Education in July 1942, London, HMSO.

75 Addison, P. (1977), *The Road to 1945* (op. cit.), pp. 173–4.

CHAPTER 2 EDUCATING SONS AT ELLESMERE COLLEGE

1 The social divisions in British society and their educational needs were a highly contentious issue. The present interpretation follows two previous author-atative studies: Honey, J. R. de S. (1977), *Tom Brown's Universe, The Development of the Public School in the Nineteenth Century*, London, Millington, pp. 151–3; Bamford, T. W. (1967), *Rise of the Public Schools*, London, Nelson.

2 Eliot, George (1966) *Felix Holt: The Radical*, London, Dent, first published 1856.

3 Gerth, H. H. and Mills, C. W. (1958) (eds), *From Max Weber: Essays in Sociology*, London, Oxford University Press; Weber, M. (1964), *Theory of Social and Economic Organisations*, Glencoe, Illinois, Free Press.

4 *Report of Her Majesty's Commissioners appointed to inquire into the Revenues and Management of Certain Schools and Colleges, and the Studies Pursued and Instruction given therein*. [*The Clarendon Report*], P.P. 1864, XX, Cmd 3288, Part I, General Report p. 56.

5 Ibid., p. 32.

6 Ibid., p. 56.

7 Ibid., p. 32.

8 Wilkinson, R. (1964), *The Prefects: British Leadership and the Public School Tradition: A Comparative Study in the Making of Rulers*, London, Oxford University Press, p. 80.

9 Davie, G. E. (1964), *The Democratic Intellect: Scotland and her Universities in the Nineteenth Century*, Edinburgh, Edinburgh University Press.

10 Bryant, M. (1980), *The Unexpected Revolution: A Study in the Education of Women and Girls*, Cambridge University Press.

11 *Report of the Royal Commission known as the Schools Inquiry Commission [The Taunton Report]* P.P. 1867, XXVIII, Cmd 3966, I, p. 18.

12 Ibid., pp. 16–20.

13 Ibid., p. 17.

14 Ibid., p. 104.

15 Ibid., p. 284.

16 Ibid., p. 302.

17 Archer, R. L. (1921), *Secondary Education in the Nineteenth Century*, London; Fletcher, S. (1980), *Feminists and Bureaucrats: A Study in the Development of Girls' Education in the Nineteenth Century*, Cambridge University Press.

18 P.P. 1867, XVIII, *Schools Inquiry Commission*, I, p. 320.

19 Kirk, K. E. (1937), *The Story of the Woodard Schools*, London, Hodder, p. 27.

20 Ibid., pp. 115–34.

21 Heeney, B. (1969) *Mission to the Middle Classes: The Woodard Schools 1848–1891*, London, SPCK.

22 Kirk, K. E. (1937). *The Story* (op. cit.), p. 166.

23 Heward, C. M. (1984), 'Parents, Sons and Their Careers: A Case Study of a Public School, 1930–50', in Walford, G. (ed.), *British Public Schools: Policy and Practice*, Sussex, Falmer, p. 140.

24 *The Ellesmerian*, 1885, vol. 1, no. 1, p. 8.

25 Ibid., p. 11.

26 Ibid., 1886, vol. 2, no. 2, p. 27.

27 Ibid., 1888, vol. 4, no. 6, p. 85.

28 Ibid., 1889, vol. 5, no. 5, p. 65.

29 Ibid., 1890, vol. 6, no. 6, p. 60.

30 Ibid., 1890, vol. 6, no. 3, p. 30.

31 Ibid., 1905, vol. 21, no. 2, p. 10.

32 Heward, C. M. (1984) 'Parents, Sons' (op. cit.), p. 143.

33 Honey, J. R. de S. (1977) *Tom Brown's Universe* (op. cit.), p. 276.

34 Archer, R. L. (1921), *Secondary Education* (op. cit.).

35 Simon, B. (1974), *Education and the Labour Movement: 1870–1920*, London, Lawrence & Wishart, pp. 176–86.

36 Ibid., pp. 208–46.

37 Eaglesham, E.J.R. (1956), *From School Board to Local Authority*, London, Routledge & Kegan Paul.

38 Honey, J. R. de S. (1977), *Tom Brown's Universe*, (op. cit.); Banks, O. (1955),

Party and Prestige in English Secondary Education: A Study in Educational Sociology, London, Routledge & Kegan Paul, p. 220.

39 Ogilvie, V. (1967), The English Public Schools, London, Batsford.

40 Hall, P. A. (1934), Fifty Years of Ellesmere 1884–1934, London, Eyre & Spottiswoode.

41 Roach, J. (1979) 'Examinations and the Secondary Schools 1900–1945, History of Education, vol. 8, no. 1, pp. 45–58.

42 Petch, J. A. (1953), Fifty Years of Examining: the Joint Matriculation Board, 1903–1953, London, Harrap, pp. 80–99 and 182–200; Board of Education 1938, Report of the Consultative Committee on Secondary Education with special reference to Grammar Schools and Technical High Schools, London, HMSO, pp. 254–67.

43 Gallie, W. B. (1949), An English School, London, Cresset, p. 42.

44 Millerson, G. (1964), The Qualifying Associations: A Study of Professionalisation, London, Routledge & Kegan Paul, pp. 120–47; Carr-Saunders, A. M. and Wilson, P. A. (1964), The Professions, London, Frank Cass, pp. 307–18.

45 Cairns. J.A.R. (1926) The Problem of a Career Solved by Thirty Six Men of Distinction, London, Arrowsmith.

46 Ibid., p. 142.

47 Ibid., p. 257.

48 Ibid., p. 111–12.

49 Ibid., p. 31.

50 A development noted favourably by the Board of Education Inspectors in 1931, Hall, P. A. (1934), Fifty Years (op. cit.), p. 154.

51 Waugh, A. (1955), The Loom of Youth, London, Bles, first published 1917; Mack, E. C. (1941), Public Schools and British Opinion since 1860, New York, Columbia University Press.

52 Graves, Robert (1929), Goodbye to All That, London, Cape.

53 Simpson, J. H. (1965), Schoolmaster's Harvest, London, Faber.

54 Hearnden, A. (1984), Red Robert: A Life of Robert Birley, London, Hamish Hamilton.

55 Hall, P. A. (1934), Fifty Years (op. cit.) p. 158.

56 The Ellesmerian, 1961, vol. 72, no. 292, p. 39.

57 Ibid., p. 40.

58 Old Ellesmerian Chronicle, 1939, vol. 54, pp. 127–8.

59 'Dover' correspondence, 18 November 1942.

60 R. Carver, oral evidence.

61 David Parton, oral evidence.

62 Addison, D. (1985), Now the War is Over: A Social History of Britain 1945–51, London, BBC, p. 165.

63 Taylor, W. (1963), The Secondary Modern School, London, Faber.

64 Public Schools Year Book, 1934.

65 Ibid.

66 Creak, W. J. (1953), History of Adams Grammar School, Wem, p. 54.

67 Gaydon, A. T. (ed.) (1973), A History of Shropshire, vol. 2, London, Oxford University Press, p. 151.

68 Shropshire Education Committee Report, 6 February 1926, 24 July 1926, 5 February 1927, in *Salop County Council Reports* 1925/26, p. 331, 1926–27, pp. 117 and 269.

69 Banks, O. (1955), *Parity and Prestige* (op. cit.).

70 *Shrewsbury Chronicle*, 16 March 1928, quoted in Baugh, G. C. (ed.) (1979), *A History of Shropshire*, vol. 3, London, Oxford University Press, p. 202.

71 Shropshire County Council Minutes, 1936–37, pp. 86–7.

72 Baugh, G. C. (ed.) (1979), *A History of Shropshire* (op. cit.), vol. 3, p. 203.

73 Canon Derry (1980), *The Ellesmerian*, vol. 92, no. 317, 'The Provost's Farewell Address'.

74 Gosden, P.H.J.H. (1976), *Education in the Second World War: A Study in Policy and Administration*, London, Methuen, pp. 48, 73–5.

75 Lyon, H. (1945), 'The Future and Function of the Boarding School' in Moore, R. W. (ed.), *Education: Today and Tomorrow*, London, Michael Joseph, pp. 79–93.

76 Diggory correspondence, 6 June 1941.

77 'Little' correspondence, 12 February 1946, 19 and 21 May 1946.

78 Davies correspondence, 17 May 1940.

79 Bamford, T. W. (1967), *Rise of the Public Schools* (op. cit.); Chandos, J. (1984), *Boys Together: English Public Schools 1800–1864*, London, Hutchinson, p. 67.

80 Bamford, T. W. (1967), *Rise of the Public Schools* (op. cit.), p. 77; Newsome, D. (1961), *Godliness and Good Learning: Four Studies on a Victorian Ideal*, London, John Murray.

81 Mangan, J. A. (1981), *Athleticism in the Victorian and Edwardian Public School*, Cambridge University Press, p. 212.

82 Norwood, C. (1929), *The English Tradition of Education*, London, John Murray, p. 60.

83 Ibid., p. 109.

84 Woolf, V. (1977), *Three Guineas*, Harmondsworth, Penguin.

85 Crichton Miller, H. (1922), *The New Psychology and the Parent*, London, Jarrold, p. 69.

86 Ibid., pp. 71–2.

87 David Parton, Nigel Dale, David Bradley, oral evidence.

88 Major Terence Thornton, oral evidence.

89 M. C. Cockin, oral evidence.

90 K. M. Lees, M. C., Cockin, D. J. Latham, oral evidence.

91 Dale, R. R. (1969, 1971, 1974), *Single Sex or Co-educational Schools*, 3 volumes, London, Routledge & Kegan Paul.

92 Deeping, W. (1925), *Sorrell & Son*, London, Cassell.

93 Baldwin, O. (1933), *Unborn Son*, London, Grayson & Grayson.

94 Woolf, V. (1977), *Three Guineas*, Harmondsworth, Penguin p. 96.

CHAPTER 3 THE MAINSTAY OF THE SCHOOL

1 Hall, P. A. (1934), *Fifty Years of Ellesmere, 1884–1934*, London, Eyre & Spottiswoode, p. 63.
2 Gallie, W. B. (1949), *An English School*, London, Cresset, p. 24.
3 Ibid., p. 26.
4 Doughty correspondence, 25 September 1944.
5 Fox, I. (1985), *Private Schools and Public Issues*, London, Macmillan.
6 Simon, B. (1974), *Education and the Labour Movement 1870–1920*, London, Lawrence & Wishart, pp. 346–9.
7 'Laker' correspondence, 29 September 1942.
8 Laughton correspondence, 6 April 1940.
9 'Laker' correspondence, 23 April 1939.
10 Frank Sutterby, oral evidence.
11 Board of Education (1943), *Report of the Secondary School Examinations Council on Curriculum & Examinations in Secondary Schools*, London, HMSO; Addison, Paul (1985), *Now the War is Over: A Social History of Britain 1945–51*, London, Quartet, follows Rubinstein, D. (1979), 'Ellen Wilkinson Reconsidered', *History Workshop Journal*, vol. 7, no. 2, pp. 161–9, in seeing the Minister of Education, Ellen Wilkinson, as largely responsible for the implementation of the 1944 Education Act by means of a tripartite rather than a multilateral system of secondary education. Such an interpretation underestimates the growing importance of concepts and measures of fixed intelligence and the consequent support for categorisation by measured intelligence in practices like streaming and segregated special education during the period under review.
12 'Laker' correspondence, 19 May 1939.
13 Leinster-Mackay, D. (1984), *The Rise of the English Prep School*, Sussex, Falmer, pp. 184, 223–30.
14 Caller correspondence, 24 March 1934.
15 Lumley Davies correspondence, passim.
16 'Laker' correspondence, 14 June 1939.
17 Coates correspondence, 25 February 1943.
18 Davis correspondence, 24 November 1937; Ellis correspondence, 8 February 1937.
19 Clarke correspondence, 8 June 1940.
20 PRO, ED. 136/129, Leeson to Holmes, 14 October 1938 quoted by Gosden, P.H.J.H. (1976), *Education in the Second World War: A Study in Policy and Administration*, London, Methuen, p. 333.
21 'Lawson' correspondence, 20 January 1936.
22 Quigly, Isabel (1982), *The Heirs of Tom Brown: The English School Story*, London, Chatto & Windus; Musgrave, P. W. (1985), *From Brown to Butler: The Life and Death of the School Story*, London, Routledge & Kegan Paul.
23 See below p. 147, ch. 7.
24 M. K. Lees, oral evidence.

25 Hughes, T. (n.d.), *Tom Brown's Schooldays*, London, Nisbet, p. 61.

26 Malcolm Lees oral evidence.

27 'Lawson' correspondence, 27 April 1938.

28 'Roper' correspondence, undated.

29 Courtenay correspondence, 14 January 1942.

30 Duplicated letters from school supplied by Nigel Dale.

31 David Parton, oral evidence.

32 'Lawson' correspondence, 9 April 1938.

33 Ibid., 28 April 1938.

34 Ibid., 29 April 1938.

35 Berger, P. L. and Luckman, T. (1967), *The Social Construction of Reality, a Treatise in the Sociology of Knowledge*, Harmondsworth, Penguin. Schutz, A. (1964), 'The Stranger: An Essay in Social Psychology' in Burderson, A. (ed.), *Collected Papers 11*, The Hague, Martinus Nijhoff, pp. 91–105.

36 Douglas, M. (1970), *Purity & Danger: An Analysis of Concepts of Pollution and Taboo*, Harmondsworth, Penguin; (1973) *Natural Symbols: Explorations in Cosmology*, Harmondsworth, Penguin.

37 Bernstein, B. (1970), 'On the Classification and Framing of Knowledge in Young, M.F.D. (ed.), *Knowledge and Control: New Directions in the Sociology of Education*, London, Macmillan.

38 Douglas, M. (1973) (ed.), *Rules and Meanings: The Anthropology of Everyday Knowledge*, Harmondsworth, Penguin, p. 207.

39 Lees correspondence, 3 May 1945.

40 Malcolm Lees, oral evidence.

41 Mike Smith, oral evidence.

42 Major Terence Thornton, oral evidence.

43 Mike Smith, oral evidence.

44 Ruby Purcell, oral evidence.

45 Malcolm Lees, oral evidence; Gallie, W. B. (1949), *An English School* (op. cit.), p. 13.

46 Hall, P. A. (1934), *Fifty Years* (op. cit.), pp. 69–70.

47 Honey, J. (forthcoming), 'Talking Proper: Schooling and the Establishment of English R.P.' in Nixon, G. and Honey, J. *An Historic Tongue: Studies in English Linguistics in Memory of Barbara Strong*, London, Croom Helm.

48 News Supplement vol. I, no. 25, 25 January 1937, unpublished wall newspaper.

49 David Parton, oral evidence.

50 Hall, P. A. (1934), *Fifty Years* (op. cit.), p. 66; Nigel Dale oral evidence.

51 'Lawson' correspondence, 2 June 1939.

52 Ibid., 31 August 1939.

53 Ibid., 11 September 1939.

54 Ibid., 23 September 1939.

55 Ibid., 27 September 1939.

56 Ibid., 6 January 1940.

57 Ibid., 2 February 1940.
58 'Laker' correspondence, 29 September 1940.
59 Ibid., 19 November 1945.

CHAPTER 4 THE POOR CHURCH MICE

1 Bamford, T. W. (1960), *Thomas Arnold*, London, Cresset Press; Archer, R. L. (1921), *Secondary Education in the Nineteenth Century*.
2 Mangan, J. A. (1981), *Athleticism in the Victorian and Edwardian Public School: the Emergence and Consolidation of an Educational Ideology*, Cambridge University Press; Newsome, D. (1961), *Godliness and Good Learning: Four Studies in a Victorian Ideal*, London, John Murray.
3 Heeney, B. (1969), *Mission to the Middle Classes: The Woodard Schools 1848–91*, London, SPCK; Newsome, D. (1961), *Godliness and Good Learning* (op. cit.), p. 208.
4 Mangan, J. A. (1981), *Athleticism* (op. cit.).
5 Norwood, C. (1928), *The English Tradition of Education*, London, John Murray.
6 Mike Smith, oral evidence.
7 Mowat, C. L. (1955), *Britain between the Wars 1918–1940*, London, Methuen, p. 224.
8 *The Public Schools Yearbook* 1933.
9 'Heywood' correspondence, 26 November 1938.
10 Ibid., 1 December 1938.
11 Woolf, V. (1938), *Three Guineas*, London, Hogarth.
12 'Heywood' correspondence, 6 December 1938.
13 Finch, J. (1983), *Married to the Job: Wives' Incorporation in Men's Work*, London, Allen & Unwin.
14 'Heywood' correspondence, 2 November 1942.
15 Ibid.
16 Ibid.
17 Gosden, P.H.J.H. (1976), *Education and the Second World War: A Study in Policy and Administration*, London, Methuen, p. 147.
18 'Heywood' correspondence, 5 November 1942.
19 Ibid., 28 April 1943.
20 Ibid., 2 April 1943.
21 Tolson, A. (1977), *The Limits of Masculinity*, London, Tavistock, 23–4.
22 Hughes, T. (n.d.), *Tom Brown's Schooldays*, London, Nisbet, p. 51.
23 Caller correspondence, n.d.
24 Hair, P.E.H. (1982), 'Children in Society 1850–1980', in Barker, T. and Drake, M. (eds), *Population and Society in Britain 1850–1980*, London, Batsford.

25 Halsey, A. H. (1972) (ed.), *Trends in British Society since 1900*, London Macmillan, p. 29; Branson, N. and Heinemann, M. (1973), *Britain in the Nineteen Thirties*, London, Granada, pp. 180–5.

26 Branson, N. and Heinemann, M. (1973), *Britain in the Nineteen Thirties* (op. cit.), pp. 200–12.

27 Stevenson, J. (1984), *British Society 1914–45*, Harmondsworth, Penguin, pp. 129–30; Branson, M. and Heinemann, M. (1973), *Britain in the Nineteen Thirties*, (op. cit.), pp. 257–61.

28 Young, M. and Wilmott, P. (1973), *The Symmetrical Family*, London, Routledge & Kegan Paul; Gavron, H. (1968), *The Captive Wife*, Harmondsworth, Penguin.

29 Hamilton, C. (1940), *The Englishwoman*, London, Longmans for the British Council.

30 Stevenson, J. (1984), *British Society 1914–45* (op. cit.), pp. 143–81.

31 Crichton Miller, H. (1922), *The New Psychology and the Parent*, London, Jarrold, p. 74.

32 Ibid., p. 90.

33 Winnicott, D. W. (1944), *Getting to Know Your Baby; Six Broadcast Talks*, London, BBC.

34 Riley, D. (1933), *War in the Nursery: Theories of the Child and Mother*, London, Virago.

35 'Roper' correspondence, 17 February 1938.

36 Ibid., undated.

37 Ibid., 18 February 1938.

38 Mrs J. Nankivell, oral evidence.

39 Gallie, W. D. (1949), *An English School*, London, Cresset, pp. 12–13.

40 Ruby Purcell, oral evidence.

41 'Roper' correspondence, undated.

42 Ruby Purcell, oral evidence.

43 *The Ellesmerian*, 1941, vol. 60, no. 248, p. 153.

44 'Roper' correspondence, 6 December 1939.

45 Ibid., undated.

46 Ibid.

47 Ibid.

48 L'Estrange correspondence, 19 January 1941.

49 Firth, J. (1983), *Married to the Job* (op. cit.).

50 'Roper' correspondence, undated.

51 Ibid., 11 April 1947.

52 Prebendary R. Taylor, oral evidence.

53 M. C. Cockin, oral evidence.

54 David Parton, oral evidence.

55 J. D. Carver, oral evidence.

56 'Davidson' correspondence, 17 September 1939.

CHAPTER 5 THE WIDOW'S MITE

1 Marwick, A. (1968), *Britain in a Century of Total War*, London, Macmillan; Summerfield, P. (1984), *Women Workers in the Second World War*, London, Croom Helm; Marwick, A. (1987), 'My Battle with the Second World War, *Times Higher Educational Supplement*, 6 March 1987, p. 11.

2 Stevenson, J. (1984), *British Society 1914–1945*, Harmondsworth, Penguin, pp. 148–62; Hall, C. (1977), 'Married Women at Home in Birmingham in the 1920s and 1930s, *Oral History*, vol. 5, no. 2, pp. 62–83.

3 'Roper' correspondence, undated.

4 Hannah, L. (1986), *Inventing Retirement: The Development of Occupational Pensions in Britain*, Cambridge University Press, pp. 117–18.

5 Bamford, T. W. (1967), *Rise of the Public Schools: A Study of Boys' Public Schools in England and Wales from 1837 to the Present Day*, London, Nelson, p. 22. Bamford terms these ladies 'socially ambitious'. It seems more likely that they were attempting to maintain their husbands' plans for their sons' education on very much reduced means.

6 Thane, P. (1982), *The Foundations of the Welfare State*, London, Longman, p. 46.

7 Wilson, E. (1977), *Women and the Welfare State*, London, Tavistock, p. 106; Thane, P. (1982), *The Foundations* (op. cit.), p. 85.

8 Thane, P. (1982), *The Foundations* (op. cit.), pp. 198–9.

9 Hannah, L. (1986), *Inventing Retirement* (op. cit.), pp. 8–10.

10 Rhodes, G. (1965), *Public Sector Pensions*, London, Allen and Unwin, pp. 61–2.

11 Hannah, L. (1986), *Inventing Retirement* (op. cit.), pp. 117–21.

12 Rhodes, G. (1965), *Public Sector Pensions* (op. cit.), p. 130.

13 *Royal Commission on Equal Pay*, 1946, Cmd 3937, London, HMSO.

14 Abel-Smith, B. (1960), *A History of the Nursing Profession*, London, Heinemann.

15 Marsh, D. C. (1950), *National Insurance and Assistance in Great Britain*, London, Pitman.

16 'Peters' correspondence, 6 May 1929.

17 Abel-Smith, B. (1960), *A History of the Nursing Profession* (op. cit.), p. 119.

18 Ibid., pp. 282–3.

19 'Peters' correspondence, Ascension Day, 1929.

20 Ibid., 29 May 1929.

21 Ibid.

22 *The Ellesmerian*, 1939, vol. 50, no. 244, p. 141.

23 'Peters' correspondence, 5 April 1939.

24 'Dover' correspondence, 22 November 1935.

25 Ibid.

26 Ibid., 7 November 1935.

27 Rhodes, G. (1965), *Public Sector Pensions*, London, Allen & Unwin, p. 60 and pp. 275–9.

28 'Dover' correspondence, 21 March 1936.

29 Ibid., 22 March 1936 and 3 April 1936.

30 Ibid., 3 April 1936.

31 Balderson, E. with Goodlad, D. (1982), *Backstairs Life in a Country House*, London, David & Charles, pp. 12–14; Hamilton, C. (1942), *Women of England*, London, Longmans for the British Council; Taylor, P. (1979), 'Daughters and Mothers – maids and mistresses: domestic service between the wars' in Clarke, J. et al. (eds), *Working Class Culture: Studies in History and Theory*, London, Hutchinson. For a thoughtful portrayal of the clash of values between pre-war British India and wartime Britain see Laura Talbot (1985), *The Gentlewoman*, London, Virago, about a governess brought up in India battling to preserve a social order abandoned by employees and staff in an aristocratic country house during the war. The book was first published by Macmillan in 1952.

32 'Dover' correspondence, 3 April 1936.

33 Ibid., 24 April 1936 and 26 April 1936.

34 Ibid., 26 September 1936.

35 Summerfield, P. (1984), *Women Workers* (op. cit.).

36 Burton, Elaine (1941), *What of the Women: A Study of Women in Wartime*, London, Fredereick Muller, pp. 26–8.

37 'Dover' correspondence, 11 November 1940.

38 Lovekin correspondence, 19 September 1939.

39 'Bishop' correspondence, 27 November 1941.

40 'Dover' correspondence, 16 November 1942 and 27 March 1943.

41 Ibid., 31 August 1939 and 18 November 1942.

42 Ibid., 16 November 1942.

43 Mayhew, P. (ed.) (1985), *One Family's War*, London, Futura; Addison, P. (1977), *The Road to 1945: British Politics and the Second World War*, London, Quartet; Mortimer, J. (1985), 'The Planning of the New Jerusalem (A review of Addison)', *The Sunday Times*, 29 September, p. 44.

44 Oral evidence, Nigel Dale, Ruby Purcell.

45 Coryn, H. D. correspondence undated.

46 *The Ellesmerian*, 1941, vol. 60, no. 248, p. 147.

47 *Ellesmerian Chronicle*, October 1963, no. 296, p. 48.

48 Nigel Dale's documents, July 1943.

49 Nigel Dale, oral evidence.

50 *Liverpool Daily Post*, 4 April 1951.

51 Malcolm Lees oral evidence.

52 'Watson' correspondence, 5 December 1937.

53 Ibid., 30 January 1938.

54 Ibid., 18 July 1941.

55 Ibid., 25 January 1939.

56 Ibid., 30 April 1939.

57 Calder, A. (1971), *The People's War: Britain 1939–45*, London, Granada; Taylor, A.J.P. (1970), *English History 1914–1945*, Harmondsworth, Penguin, pp. 609–13.

58 'Watson' correspondence, 22 March 1941.
59 Ibid., 24 April 1941.
60 Ibid., 18 July 1941.
61 Ibid., 12 September 1941.

CHAPTER 6 PROFESSIONAL FATHERS AND SONS

1 G.B. General Register Office (1956), *Report of 1951 Census*, Occupation Tables, p. 660.
2 Lyle brothers correspondence, 16 February 1943.
3 Routh, G. (1980), *Occupation and Pay in Great Britain 1906–79* (2nd ed) London, Macmillan, pp. 154–5, p. 179; Addison, D. (1985), *Now the War is Over*, London, Cape, p. 28.
4 Millerson, G. (1964), *The Qualifying Association: A Study in Professionalization*, London, Routledge & Kegan Paul, pp. 62–3.
5 'Davidson' correspondence, 18 January 1939.
6 Board of Education (1944), *The Public Schools and the General Educational System (The Fleming Report)*, London, HMSO, pp. 47–8.
7 'Jarvis' correspondence, 19 April 1941.
8 Major T. C. Thornton, oral evidence.
9 D. J. Latham, oral evidence.
10 Corbett correspondence, 17 February 1944.
11 R. M. Carver, oral evidence.
12 Malcolm Lees, oral evidence.
13 D. J. Latham, oral evidence.
14 M. C. Cockin, oral evidence.
15 Ruby Purcell, oral evidence.
16 Peter Snape, oral evidence.
17 Board of Education, 1944, *The Public Schools* (op. cit.), pp. 37–8.
18 Wakeford, J. (1969), *The Cloistered Elite: A Sociological Analysis of the English Public Boarding School*, London, Macmillan, pp. 128–59. Goffman, E. (1961), *Asylums: Essays on the Social Situation of Mental Patients and Other Inmates*, New York, Doubleday.
19 Lacey, C. (1970), *Hightown Grammar: The School as a Social System*, Manchester University Press.
20 Connell, R. W. et al., (1982), *Making the Difference: Schools, Families and Social Division*, London, Allen & Unwin; Lloyd-Smith, M. (1986), 'School Processes and the Creation of Deviance', unpublished, mimeographed. The research on public schools has been recently reviewed and extended in Walford, G. (1986), *Life in Public Schools*, Sussex, Falmer.
21 Wakeford, J. (1969), *The Cloistered Elite* (op. cit.), pp. 177–9.
22 'Watson' correspondence, 2 November 1941.
23 Gallie, W. B. (1949), *An English School*, London, Cresset, pp. 11–16.

24 Tolson, A. (1977), *The Limits of Masculinity*, London, Tavistock, p. 87.
25 'Davidson' correspondence, 24 January 1983.
26 'Mason' correspondence, 12 July 1941.
27 Deeping, W. (1925), *Sorrell & Son*, London, Cassell, p. 115. Winchester College finally abandoned boxing in 1986.
28 'Mason' correspondence, 18 July 1941.
29 Ibid.
30 Ibid., 20 October 1945 and 16 November 1945.
31 Ibid., 1 June 1946.
32 Ibid., 26 January 1948.
33 Lees, oral evidence.
34 Gallie, W. B. (1949), *An English School* (op. cit.), p. 13.
35 Lees, oral evidence.
36 Lees correspondence, 11 May 1945.
37 Ibid., 23 May 1945.
38 Lees, oral evidence.
39 Lees correspondence, 3 June 1945.
40 Cooper, S. (1963), 'Snoek Piquante', in Sissons, M. and French, P., *Age of Austerity*, London, Hodder & Stoughton; Addison, P. (1985), *Now the War is Over: A Social History of Britain 1945–51*, London, Cape, pp. 28–9.
41 Lees, oral evidence.
42 Lees correspondence, 2 October 1950.
43 Ibid., 28 October 1945.
44 Ibid., 15 December 1945.
45 Ibid., 20 July 1948.
46 Ibid., 2 November 1947.
47 Ibid., 1 November 1949.
48 Ibid., n.d., Michaelmas 1947.
49 Ibid.
50 Ibid.
51 Ibid., 20 July 1948.
52 Ibid., 24 June 1948.
53 Lees, oral evidence.
54 Lees correspondence, 11 November 1947.
55 Ibid., 27 January 1949.
56 M. C. Cockin and D. J. Latham, oral evidence.
57 Lees correspondence, 11 November 1947.
58 Carlile correspondence, 5 May 1941; 'Owen' correspondence, 6 February 1940.
59 Malcolm Lees, oral evidence.
60 *Old Ellesmerian Chronicle*, 1980, no. 210, p. 58.
61 Mike Smith, oral evidence.
62 D. J. Latham, oral evidence.
63 Ibid.
64 Major Terence Thornton, oral evidence.

65 David Bradley, oral evidence.
66 D. J. Latham, oral evidence.
67 David Parton and David Bradley, oral evidence.
68 Hargreaves, D. H. (1967), *Social Relations in a Secondary School*, London, Routledge & Kegan Paul; Lacey, C. (1970), *Hightown Grammar: The School as a Social System*, Manchester University Press; Burgess, R. G. (1983), *Experiencing Comprehensive Education: A Study of Bishop McGregor School*, London, Methuen.
69 *Old Ellesmerian Chronicle* in *The Ellesmerian*, vol. 92, no. 317, November 1980, no page numbers.
70 Nigel Dale, oral evidence.
71 David Parton, oral evidence.
72 David Bradley, oral evidence.

CHAPTER 7 BEING A FARMER'S BOY

1 Gregory correspondence, 30 May 1942.
2 'Cant' correspondence, 9 May 1947.
3 Calder, A. (1971), *The People's War*, London, Granada, pp. 482–3.
4 Ibid., p. 485.
5 Maurice Evans, Farmer at Bryn Mawr, Ale Oak, Newcastle on Clun, Shropshire, oral evidence.
6 Calder, A. (1971), *The People's War* (op. cit.), p. 484.
7 *The Ellesmerian*, 1942, vol. 52, no. 250, p. 20.
8 *The Ellesmerian*, 1943, vol. 53, no. 251, p. 29.
9 *The Ellesmerian*, 1942, vol. 52, no. 250, p. 20.
10 *The Ellesmerian*, 1943, vol. 53, no. 251, p. 29.
11 Archival film of public schoolboys who went down the mines as Bevin boys shown on 'Home Fires – Britain 1940–44', *The World At War*, Channel Four, 15 March 1987.
12 Longmate, N. (ed.) (1981), *The Home Front*, London, Chatto & Windus, p. 158.
13 Orwell, G. (1940) Boys' Weeklies, *Horizon*, March.
14 *Boys' Own Annual, 1940–41*, vol. 63, London, passim.
15 Collier correspondence, 1 June 1941.
16 Foster correspondence, 18 September 1942.
17 'Hannay' correspondence, 10 January 1942.
18 Ibid., 20 January 1942.
19 Ibid., 24 October 1942.
20 Ibid., 24 September 1944.
21 'Wood' correspondence, 14 May, 1942.
22 Ibid., 28 April 1945.
23 Ibid., 28 September 1946.
24 Ibid., 3 October 1946.

25 Cooper, S. (1963), 'Snoek Piquante', in Sissons, M. and French, P. (eds), *Age of Austerity*, London, Hodder, pp. 47–9.

26 M. Lees, oral evidence.

27 M. Cockin, oral evidence.

28 'Wood' correspondence, 16 October 1947.

29 Ibid., 2 November 1947, 3 November 1947, 19 November 1947.

30 Ibid., 31 March 1949.

31 Mike Smith, oral evidence.

32 Gathorne-Hardy, J. (1979), *The Public School Phenomenon, 597–1977*, Harmondsworth, Penguin, pp. 46–9; Chandos, J. (1984), *Boys Together: English Public School 1800–1864*, London, Hutchinson, pp. 221–46.

33 Kendall, G. (1937), *A Headmaster Reflects*, London, William Hodge.

34 'Barnes' correspondence, 8 February 1939.

35 Ibid., 9 February 1939.

36 Norwood, C. (1929), *The English Tradition of Education*, London, John Murray, p. 65.

37 Ibid., p. 78.

38 'Lawson' correspondence, 29 April 1938.

39 'Stevens' correspondence, 6 January 1942.

40 Ibid., 2 August 1940.

41 Ibid., 5 May 1941.

42 Ibid., 22 December 1941.

43 R.S.M. Page, oral evidence.

44 'King' correspondence, 1 August 1944 and 2 August 1944.

45 Ryan, T. (1985), 'Roots of Masculinity' in Metcalf, A. and Humphries, M. (eds), *The Sexuality of Men*, London, Pluto.

46 Nigel Dale, oral evidence.

47 'Rivers' correspondence, 8 November 1942.

48 Ibid.

49 Driberg, G. T. (1977), *Ruling Passions*, London, Cape, p. 47.

50 Gathorne-Hardy, J. (1977), *The Public School Phenomenon* (op. cit.), p. 177.

51 Gallie, W. D. (1949), *An English School* (op. cit.), pp. 114–15.

52 Ibid., p. 103.

53 Graves, R. (1929), *Goodbye to All That*, London, Cape, p. 66.

54 Gathorne-Hardy, J. (1979), *The Public School Phenomenon* (op. cit.), pp. 188–97; Wakeford, J. (1969), *The Cloistered Elite*, London, Macmillan.

55 Gallie, W. D. (1949), *An English School* (op. cit.), p. 56.

56 Deeping, W. (1925), *Sorrell & Son*, London, Cassell, pp. 191–204.

57 Wilkinson, R. (1964), *The Prefects: British Leadership and the Public School Tradition: A Comparative Study in the Making of Rulers*, London, Oxford University Press, p. 106 and p. 116; Graves, R. (1929), *Goodbye to All That* (op. cit.).

CHAPTER 8 SCHOLARSHIP BOYS

1 Board of Education (1938), *Report of the Consultative Committee on Secondary Education with Special Reference to Grammar Schools and Technical High Schools* (Chairman Lord Spens), London, HMSO, p. 305.

2 Campbell, F. (1956), *Eleven Plus and All That: The Grammar School in a Changing Society*, London, Watts, reprinted in Silver, H. (ed.) (1973), *Equal Opportunity in Education*, London, Methuen, pp. 167–8.

3 P.P. 1864 XX (3288), *Report of the Commissioners on the Revenues and Management of certain Colleges and Schools*, vol. 1 Report, p. 59 and pp. 135–6; P.P. 1867–8 XXVIII, *Schools Inquiry Commission*, vol. 1, pp. 224–31.

4 Perkin, H. (1969), *The Origins of Modern English Society 1780–1880*, London, Routledge & Kegan Paul; Bamford, T. W. (1967), *Rise of the Public Schools*, London, Nelson.

5 Honey, J. R. de S. (1977), *Tom Brown's Universe: The Development of the Public School in the Nineteenth Century*, London, Millington.

6 Rubinstein, D. (1986), 'Education and the Social Origins of British Elites 1880–1970', *Past and Present*, vol. 112, pp. 163–207.

7 Banks, O. (1955), *Parity and Prestige: A Study in Educational Sociology*, London, Routledge & Kegan Paul, pp. 3–4.

8 P.P. 1895 XLII, *Royal Commission on Secondary Education* (7862), vol. VI, Report on Certain Burgh Schools and Schools of Secondary Education in Scotland, by D. R. Fearon, HMI, p. 34; Gray, J. L. Macpherson, A. and Raffe, D. (1983), *Reconstruction of Secondary Education: Theory, Myth and Practice Since the War*, London, Routledge & Kegan Paul, p. 39, pp. 45–6.

9 Banks, O. (1955), *Parity and Prestige* (op. cit.), p. 3.

10 Heward, C. (1982), 'Education, Examinations and the Artisans: The Department of Science and Art in Birmingham, 1853–1902, in Macleod, R. (ed.), *Days of Judgement*, Driffield, Nafferton.

11 P.P. 1895, XLIII, *Royal Commission on Secondary Education* (7862), Chairman Mr James Bryce, vol. 1, Report, pp. 63–4 and 168–70.

12 Webb, S. (1901), *The Educational Muddle and the Way Out*, London, Fabian Society Tract 106.

13 Brennan, E.J.T. (1975), *Education for National Efficiency: The Contribution of Sidney and Beatrice Webb*, London, Athlone, pp. 96–104, 109, 116–121; Simon, B. (1965), *Education and the Labour Movement 1870–1920*, London, Lawrence & Wishart.

14 Eaglesham, E.J.R. (1956), *From School Board to Local Authority*, London, Routledge & Kegan Paul.

15 Board of Education 1938, *Spens Report* (op. cit.), pp. 306–7.

16 Gray, J. L. and Moshinsky, P. (1938), 'Ability and Opportunity in English Education', in Hogben, L. (ed.) *Political Arithmetic*, London, Allen & Unwin.

17 Lindsay, K. (1926), *Social Progress and Educational Waste: Being a Study of the 'Free Place' and Scholarship System*, London, Routledge & Kegan Paul; Campbell, F.

(1956), *Eleven-Plus and All That: The Grammar School in a Changing Society*, London, Watts.

18 Burnett, J. (1969), *A Social History of the Cost of Living*, Harmondsworth, Penguin.

19 Mack, E. C. (1941), *Public Schools and British Opinion Since 1860*, New York, Columbia University Press.

20 Banks, O. (1955), *Parity and Prestige* (op. cit), p. 226.

21 Kendall, G. (1938), *A Headmaster Reflects*, London, Hodge, p. 24.

22 Orwell, G. (1968), 'Such, Such were the Joys', in Orwell, S. and Angus, I., *The Collected Essays, Journalism and Letters of George Orwell*, vol. IV, *In Front of Your Nose 1945–1950*, London, Secker & Warburg.

23 'Roberts' correspondence, 28 October 1935.

24 Ibid., 9 July 1942.

25 Ibid., 29 July 1942.

26 Ibid., 26 August 1942.

27 'Hawkins' correspondence, 5 October 1943.

28 Farrow correspondence, 6 May 1944, 10 May 1944, 22 May 1944.

29 Farrow correspondence, 26 April 1948.

30 Rubinstein D. (1986), *Education and the Social Origins*, (op. cit.).

31 Addison, P. (1977) *The Road to 1945* (op. cit.), pp. 168–73.

32 *Picture Post*, 1 January 1941; B. L. Coombes was a noted member of the British Communist Party. His autobiography *These Poor Hands* was published by Gollancz in 1939 for the Left Book Club. *Picture Post* was launched in 1938 by its first editor Stefan Lorant, a Hungarian refugee who went to Canada in 1940. His backer, the owner of the paper, was Edward Hulton, a radical liberal. It represented the highest standards of photo journalism and popular intellectualism, to which such writers as A.J.P. Taylor and Quentin Hogg contributed. The new editor in 1940, Tom Hopkinson, vigorously espoused social reconstruction and the paper backed the Labour Party in 1945. Its circulation rose from 2 million in 1939 to 9 million in 1949; Addison, P. (1982), *The Road to 1945* (op. cit.), p. 152; Stevenson, J. (1984), *British Society 1914–45*, Harmondsworth, Penguin, p. 273.

33 Gathorne-Hardy, J. (1977), *The Public School Phenomonon 597–1977*, Harmondsworth, Penguin, p. 273.

34 *Picture Post* 1 January 1941, p. 30.

35 Mack, E. C. (1941), *Public Schools and British Opinion Since 1860* (op. cit.), pp. 455–63.

36 Worsley, T. C. (1940), *Barbarians and Philistines: Democracy and the Public Schools*, London; Simon, B. (1986), 'The 1944 Education Act: A Conservative Measure?' *History of Education*, vol. 15, no. 1, pp. 31–43.

37 Spencer, F. H. (1941), *Education for the People*, London, Routledge & Kegan Paul, p. 180.

38 Gosden, P.H.J.H. (1976), *Education in the Second World War; A Study in Policy and Administration*, London, Methuen, pp. 269–70; Simon, B. (1986), *The 1944 Education Act* (op. cit.); Addison, P. (1977), *The Road to 1945: British Politics and the*

Second World War, London Quartet, p. 173; Howard, A. (1987), *RAB, the Biography of R. A. Butler*, London, Cape, p. 122.

39 Board of Education (1944), *The Public Schools and the General Educational System. Report of the Committee on Public Schools Appointed by the President of the Board of Education in July 1942*, London, HMSO.

40 Banks, O. (1955), *Parity and Prestige* (op. cit.), pp. 233–8.

41 Bernbaum, G. (1967), *Social Change and the Schools 1918–1944*, London, Routledge & Kegan Paul; Simon, B. (1974), *Politics of Educational Reform 1920–1940*, London, Lawrence & Wishart; Banks, O. (1955), *Parity and Prestige* (op. cit.).

42 Halsey, A. H. et al. (1980), *Origins and Destinations: Family, Class and Education in Modern Britain*, Oxford, Clarendon.

43 Board of Education (1943), *Report of the Secondary School Examinations Council on Curriculum and Examinations in Secondary Schools (Chairman: Sir Cyril Norwood)*, London, HMSO.

44 Taylor, W. (1963), *The Secondary Modern School*, London, Faber.

45 Halsey, A. H., et al. (1980), *Origins and Destinations* (op. cit.).

46 'Tyson' correspondence, 7 August 1947.

47 Ibid.

48 Ibid., 15 August 1947.

49 Tolson, A. (1977), *The Limits of Masculinity*, London, Tavistock, pp. 34–7.

50 *The Ellesmerian*, January vol. 66, p. 1.

51 Kendall, G. (1938) A Headmaster Reflects (op. cit.), pp. 29 and 134.

52 'Booth' correspondence, 15 May 1946.

53 Ibid., 29 September 1946.

54 Ibid., 22 May 1947.

55 Rothblatt, S. (1982), 'Failure in Early Nineteenth Century, Oxford and Cambridge', *History of Education*, vol. 11, no. 1, pp. 1–21.

56 'Hawkins' correspondence, 15 January 1952.

57 Orwell, G. (1968), 'Such, Such were the Joys (op. cit.), note 22.

58 'Gray' correspondence, 27 April 1943.

59 Ibid., 17 July 1945. I am indebted to Dr Joan Hay, Consultant Child Psychiatrist, Alexandra Hospital, Walderslade, Kent for her comments on this case and information about the incidence and treatment of nocturnal enuresis.

60 'Gray' correspondence, 4 March 1946.

61 Ibid., 19 March 1946.

62 Ibid., 22 February 1946.

CHAPTER 9 THE SCHOOL AS FATHER AND MOTHER

1 Young, M. and Willmott, P. (1973), *The Symmetrical Family*, London, Routledge & Kegan Paul; Pahl, J. M. and Pahl, R. E. (1972), *Managers and Their Wives*, Harmondsworth, Penguin.

2 Rowbotham, S. (1973), *Women's Consciousness, Man's World*, Harmondsworth,

Penguin; Barratt, M. (1980), *Women's Oppression Today: Problems in Marxist Feminist Analysis*, London, New Left Books.

3 *The Times Educational Supplement* (1944), 12 August, p. 386.

4 'Barnes' correspondence; 'Stevens' correspondence, 5 May 1941.

5 Mowat, C. L. (1955), *Britain Between the Wars, 1918–40*, London, Methuen, pp. 609–60.

6 'Davidson' correspondence, 17 October 1938.

7 Kee, R. (1985), *The World We Left Behind: A Chronicle of the Year 1939*, London, Sphere, pp. 49, 237–8.

8 Crohn correspondence, 26 and 28 November 1938, 2 November 1938, 17 December 1938, 16 July 1939.

9 Luft correspondence, 5 July 1939, 16 July 1939.

10 Ibid., 20 July 1939, 22 July 1939.

11 Ibid., 13 September 1939.

12 Kodicek, J. (1940), 'Two Ways of Education – Their Differences and Similarities', *The Ellesmerian*, vol. 60, no. 245, pp. 18–19.

13 Roy Carver, oral evidence: Lowry correspondence, 1940.

14 Luft correspondence, 11 September 1940, 17 September 1940.

15 'Richardson' correspondence, 14 September 1939.

16 Ibid., 4 February 1939.

17 Ibid., 17 April 1939.

18 Honey, J. R. de S. (1977), *Tom Brown's Universe*, London, Millington; Bamford, T. W. (1967), *Rise of the Public Schools*, London, Nelson.

19 'Richardson' correspondence, 17 April 1939.

20 Ibid., 18 September 1939.

21 Ibid., 3 September 1941.

22 Ibid., 5 September 1941.

23 Ibid., 3 September 1941.

24 Ibid., 5 September 1941.

25 Ibid., 3 September 1941.

26 Ibid., 6 August 1942.

27 Ibid.

28 Ibid., 28 April 1943.

29 *Old Ellesmerian Chronicle*, October 1966, vol. 302, p. 119.

30 'Wilkinson' correspondence, 18 November 1939.

31 Ibid., 12 July 1942.

32 Ibid.

33 Ibid., 14 November 1943.

34 Ibid., 23 November 1943 and 12 January 1944.

35 Ibid., 28 July 1942 and 28 July 1942.

36 Ibid., 30 August 1941.

37 Ibid., 17 August 1941.

38 'Laker' correspondence, 17 July 1944.

39 Gallie correspondence, 3 November 1944.

40 'Hampshire' correspondence, 5 May 1948.

41 Ibid., 3 May 1944.
42 Ibid., 5 May 1944.
43 *The Ellesmerian* 1947, vol. 62, no. 269, pp. 14–15.
44 'Lopez' correspondence, 22 December 1941.
45 Graydon correspondence, 24 February 1939.
46 Forster correspondence, 2 October 1947.
47 'Driffield' correspondence; Malcolm Lees, oral evidence.
48 Graves, R. (1929), *Goodby to All That*, London, Murray.
49 M. C. Cockin, oral evidence.
50 Gallie, W. B. (1949), *An English School*, London, Cresset, p. 74.
51 Wilkinson, R. (1962), *The Prefects: British Leadership and the Public School Tradition*, London, Oxford University Press, p. 116.

CHAPTER 10 CONCLUSIONS

1 Routh, G. (1980), *Occupation and Pay in Great Britain 1906–79* (2nd ed.), London, Macmillan, p. 1.
2 *Census of Great Britain 1851* (1852), Population Tables, vol. I, London, HMSO, p. xxxiv.
3 Heward, C. (1985), 'Home, School and Work: Changes in Growing Up in the Birmingham Jewellery Quarter 1851–81', Unpublished M. A. thesis, Warwick University.
4 Bamford, T. W. (1967), *Rise of the Public Schools: A Study of Boys Public Boarding Schools in England and Wales from 1837 to the Present Day*, London, Nelson; Honey, J. R. de S. (1977), *Tom Brown's Universe: The Development of the Public School in the Nineteenth Century*, London, Millington.
5 Chodorow, N. (1978), *The Reproduction of Mothering: Psycho-analysis and the Sociology of Gender*, London and Los Angeles, University of California Press.
6 Salter, B. and Tapper, T. (1985), *Power and Policy in Education*, Sussex, Falmer, p. 67.
7 Connell, R. W. et al. (1982), *Making the Difference: Schools, Families and Social Division*, London, Allen & Unwin; Mahoney, P. (1985), *Schools for the Boys?, Coeducation Reassessed*, London, Hutchinson; Spender, D. (1982), *Invisible Women, the Schooling Scandal*, London, Writers' and Readers' Publishing Cooperative.
8 Willis, P. (1977), *Learning to Labour: How Working Class Kids get Working Class Jobs*, Farnborough, Saxon House.
9 Delamont, S. (1984), 'Debs, Dollies, Swots & Weeds: Classroom Styles at St. Luke's', in Walford, G. (ed.) *British Public Schools: Policy and Practice*, Sussex, Falmer.
10 For a review of the argument and literature see Rubinstein, D. (1986), 'Education and the Social Origins of British Elites 1880 to 1970', *Past and Present*, vol. 112, pp. 163–7.

11 Weber, M. (1947), *Theory of Social and Economic Organisation*, Glencoe, Illinois, Free Press.

12 Perkin, H. (1969), *The Origins of Modern English Society 1780–1880*, London, Routledge & Kegan Paul, pp. 291–339.

13 Honey, J. R. de S. (1977), *Tom Brown's Universe* (op. cit.); Bamford, T. W. (1967), *Rise of the Public Schools* (op. cit.); Rothblatt, S. (1968), *The Revolution of the Dons*, Cambridge University Press.

14 Mangan, J. A. (1981), *Athleticism in the Victorian and Edwardian Public Schools: The Emergence and Consolidation of an Educational Ideology*, Cambridge University Press.

15 Rubinstein, D. (1986), *Education and the Social Origins* (op. cit.).

16 Bridgeman and Fox, I. (1978), 'Why People Choose Private Schools', *New Society*, 29 June, pp. 702–5; Fox, I. (1985), *Private Schools and Public Issues: The Parents' View*, London, Macmillan.

17 Salter, B. and Tapper, T. (1985), *Power and Policy* (op. cit.); Walford, G. (1986), *Life in Public Schools*, London, Methuen.

18 Kalton, G. (1966), *The Public Schools: A Factual Survey*, London, Longmans, Green, pp. 102–3.

19 Cockshoot correspondence, 22 September 1941.

20 Goldthorpe, J. H. et al. (1980), *Social Mobility and Class Structure in Modern Britain*, Oxford, Clarendon.

21 Halsey, A. H. et al. (1980), *Origins and Destinations: Family, Class and Education in Modern Britain*, Oxford, Clarendon.

22 Heath, A. and Ridge, J. (1983), 'Schools, Examinations and Occupational Attainment', in Purvis, J. and Hales, M. (eds) *Achievement and Inequality in Education*, London, Routledge & Kegan Paul, pp. 239–57.

BIBLIOGRAPHY

MANUSCRIPT SOURCES FROM ELLESMERE COLLEGE

'Barnes' correspondence, 18 July 1943 – 9 June 1948.
'Bishop' correspondence, 18 January 1935 – 4 October 1955.
'Booth' correspondence, 28 December 1940 – 22 May 1947.
Caller correspondence, 9 March 1934 – 3 October 1942.
'Cant' correspondence, 10 May 1943 – 2 May 1950.
Carlile correspondence, 8 July 1935 – 16 January 1942.
Clarke correspondence, 8 June 1940 – 30 September 1948.
Coates correspondence, 2 August 1940 – 7 November 1945.
Cockshoot correspondence, 22 September 1941 – 29 July 1942.
Collier correspondence, 17 June 1937 – 4 August 1950.
Corbett correspondence, 27 September 1943 – 17 February 1944.
Coryn correspondence, 11 October 1940 – 19 November 1948.
Crohn correspondence, 28 September 1938 – 25 July 1939.
'Davidson' correspondence, 11 May 1937 – 20 July 1945.
Davies correspondence, 11 May 1940 – 5 November 1943.
Davis correspondence, 29 November 1937 – 28 July 1940.
Diggory correspondence, 6 June 1941 – 31 December 1948.
Doughty correspondence, 15 March 1944 – 1 February 1951.
'Dover' correspondence, 7 November 1935 – 27 March 1943.
'Driffield' correspondence, 13 July 1943 – 11 July 1945.
Ellis correspondence, 16 February 1937 – 2 September 1946.
Farrow correspondence, 14 October 1943 – 22 May 1954.
Foster correspondence, 23 September 1940 – 26 January 1943.
Gallie correspondence, 2 November 1939 – 3 November 1944.
'Gray' correspondence, 24 February 1943 – 15 May 1946.
Graydon correspondence, 2 July 1936 – 5 March 1939.
Gregory correspondence, 30 May 1942 – 23 April 1945.
'Hampshire' correspondence, 29 July 1946 – 16 August 1948.
'Hawkins' correspondence, 10 May 1944 – 18 September 1946.
'Hannay' correspondence, 6 June 1937 – 29 December 1944.
'Heywood' correspondence, 6 December 1938 – 28 April 1943.
'Jarvis' correspondence, 21 June 1937 – 8 September 1947.

'King' correspondence, 27 October 1941 – 25 August 1944.
'Laker' correspondence, 23 April 1939 – 19 March 1945.
Laughton correspondence, 10 August 1939 – 4 July 1941.
'Lawson' correspondence, 17 February 1936 – 8 February 1940.
L'Estrange correspondence, 2 June 1933 – 24 January 1941.
Lees correspondence, 31 August 1944 – 29 November 1951.
'Little' correspondence, 18 January 1939 – 14 January 1972.
Loewy correspondence, 22 July 1940 – 20 October 1941.
'Lopez' correspondence, 9 July 1935 – 26 September 1942.
Lovekin correspondence, 15 March 1934 – 20 October 1943.
Luft correspondence, 5 July 1939 – 21 February 1942
Lumley Davies correspondence, 28 January 1943 – 23 April 1945.
Lyle correspondence, 2 August 1939 – 25 August 1949.
'Mason' correspondence, 22 January 1941 – 12 March 1948.
'Owen' correspondence, 17 August 1938 – 16 February 1942.
'Peters' correspondence, 21 May 1929 – 11 August 1939.
'Richardson' correspondence, 6 July 1938 – 11 March 1948.
'Rivers' correspondence, 20 April 1939 – 28 June 1948.
'Roberts' correspondence, 12 February 1936 – 26 August 1942.
'Roper' correspondence, 19 January 1937 – 20 July 1952.
'Stevens' correspondence, 2 August 1940 – 7 November 1945.
'Tyson' correspondence, 13 March 1945 – 15 August 1947.
'Watson' correspondence, 14 November 1937 – 30 December 1946.
'Wilkinson' correspondence, 5 July 1932 – 11 December 1948.
'Wood' correspondence, 26 June 1937 – 19 November 1947.

ORAL SOURCES

David Bradley, pupil 1945–52.
R. M. Carver, pupil 1943–9.
M. C. Cockin, pupil 1946–9.
Nigel Dale, pupil 1943–6.
Maurice Evans, farmer in Shropshire.
D. J. Latham, pupil 1944–53.
Malcolm Lees, pupil 1945–50.
Mrs J. Nankivell, wife of J. W. Nankivell, headboy 1912, master 1935–68.
R. S. M. Page, staff 1955–81.
David Parton, pupil 1946–52.
Ruby Purcell, staff 1938–present.
M. T. Smith, pupil 1944–51.
Peter Snape, pupil 1924–9.
Frank Sutterby, master 1953–84.
Prebendary Richard Taylor, pupil 1936–8.
Major Terence Thornton, pupil 1935–40.

THESES

Heward, C. (1985), 'Home, School and Work: Changes in Growing Up in the Birmingham Jewellery Quarter 1851–81', Unpublished M.A. thesis, Warwick University.

PRINTED SOURCES

Official publications
G. B. General Register Officer (1852), *Census of Great Britain 1851*, London, HMSO.
P.P. 1864, XX, *Report of Her Majesty's Commissioners appointed to inquire into the Revenues and Management of Certain Schools and Colleges, and the Studies Pursued and Instruction given therein*. [*The Clarendon Report*], Cmd 3288, London, HMSO.
P.P. 1867, XXVIII, *Report of the Royal Commission known as the Schools Inquiry Commission* [*The Taunton Report*], Cmd 3966, London, HMSO.
P.P. 1895, XLIII, *Report of the Royal Commission on Secondary Education* (7862) (Chairman Mr James Bryce), London, HMSO.
Board of Education (1926), *Report of the Consultative Committee of the Board of Education on the Education of the Adolescent* (Chairman Sir W. H. Hadow), London, HMSO.
Board of Education (1938), *Report of the Consultative Committee on Secondary Education with Special Reference to Grammar Schools and Technical High Schools* (Chairman, Mr Will Spens), London, HMSO.
Board of Education (1943), *Report of the Secondary School Examinations Council on Curriculum and Examinations in Secondary Schools* (Chairman: Sir Cyril Norwood), London, HMSO.
Board of Education (1944), *The Public Schools and the General Educational System. Report of the Committee on Public Schools appointed by the President of the Board of Education in July 1942*, (Chairman: Lord Fleming), London, HMSO.
Report of the Royal Commission on Equal Pay (1946), Cmd 6937, London, HMSO.
G. B. General Register Office (1956), *Report of 1951 Census*, London, HMSO.

Local Records
Shropshire County Records Office
Shropshire Education Committee Reports, 6 February 1926, 24 July 1926, 5 February 1927, in Salop County Council Reports 1925/26, p. 331, 1926–27, pp. 117 and 269.

Ellesmere College: *The Ellesmerian*, 1885, vol. 1 – present.
The Old Ellesmerian Chronicle.

The News Supplement: Wall Newspaper 1937–9.

Victoria County History, Gaydon, A. T. (ed.) (1973), *A History of Shropshire*, vol. 2, London, Oxford University Press; Baugh, G. C. (ed.) (1979), *A History of Shropshire*, vol. 3, London, Oxford University Press.

Books

Abel-Smith, B. (1960), *A History of the Nursing Profession,*, London, Heinemann.

Addison, P. (1977), *The Road to 1945: British Politics and the Second World War*, London, Quartet.

Addison, P. (1985), *Now the War is over: A Social History of Britain 1945–51*, London, BBC.

Archer, R. L. (1921), *Secondary Education in the Nineteenth Century*, Cambridge University Press.

Balderson, E. with Goodlad, D. (1982), *Backstairs Life in a Country House*, London, David & Charles.

Baldwin, O. (1933), *Unborn Son*, London, Grayson & Grayson.

Bamford, T. W. (1967), *Rise of the Public Schools: A Study of Boys' Public Boarding Schools in England & Wales from 1837 to the Present Day*, London, Nelson.

Banks, O. (1955), *Parity and Prestige in English Secondary Education: A Study in Educational Sociology*, London, Routledge & Kegan Paul.

Barker, T. and Drake, M. (1982), *Population and Society in Britain 1850–1980*, London, Batsford.

Barratt, M. (1980), *Women's Oppression Today: Problems in Marxist Feminist Analysis*, London, New Left Books.

Berger, P. L. and Luckman, T. (1967), *The Social Construction of Reality: A Treatise in the Sociology of Knowledge*, Harmondsworth, Penguin.

Bernbaum, G. (1967), *Social Change and the Schools 1918–1944*, London, Routledge & Kegan Paul.

Branson, N. and Heinemann, M. (1973), *Britain in the 1930's*, London, Granada.

Brennan, E.J.T. (1975), *Education for National Efficiency: The Contribution of Sidney and Beatrice Webb*, London, Athlone.

Broad, R. and Fleming, S. (eds) (1981), *Nella Last's War*, Bristol, Fallingwall Press.

Bryant, M. (1980), *The Unexpected Revolution: A Study in the Education of Women and Girls*, Cambridge University Press.

Burgess, R. G. (1983), *Experiencing Comprehensive Education: A Study of Bishop McGregor School*, London, Methuen.

Burnett, J. (1969), *A Social History of the Cost of Living*, Harmondsworth, Penguin.

Burton, Elaine (1941), *What of the Women: A Study of Women in Wartime*, London, Frederick Muller.

229

Cairns, J.A.R. (1926), *The Problem of a Career Solved by Thirty Six Men of Distinction*, London, Arrowsmith.

Calder, A. (1971), *The People's War: Britain 1939–1945*, London, Granada.

Campbell, F. (1956), *Eleven-Plus and All That: The Grammar School in a Changing Society*, London, Watts.

Carr-Saunders, A. M. and Wilson, P. A. (1933), *The Professions*, London, Frank Cass.

Chandos, J. (1984), *Boys Together: English Public Schools 1800–1864*, London, Hutchinson.

Chodorow, N. (1978), *The Reproduction of Mothering: Psycho-analysis and the Sociology of Gender*, London and Los Angeles, University of California Press.

Clarke, J. et al. (eds) (1979), *Working Class Culture: Studies in History and Theory*, London, Hutchinson.

Connell, R. W. et al. (1982), *Making the Difference: Schools, Families and Social Division*, London, Allen & Unwin.

Creak, W. J. (1953), *History of Adams Grammar School*, Wem.

Crichton Miller, H. (1922), *The New Psychology and the Parent*, London, Jarrold.

Dale, R. R. (1969, 1971 & 1974), *Single Sex or Co-educational Schools*, 3 vols, London, Routledge & Kegan Paul.

Davie, G. E. (1964), *The Democratic Intellect: Scotland and her Universities in the Nineteenth Century*, Edinburgh University Press.

Deeping, W. (1925), *Sorrell & Son*, London, Cassell.

Douglas, M. (1970), *Purity & Danger: An Analysis of Concepts of Pollution and Taboo*, Harmondsworth, Penguin.

Douglas, M. (1973), *Rules & Meanings: An Anthropology of Everyday Knowledge*, Harmondsworth, Penguin.

Douglas, M. (1973), *Natural Symbols: Explorations in Cosmology*, Harmondsworth, Penguin.

Driberg, G. T. (1977), *Ruling Passions*, London, Cape.

Eaglesham, E.J.R. (1956), *From School Board to Local Authority*, London, Routledge & Kegan Paul.

Eliot, George (1966), *Felix Holt: The Radical*, London, Dent, first published 1856.

Finch, J. (1983), *Married to the Job: Wives' Incorporation in Men's Work*, London, Allen & Unwin.

Fletcher, S. (1980), *Feminists and Bureaucrats: A Study in the Development of Girls' Education in the Nineteenth Century*, Cambridge University Press.

Floud, J., Halsey, A. H., and Martin, F. M. (1956), *Social Class & Educational Opportunity*, London, Heinemann.

Fraser, D. (1984) (2nd ed.), *The Evolution of the British Welfare State*, London, Macmillan.

Gallie, W. B. (1949), *An English School*, London, Cresset.

Garfinkel, H. (1967), *Studies in Ethnomethodology*, Englewood Cliffs, N. J., Prentice Hall.

Gathorne-Hardy, J. (1979), *The Public School Phenomenon, 597–1977*, Harmondsworth, Penguin.

Gavron, H. (1968), *The Captive Wife*, Harmondsworth, Penguin.

Gerth, H. H. and Mills, C. W. (1958) (eds), *From Max Weber: Essays in Sociology*, London, Oxford University Press.

Goffman, E. (1961) *Asylums: Essays on the Social Situation of Mental Patients and Other Inmates*, New York, Doubleday.

Goldthorpe, J. (with Llewellyn, C. and Payne, C.) (1980), *Social Mobility and Class Structure in Modern Britain*, Oxford, Clarendon.

Gosden, P.H.J.H. (1976), *Education in the Second World War: A Study in Policy and Administration*, London, Methuen.

Graves, R. (1929), *Goodbye to All That*, London, Jonathan Cape.

Gray, J. L. and Moshinsky, P. (1938), 'Ability and Opportunity in English Education', in Hogben, L. (ed.), *Political Arithmetic*, London, Allen & Unwin.

Gray, J. Macpherson, A. and Raffe, D. (1983), *Reconstruction of Secondary Education, Theory, Myth and Practice Since the War*, London, Routledge & Kegan Paul.

Greene, G. (ed.) (1934), *The Old School*, London, Jonathan Cape.

Hall, P. A. (1934), *Fifty Years of Ellesmere 1884–1934*, London, Eyre & Spottiswoode.

Halsey, A. H. (1972) (ed.), *Trends in British Society Since 1900*, London Macmillan.

Halsey, A. H., Heath, A. F. and Ridge, J. M. (1980), *Origins and Destinations: Family, Class and Education in Modern Britain*, Oxford, Clarendon.

Hamilton, C. (1940), *The Englishwoman*, London, Longmans, for the British Council. Council.

Hannah, L. (1986), *Inventing Retirement: The Development of Occupational Pensions in Britain*, Cambridge University Press.

Hargreaves, D. H. (1967), *Social Relations in a Secondary School*, London, Routledge & Kegan Paul.

Hearnden, A. (1984), *Red Robert: A Life of Robert Birley*, London, Hamish Hamilton.

Heeney, B. (1969), *Mission to the Middle Classes: The Woodard Schools 1848–1891*, London, SPCK.

Honey, J. R. de S. (1977), *Tom Brown's Universe: The Development of the Public School in the Nineteenth Century*, London, Millington.

Howard, A. (1987), *RAB, the Biography of R. A. Butler*, London, Cape.

Hughes, T. (n.d.), *Tom Brown's Schooldays*, London, Nisbet (first published 1857).

Kalton, G. (1966), *The Public Schools: A Factual Survey*, London, Longmans, Green.

Kee, R. (1985), *The World We Left Behind: A Chronicle of the Year 1939*, London, Sphere.

Kendall, G. (1937), *A Headmaster Reflects*, London, William Hodge.

Kirk, K. E. (1937), *The Story of the Woodard Schools*, London, Hodder.

Lacey, C. (1970), *Hightown Grammar: The School as a Social System*, Manchester University Press.

Leinster-Mackay, D. (1984), *The Rise of the English Prep School*, Sussex, Falmer.

Lindsay, K. (1926), *Social Progress and Educational Waste: Being a Study of the 'Free Place' and Scholarship System*, London, Routledge & Kegan Paul.

Longmate, N. (ed.) (1981), *The Home Front*, London, Chatto & Windus, p. 158.

Mack, E. C. (1941), *Public Schools and British Opinion since 1860*, New York, Columbia University Press.

Macleod, R. (ed) (1982), *Days of Judgement*, Driffield, Nafferton.

Mahoney, P. (1985), *Schools for the Boys? Coeducation Reassessed*, London, Hutchinson.

Marsh, D. C. (1950), *National Insurance and Assistance in Great Britain*, London, Pitman.

Marsh, D. C. (1965), *The Changing Social Structure of England and Wales 1871–1961*, London, Routledge & Kegan Paul.

Marwick, A. (1963), *The Explosion of British Society 1914–62*, London, Pan.

Marwick, A. (1968), *Britain in a Century of Total War*, London, Macmillan.

Marwick, A. (1971), *The Explosion of British Society 1914–1970*, (2nd ed.), London, Macmillan.

Marwick, A. (1982), *British Society Since 1945*, London, Allen Lane.

Mangan, J. A. (1981), *Athleticism in the Victorian and Edwardian Public School*, Cambridge University Press.

Mayhew, P. (ed.) (1985), *One Family's War*, London, Futura.

Metcalf, A. and Humphries, M. (eds) (1985), *The Sexuality of Men*, London, Pluto.

Millerson, G. (1964), *The Qualifying Associations: A Study of Professionalisation*, London, Routledge & Kegan Paul.

Moore, R. W. (ed.) (1945), *Education: Today and Tomorrow*, London, Michael Joseph.

Mowat, C. L. (1955), *Britain between the Wars*, London, Methuen.

Musgrave, P. W. (1985), *From Brown to Bunter: The Life and Death of the School Story*, London, Routledge & Kegan Paul.

Newsome, D. (1961), *Godliness and Good Learning; Four studies in a Victorian Ideal*, London, John Murray.

Nixon, G. and Honey, J. R. de S. (forthcoming) *An Historic Tongue: Studies in English Linguistics in Memory of Barbara Strong*, London, Croom Helm.

Norwood, C. (1929), *The English Tradition of Education*, London, John Murray.

Ogilvie, V. (1967), *The English Public Schools*, London, Batsford.

Orwell, S. and Angus, I. (1968), *The Collected Essays, Journalism and Letters of George Orwell*, 4 vols, London, Secker & Warburg.

Pahl, J. M. and Pahl, R. E. (1972), *Managers and Their Wives*, Harmondsworth, Penguin.

Parsons, C. (1978), *Schools in an Urban Community; A Study of Carbrook 1870–1965*, London, Routledge & Kegan Paul.

Pelling, Henry (1970), *Britain and the Second World War*, London, Collins.

Perkin, H. (1969), *The Origins of Modern English Society 1780–1880*, London, Routledge & Kegan Paul.

Petch, J. A. (1953), *Fifty Years of Examining: The Joint Matriculation Board, 1903–1953*, London, Harrap.

Pleck, J. and Sawyer, J. (eds) (1974), *Men and Masculinity*, Englewood Cliffs, N.J., Prentice Hall.

Pollard, Sydney (1969) (2nd ed.), *The Development of the British Economy 1914–1967*, London, Edward Arnold.

Purvis, J. and Hales, M. (1983), *Achievement and Inequality in Education*, London, Routledge & Kegan Paul.

Quigly, Isabel (1982), *The Heirs of Tom Brown: The English School Story*, London, Chatto & Windus.

Rhodes, G. (1965), *Public Sector Pensions*, London, Allen & Unwin.

Riley, D. (1983), *War in the Nursery: Theories of the Child and Mother*, London, Virago.

Roberts, R. (1973), *The Classic Slum: Salford Life in the First Quarter of the Century*, Harmondsworth, Penguin.

Rothblatt, S. (1968), *The Revolution of the Dons*, Cambridge University Press.

Routh, G. (1980), *Occupation and Pay in Great Britain 1906–79* (2nd ed.), London, Macmillan.

Rowbotham, S. (1973), *Women's Consciousness, Man's World*, Harmondsworth, Penguin.

Ryan, M. D. (1981), *Cradle of the Middle Class. The Family in Oneida County New York 1790–1865*, Cambridge University Press.

Salter, B. and Tapper, T. (1985), *Power and Policy in Education*, Sussex, Falmer.

Schutz, A. (1964), 'The Stranger: An Essay in Social Psychology' in Burderson, A. (ed.), *Collected Papers 11*, The Hague, Martinus Nijhoff.

Simon, B. (1974), *Education and the Labour Movement: 1870–1920*, London, Lawrence & Wishart.

Simon, Brian (1974), *The Politics of Educational Reform 1920–1940*, London, Lawrence & Wishart.

Simpson, J. H. (1954), *A Schoolmaster's Harvest: Some Findings of Fifty Years*, London, Faber.

Sissons, M. and French, P. (1963), *Age of Austerity*, London, Hodder & Stoughton.

Spencer, F. H. (1941), *Education for the People*, London, Routledge & Kegan Paul.

Spender, D. (1982), *Invisible Women, the Schooling Scandal*, London, Writers' and Readers' Publishing Cooperative.

Steedman, Carolyn (1986), *Landscape for a Good Woman*, London, Virago.

Stevenson, J. (1984), *British Society 1914–1945*, Harmondsworth, Penguin.

Summerfield, P. (1984), *Women Workers in the Second World War*, London, Croom Helm.

Taylor, A.J.P. (1970), *English History 1914–45*, Harmondsworth, Penguin.

Taylor, W. (1963), *The Secondary Modern School*, London, Faber.

Thane, P. (1982), *The Foundations of the Welfare State*, London, Longman.

Tolson, A. (1977), *The Limits of Masculinity*, London, Tavistock.

Wakeford, J. (1969), *The Cloistered Elite: A Sociological Analysis of the English Public Boarding School*, London, Macmillan.

Walford, G. (ed.) (1984), *British Public Schools: Policy and Practice*, Sussex, Falmer.

Walford, G. (1986), *Life in Public Schools*, Sussex, Falmer.

Walker, T. (1982), *The High Path*, London, Routledge & Kegan Paul.

Waugh, A. (1955), *The Loom of Youth*, London, Richards Press, First published 1917.

Waugh, E. (1984), *The Sword of Honour Trilogy*, Harmondsworth, Penguin.

Webb, S. (1901), *The Educational Muddle and the Way Out*, London, Fabian Society Tract 106.

Weber, M. (1947), *Theory of Social and Economic Organisation*, Glencoe, Illinois, Free Press.

Weeks, J. (1981), *Sex, Politics and Society, the Regulation of Sexuality since 1800*, London, Longman.

White, J. (1980), *Rothschild's Buildings: Life in an East End Tenement Block*, 1887–1920, London, Routledge & Kegan Paul.

Wilkinson, R. (1964), *The Prefects: British Leadership and the Public School Tradition: A Comparative Study in the Making of Rulers*, London, Oxford University Press.

Williams, G. (1945), *Women & Work*, London, Nicholson & Watson.

Willis, P. (1977), *Learning to Labour, How Working Class Kids get Working Class Jobs*, Farnborough, Saxon House.

Wilson, E. (1977), *Women and the Welfare State*, London, Tavistock.

Winnicott, D. W. (1944), *Getting to Know Your Baby*, Six Broadcast Talks, London, BBC.

Woolf, V. (1977), *Three Guineas*, Harmondsworth, Penguin.

Worsley, T. C. (1940), *Barbarians and Philistines: Democracy and the Public Schools*, London, Hale.

Young, M. F. D. (ed.) (1970), *Knowledge and Control, New Directions in the Sociology of Education*, London, Macmillan.

Young, M. and Wilmott, P. (1973), *The Symmetrical Family*, London, Routledge & Kegan Paul.

Articles

Bridgeman and Fox, I. (1978), 'Why People Choose Private Schools', *New Society*, 29 June, pp. 702–5.

Holley, J. (1981), 'The Two Family Economies of Industrialism', *Journal of Family History*, 6, pp. 57–68.

Hall, C. (1977), 'Married Women at Home in Birmingham in the 1920s and 1930s', *Oral History*, vol. 5, no. 2, pp. 62–83.

Marwick, A. (1987), 'My Battle with the Second World War', *Times Higher Educational Supplement*, 6 March 1987, p. 11.

Roach, J. (1979), 'Examinations and the Secondary Schools 1900–1945', *History of Education*, vol. 8, no. 1, pp. 45–58.

Rothblatt, S. (1982), 'Failure in Early Nineteenth Century Oxford and Cambridge', *History of Education*, vol. 11, no. 1, pp. 1–21.

Rubinstein, D. (1979), 'Ellen Wilkinson Reconsidered', *History Workshop Journal*, vol. 7, no. 2, pp. 161–9.

Rubinstein, D. (1986), 'Education and the Social Origins of British Elites, 1880–1970', *Past and Present*, vol. 112, pp. 163–7.

Simon, B. (1986), 'The 1944 Education Act: A Conservative Measure?', *History of Education*, vol. 15, no. 1, pp. 31–43.

Miscellaneous Periodicals
Boys' Own Annual, 1940–41, vol. 63.
Liverpool Daily Post, 4 April 1951.
New Society, 29 June 1978.
Picture Post, 1 January 1941.
Public Schools Yearbook, 1933, 1934.
Sunday Times, 29 September 1985.
Times Educational Supplement, 12 August 1944.
Times Higher Educational Supplement, 6 March 1987.
Universities Quarterly, 1947, vol. 2, no. 1.

Index